T0100253

DevOps Tools for Java Developers

*Best Practices from Source Code
to Production Containers*

*Stephen Chin, Melissa McKay,
Ixchel Ruiz, and Baruch Sadogursky*

Beijing · Boston · Farnham · Sebastopol · Tokyo

DevOps Tools for Java Developers

by Stephen Chin, Melissa McKay, Ixchel Ruiz, and Baruch Sadogursky

Published by O'Reilly Media, Inc., 1005 Gravenstein Highway North, Sebastopol, CA 95472.

O'Reilly books may be purchased for educational, business, or sales promotional use. Online editions are also available for most titles (*http://oreilly.com*). For more information, contact our corporate/institutional sales department: 800-998-9938 or *corporate@oreilly.com*.

Acquisitions Editor: Suzanne McQuade	**Indexer:** Sue Klefstad
Development Editor: Corbin Collins	**Interior Designer:** David Futato
Production Editor: Elizabeth Faerm	**Cover Designer:** Karen Montgomery
Copyeditor: Sharon Wilkey	**Illustrator:** Kate Dullea
Proofreader: Piper Editorial Consulting, LLC	

April 2022:   First Edition

Revision History for the First Edition

2022-04-15:   First Release

See *http://oreilly.com/catalog/errata.csp?isbn=9781492084020* for release details.

978-1-492-08402-0

[LSI]

Table of Contents

Foreword

When we began writing *Continuous Delivery in Java* in 2017, both Abraham Marín-Pérez and I knew that DevOps would be a big part of our book. Since then, the importance for Java developers to know and understand operational concepts has only increased. With the rise of technologies such as cloud and containers, and supporting concepts of observability and site reliability engineering (SRE), the vast majority of us are no longer "just" developers; we're now often responsible for the coding, shipping, and running of our applications. Therefore, it makes sense for developers to embrace ops and vice versa.

The term *DevOps* is not new; it has been in use for 15 or so years. The concept was originally based around *agile infrastructure*, which emerged from the 2008 Agile Conference in Toronto where Patrick Debois, Andrew Clay Shafer, and many others met to discuss the challenges within traditional sysadmin approaches. The desire to "program" infrastructure meant that there has always been the influence of software engineering in this space. At the 2009 O'Reilly Velocity conference, John Allspaw and Paul Hammond presented their now-famous talk entitled, "10 Deploys a Day: Dev and Ops Cooperation at Flickr," which cemented the importance of devs collaborating with ops.

In my day job at Ambassador Labs, I see an increasing number of organizations building platforms to enable developers to rapidly get their ideas and code into production and in front of customers. The two most important goals are obtaining fast feedback and doing so safely, without crashes or security incidents. In my mind, these platforms are the products resulting from the effective collaboration of dev and ops.

We know from the research by Dr. Nicole Forsgren, Jez Humble, and Gene Kim, which was captured in the must-read book, *Accelerate* (IT Revolution Press, 2018), that high-performing organizations have a higher deployment frequency, lower lead time for changes, smaller change failure rate, and lower mean time to restore production issues. All of these factors are influenced by your platform, processes, and people. Developers have to think like operators, and operators have to embrace development principles. It's all about shared ownership, and this starts with shared understanding. This book will help you develop this shared understanding.

As a developer, you've no doubt been using version control to store and manage your application code for the past decade. Modern DevOps practices like GitOps take this one step further and store application and infrastructure code and configuration in version control. It is, therefore, vital to learn version control systems skills as presented in the early chapters.

The rise of microservices has presented many opportunities for developers, and also many challenges. Some of these challenges can be mitigated by using appropriate technology. Containers and related scheduling frameworks, like Kubernetes, help with packaging and running microservice in a standardized and automated fashion.

Of course, you will also need to understand the impact of these "cloud native" technologies on continuous integration and continuous delivery practices. The authors of this book have done an excellent job of walking you through all the related steps, from package management to securing artifacts and deploying.

I've been fortunate to learn firsthand from all of the authors. I've lost count of the number of times that I've been attending a DevOps conference with crowds of people wandering around only to see Baruch's distinctive top hat moving slowly through the crowd, or to bump up against a leather jacket-wearing motorbiker, only to realize it's Stephen. From this point on, I know I will soon be engrossed in interesting conversations about continuous delivery and the Java ecosystem.

I've also keenly followed Melissa's teachings on building and securing containers as part of her work at JFrog. And seeing her receive her Java Champion recognition live (and unexpectedly!) at Jfokus 2021 was a great moment. Ixchel has long been a guiding influence in the Java and JVM spaces. Since I first attended JavaOne, back in 2013—where I saw her copresent with Andres Almiray on the future of the polyglot JVM—I have learned many things from her that have made me a better developer.

I've also had the privilege of sitting on several panels alongside Ana-Maria Mihalceanu (who wrote Chapter 8) over the years, most recently covering topics such as containers, Kubernetes, and Quarkus. I always enjoy hearing her take on the operational impact of new technologies on the Java platform, and I typically leave our conversation with a bunch of new tools to research.

Whether you're a seasoned Java programmer who is new to the DevOps space, or a novice programmer keen to build on your existing knowledge about containers and cloud, I know you'll learn many things from this book. So, what are you waiting for? Sit down, grab your favorite brew (maybe a cup of Java?), and prepare to level up in all things related to DevOps tooling for Java developers.

— Daniel Bryant
Head of DevRel at Ambassador Labs
Java Champion
March 2022

Preface

This book was written in a time of immense change as the world was thrown upside down by the largest pandemic in a century. However, this work was never needed more as the software industry embraced DevOps and cloud native development to handle the accelerated pace of software delivery.

We organized this book so that the topics are in an incremental order of lifecycle, complexity, and maturity. However, DevOps is a broad enough journey that you may find some chapters more relevant than others for your project needs. As a result, we designed the chapters so that you can start in any order and focus on a particular subject for which you need expertise, examples, and best practices to advance your knowledge.

We hope you enjoy reading this title as much as we have enjoyed putting the content together. Our one ask is that you share your newfound knowledge with a friend or colleague so that we can all become better developers.

Conventions Used in This Book

The following typographical conventions are used in this book:

Italic
Indicates new terms, URLs, email addresses, filenames, and file extensions.

`Constant width`
Used for program listings, as well as within paragraphs to refer to program elements such as variable or function names, databases, data types, environment variables, statements, and keywords.

`Constant width bold`
Shows commands or other text that should be typed literally by the user.

Constant width italic

Shows text that should be replaced with user-supplied values or by values determined by context.

This element signifies a tip or suggestion.

This element signifies a general note.

This element indicates a warning or caution.

Using Code Examples

Supplemental material (code examples, exercises, etc.) is available for download at *https://github.com/devops-tools-for-java-developers*.

If you have a technical question or a problem using the code examples, please send email to *bookquestions@oreilly.com*.

This book is here to help you get your job done. In general, if example code is offered with this book, you may use it in your programs and documentation. You do not need to contact us for permission unless you're reproducing a significant portion of the code. For example, writing a program that uses several chunks of code from this book does not require permission. Selling or distributing examples from O'Reilly books does require permission. Answering a question by citing this book and quoting example code does not require permission. Incorporating a significant amount of example code from this book into your product's documentation does require permission.

We appreciate, but generally do not require, attribution. An attribution usually includes the title, author, publisher, and ISBN. For example: "*DevOps Tools for Java Developers* by Stephen Chin, Melissa McKay, Ixchel Ruiz, and Baruch Sadogursky (O'Reilly). Copyright 2022 Stephen Chin, Melissa McKay, Ixchel Ruiz, and Baruch Sadogursky, 978-1-492-08402-0."

If you feel your use of code examples falls outside fair use or the permission given above, feel free to contact us at *permissions@oreilly.com*.

O'Reilly Online Learning

 For more than 40 years, *O'Reilly Media* has provided technology and business training, knowledge, and insight to help companies succeed.

Our unique network of experts and innovators share their knowledge and expertise through books, articles, conferences, and our online learning platform. O'Reilly's online learning platform gives you on-demand access to live training courses, in-depth learning paths, interactive coding environments, and a vast collection of text and video from O'Reilly and 200+ other publishers. For more information, please visit *http://oreilly.com*.

How to Contact Us

Please address comments and questions concerning this book to the publisher:

O'Reilly Media, Inc.
1005 Gravenstein Highway North
Sebastopol, CA 95472
800-998-9938 (in the United States or Canada)
707-829-0515 (international or local)
707-829-0104 (fax)

We have a web page for this book, where we list errata, examples, and any additional information. You can access this page at *https://oreil.ly/EHNuR*.

Email *bookquestions@oreilly.com* to comment or ask technical questions about this book.

For more information about our books, courses, conferences, and news, see our website at *http://www.oreilly.com*.

Find us on LinkedIn: *https://linkedin.com/company/oreilly-media*

Follow us on Twitter: *http://twitter.com/oreillymedia*

Watch us on YouTube: *http://youtube.com/oreillymedia*

Acknowledgments

This book wouldn't have been possible without the support of our family and friends who stood with us and supported our dedication and focus on this subject. While we passionately worked to put this title together, they helped to take care of our loved ones and personal health so we could deliver the broad range of content required to cover the entire DevOps and Java ecosystem.

Also, a special thanks to Shlomi Ben Haim, CEO of JFrog. When other companies were pulling back and tightening budgets, Shlomi extended personal support for this title and gave us the freedom and flexibility to focus on the intense task of covering this extremely broad subject.

Special thanks to Ana-Maria Mihalceanu, for Chapter 8, and to Sven Ruppert, for his contribution to Chapter 7.

We would like to thank our technical reviewers, Daniel Pittman, Cameron Pietrafeso, Sebastian Daschner, and Kirk Pepperdine, for improving the accuracy of this book.

And finally a huge thanks to you, the reader, who has taken the initiative to improve your knowledge of the entire DevOps pipeline and be a change agent for improvements in automation, process, and culture.

## CHAPTER 1

DevOps for (or Possibly Against) Developers

Baruch Sadogursky

While you here do snoring lie,
Open-eyed conspiracy His time doth take.
If of life you keep a care,
Shake off slumber, and beware:
Awake, awake!
    —William Shakespeare, *The Tempest*

Some might ask if the DevOps movement is simply an ops-inspired plot against developers. Most (if not all) who would do so wouldn't expect a serious response, not least because they intend the question as tongue-in-cheek teasing. It's also because—and regardless of whether your origins are on the development or the operations side of the equation—when anyone strikes up a conversation about DevOps, it will take approximately 60 seconds before someone inquires, "But what is DevOps *really*?"

And you'd think, 11 years after the coining of the term (a decade within which industry professionals have spoken, debated, and shouted about it), that we'd all have arrived at a standard, no-nonsense, commonly understood definition. But this simply isn't the case. In fact, despite an exponentially increasing corporate demand for DevOps personnel, it's highly doubtful that any five DevOps-titled employees, chosen at random, could tell you *precisely* what DevOps is.

So, don't be embarrassed if you still find yourself scratching your head when the subject comes up. Conceptually, DevOps may not be easy to grok, but it's not impossible either.

But regardless of how we discuss the term or what definition(s) we might agree upon, there's one thing, above all else, that's critical to bear in mind: DevOps is an entirely invented concept, and the inventors came from the ops side of the equation.

DevOps Is a Concept Invented by the Ops Side

My premise about DevOps may be provocative, but it's provable too. Let's start with the facts.

Exhibit 1: The Phoenix Project

The Phoenix Project by Gene Kim et al. (IT Revolution) became a classic since published almost a decade ago. It's not a how-to manual (not in the traditional sense, anyway). It's a novel that tells the story of a highly problematic company and its IT manager who is suddenly assigned the task of implementing a make-or-break corporate initiative that's already way over budget and months behind schedule.

If you dwell in the realms of software, the rest of the book's central characters will be familiar to you. For the moment, though, let's have a look at their professional titles:

- Director, IT service support
- Director, distributed technology
- Manager, retail sales
- Lead systems administrator
- Chief information security officer
- Chief financial officer
- Chief executive officer

Notice the connective tissue between them? They're the protagonists of one of *the* most important books about DevOps ever written and *not one* of them is a developer. Even when developers do figure into the plotline, well…let's just say they're not spoken of in particularly glowing terms.

When victory comes, it's the hero of the story (together with a supportive board member) who invents DevOps, pulls the project's fat out of the fire, turns his company's fortunes around, and gets rewarded with a promotion to chief information officer (CIO) of the enterprise. And everyone lives happily—if not ever after, then for at least the two or three years such successes tend to buy you in this business before it's time to prove your worth all over again.

Exhibit 2: The DevOps Handbook

It's better to read *The Phoenix Project* before *The DevOps Handbook* by Gene Kim et al. (IT Revolution) because the former places you within a highly believable, human scenario. It's not difficult to immerse yourself in the personality types, the professional predicaments, and the interpersonal relationships of the characters. The hows and whys of DevOps unfold as inevitable and rational responses to a set of circumstances, which could have just as easily led to business collapse. The stakes, the characters, and the choices they make all seem quite plausible. Parallels to your own experience may not be too hard to draw.

The DevOps Handbook allows you to explore the component conceptual parts of DevOps principles and practices in greater depth. As its subtitle suggests, the book goes a long way toward explaining *How to Create World-Class Agility, Reliability, and Security in Technology Organizations*. But shouldn't that be about development? Whether it should or shouldn't may be open to debate. What's incontrovertible is that the book's authors are bright, super-talented professionals who are, arguably, the fathers of DevOps. However, Exhibit 2 isn't included here to praise them so much as to take a close look at their backgrounds.

Let's start with Gene Kim. He founded the software security and data integrity firm Tripwire, serving as its chief technology officer (CTO) for over a decade. As a researcher, he's devoted his professional attention to examining and understanding the technological transformations that have and are occurring within large, complex businesses and institutions. In addition to coauthoring *The Phoenix Project*, in 2019 he coauthored *The Unicorn Project* (which I'll have more to say about later). Everything about his career is steeped in ops. Even when *Unicorn* says it's "about Developers," it's still developers as seen through the eyes of an ops guy!

As for the other three authors of the *Handbook*:

- Jez Humble has held positions including site reliability engineer (SRE), CTO, deputy director of Delivery Architecture and Infrastructure Services, and Developer Relations. An ops guy! Even though the last of his titles references development, the job isn't *about* that. It's about relations *with* developers. It's about narrowing the divide between dev and ops, about which he has written, taught, and lectured extensively.

- Patrick Debois has served as a CTO, director of Market Strategy, and director of Dev♥Ops Relations (the heart is his addition). He describes himself as a professional who is "bridging the gap between projects and operations by using Agile techniques in development, project management, and system administration." That sure sounds like an ops guy.

- John Willis, as of this writing, holds the title of VP of DevOps and Digital Practices. Previously, he's been a director of Ecosystem Development, a VP of Solutions, and notably a VP of Training and Services at Opscode (now known as Progress Chef). And while John's career has been a bit more deeply involved with development, most of his work has been about ops, particularly to the degree that he has focused his attention on tearing down the walls that had once kept developers and operations personnel in distinct and separate camps.

As you can see, all the authors have an ops background. Coincidence? I think *not*.

Still not convinced that DevOps is ops driven? How about we have a look at the leaders trying to sell us on DevOps today.

Google It

As of this writing, if you typed "What is DevOps?" in a Google search just to see what would come up, your first page of results would likely include the following:

- Agile Admin, a system administration company
- Atlassian, whose products include project and issue tracking, list making, and team collaboration platforms
- Amazon Web Services (AWS), Microsoft Azure, and Rackspace Technology, all of which sell cloud ops infrastructure
- Logz.io, which sells log management and analysis services
- New Relic, whose specialty is application monitoring

All of these are very ops-focused. Yes, that first page contained one firm that was a bit more on the development side and one other that really wasn't directly related to the search. The point is that when you try to look for DevOps, most of what you'll find tends to skew toward ops.

What Does It Do?

DevOps *is* a thing! It's in *big* demand. And with this, many will want to know, concretely, what DevOps *does*, what it substantively produces. Rather than go down that route, let's look at it structurally, conceptualizing it as you would the sideways, figure-eight-shaped infinity symbol. In this light, we see a loop of processes that goes from coding to building to testing to release to deployment to operations to monitoring, and then back again to begin planning for new features, as shown in Figure 1-1.

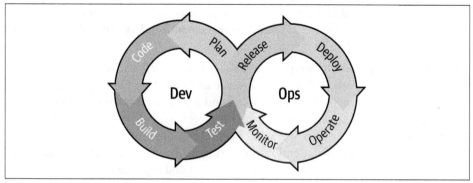

Figure 1-1. DevOps infinity loop

And if this looks familiar to some readers, it should because it bears a conceptual similarity to the Agile development cycle (Figure 1-2).

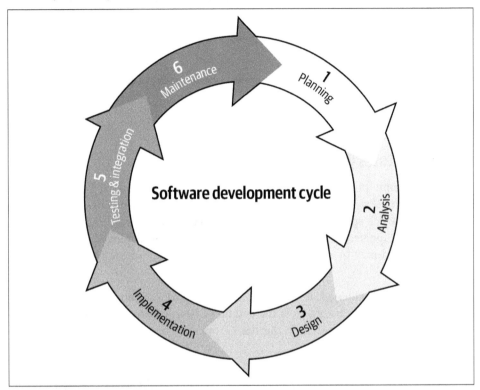

Figure 1-2. Agile development cycle

There's no profound difference between these two never-ending stories other than the fact that ops folks grafted themselves onto the old world of the Agile circle, essentially stretching it into two circles and shoehorning their concerns and pains into the domain that was once considered solely the province of developers.

State of the Industry

Since 2014, further proof that DevOps is an ops-driven phenomenon has come packaged in the form of an easy-to-read annual digest of data collected, analyzed, and summarized from tens of thousands of industry professionals and organizations worldwide. The "Accelerate: State of DevOps" report was primarily the work of DevOps Research and Assessment (DORA) and is *the* most important document in the software industry to gauge where DevOps is and where it's likely going. In the 2018 edition (*https://oreil.ly/jWjvX*), for example, we can see a serious focus on questions such as these:

- How often do organizations deploy code?
- How long does it typically take to go from code commits to successfully running in production?
- When impairments or outages occur, how long does it generally take to restore service?
- What percentage of deployed changes result in degraded service or require remediation?

Notice that all of those are very ops-centered concerns.

What Constitutes Work?

Now let's examine how *work* is defined by the "Accelerate: State of DevOps" report and *The Phoenix Project*. Well, first, *planned* work focuses on business projects and new features, which span both ops and dev. Internal projects, including server migrations, software updates, and changes driven by feedback on deployed projects can be broad-based and may or may not weight more to one side of the DevOps equation than the other.

But what about *unplanned* activities, such as support escalations and emergency outages? Those are ops heavy, as is the coding of new features, bug fixes, and refactoring—which are all about how the life of ops can be made easier by *including* developers in the DevOps story.

If We're Not About Deployment and Operations, Then Just What Is Our Job?

Clearly, DevOps isn't anything developers were (or are) demanding. It's an ops invention to make everyone else work harder. And assuming this truth, let's ponder what would happen if developers were to rise up as one and say, "Your ops concerns are *yours*, not ours." Fine. But in that case, it would be only right and proper to ask the rebelling developers for their definition of "done." What standards do they believe they need to achieve to say, "We did our job well and our part is now complete"?

This isn't a flippant question, and there are sources we can look to for answers. One, although imperfect and not infrequently criticized, is the Manifesto for Software Craftsmanship (*https://oreil.ly/mTAUe*), which puts forth four fundamental values that should motivate developers. Let's consider them:

Well-crafted software
Yes, indeed, quality is important.

Steadily adding value

No argument there. Of course we want to provide services and features that people need, want, or would like.

Community of professionals

In broad strokes, who could oppose this? Cordiality among industry peers is just being professionally neighborly.

Productive partnerships

Collaboration is certainly the name of the game. Developers aren't against quality assurance (QA), ops, or the products themselves. So, in context, this is just about being friendly with everybody (so long as other teams don't start dictating what their jobs are supposed to be).

Just What Constitutes "Done"?

With all that we've established so far, we can safely say that we need to produce code that's simple, readable, understandable, and easy to deploy. We must be certain that nonfunctional requirements (e.g., performance, throughput, memory footprint, security, privacy, etc.) are satisfied. We should work diligently to avoid incurring any technical baggage and, if we're lucky, shed some along the way. We have to be sure that all tests pass. And we're obligated to maintain fruitful relations with QA teams (when they're happy, we're happy).

With good-quality code, plus positive team leader and peer reviews, everything should be fine out of the gate. With a product team that defines standards for value and added value, benchmarks can be firmly established. Through their feedback, product owners help to determine whether those benchmarks are (or aren't) being met and by how much. That's a pretty good thumbnail definition of a good software developer having "done" what they needed to do. It also demonstrates that "well done" can never adequately be measured (or even known) without the involvement of and clear communications with ops personnel.

Rivalry?

So yes, although it *can* be proven that DevOps really wasn't anything for which developers were clamoring, it can equally be shown that its infinite practice benefits everyone. And still there are holdouts; those who imagine a rivalry, even an antagonism, between developers and, for example, QA testers. Developers work hard on their creations and then feel like the QA teams are almost like hackers, out to prove something, just digging and digging until they find a problem.

This is where DevOps counseling comes in. Every conscientious developer wants to be proud of what they're producing. Finding flaws can seem like criticism, when it's really just conscientious work coming from another direction. Good, clear, open, and continuous communication between developers and QA personnel helps reinforce the benefits of DevOps, but it also makes plain that *everyone* is ultimately working toward the same goal. When QA folks identify bugs, all they're doing is helping their developer colleagues to write better code, to be *better* developers. And this example of interplay between those on the ops side and others on the dev side demonstrates the useful blurring of the distinctions and separations between the two worlds. Their relationship is necessarily symbiotic and, once again, works along an endless continuum of activities, with one informing the other for the mutual benefit of all.

More Than Ever Before

The increasing demand for DevOps is coming as much from external forces as it is from within software companies themselves. And this is because our expectations, *all* of our expectations, as people living in a 21st century world, continue to change rapidly. The more reliant we become on ever-improving software solutions, the less time we have to waste on information and communication gaps, and delays between developers and operations personnel.

Take, for example, banking. A decade ago, most major banks had reasonably adequate websites. You could log in to have a look at your accounts, your statements, and recent transactions. Maybe you were even beginning to make payments electronically through the e-services your bank was offering. And while those services were nice and offered a certain amount of convenience, you likely still needed to go (or, at least, felt more comfortable going) to your local branch to handle your banking affairs.

What didn't exist is today's fully digital experience—complete with mobile apps, automated account monitoring and alerts, and enough services that make it more and more common for average account holders to do *everything* online. You may even be among those who not only don't care if you ever see the inside of your bricks-and-mortar branch ever again, but also don't even *know* where that branch is! What's more, banks are reacting to these rapidly changing banking habits by consolidating and closing physical branches, and offering incentives for their customers to shift their banking to the online sphere. This accelerated even more during the COVID-19 crisis, when access to branches was restricted to appointment-only services, limited walk-in access, and shorter hours.

So, 10 years ago, if your bank's website went down for 12 hours of maintenance while the bank was deploying a better, more secure site, you'd probably have taken that in stride. What's a dozen hours if it's going to result in higher-quality services? You didn't need 24/7, online banking—and, besides, the local branch was there for you. Today, that's simply not the case. Half a day's worth of downtime is unacceptable. In essence, you expect your bank to *always* be open and available. This is because your (and the world's) definition of *quality* has changed. And that change requires DevOps more than ever before.

Volume and Velocity

Another pressure impelling the growth of DevOps is the amount of data that's being stored and handled. And that's only logical. If more and more of our daily lives are reliant on software, a tremendous rise in the amount of data it generates will obviously occur. In 2020, the entire global datasphere amounted to nearly 10 zettabytes. A decade prior, it was 0.5 zettabytes. By 2025, it's reasonably estimated (*https://oreil.ly/hvghC*) that it will balloon exponentially to over 50 zettabytes!

This isn't only about behemoths like Google, Netflix, Facebook, Microsoft, Amazon, Twitter, and others getting bigger and better, and therefore needing to process larger amounts of data. This projection affirms that more and more companies will be graduating into the world of big data. With that comes the demands of vastly increased data loads, as well as the shift away from traditional staging-server environments, which offered exact replicas of given production environments. And this shift is predicated on the fact that maintaining such pair-to-pair schemes is no longer feasible in terms of size or speed.

Happy were the days of yore when everything could be tested before going into production, but this isn't possible anymore. Things are and will increasingly be released into production about which software firms don't have 100% confidence. Should this cause us to panic? No. The necessity to release fast and remain competitive should inspire innovation and creativity in the ways required to best execute controlled rollovers, test procedures, and more *in*-production testing—what's now referred to as *progressive delivery*. This comes along with feature flags and observability tools, such as distributed tracing.

Some equate progressive delivery with the blast radius of an explosive device. The idea is that when we deploy to an in-production environment, explosions should be expected. Therefore, to optimize such rollouts, the best we can hope for is to minimize casualties, to keep the size of the blast radius as small as is possible. This is consistently accomplished through improvements in the quality of servers, services, and products. And if we agree that quality is a concern of developers and its achievement is part of a developer's definition of "done," then it means *there can be no pause or disconnect between that dev moment of done and the next, ops moment of production.* Because no sooner does this happen than we're looping back into development, as bugs are fixed, services restored due to outages, and so on.

Done and Done

Maybe it's becoming clear that the expectations and demands that were and continue to be generated from the ops environment, of necessity, drove the push to DevOps. And as a result, the increased expectations and demands on developers aren't coming from some festering hatred that ops folks have for their developer colleagues, nor is it part of a plot to deprive them of sleep. Rather, *all* of this, all of what DevOps represents, is a realpolitik business response to our changing world and the changes they've forced on the software industry across the board.

The fact is that everyone has new responsibilities, some of which require professionals (certainly many departments) to be at the ready to respond *whenever* duty calls because ours is a nonstop world. Here's another way of putting this: our old definitions of "done" are done!

Our new definition is *site reliability engineering* (*SRE*). This Google-coined term forever weds dev to ops by bridging any lingering perceived gaps between the two. And while SRE areas of focus may be taken up by personnel on either or both sides of the DevOps equation, these days companies often have dedicated SRE teams that are specifically responsible for examining issues related to performance, efficiency, emergency responsiveness, monitoring, capacity planning, and more. SRE professionals think like software engineers in devising strategies and solutions for system administration issues. They're the folks who are increasingly making automated deployments work.

When SRE staff are happy, it means builds are becoming ever more reliable, repeatable, and fast, particularly because the landscape is one of scalable, backward- and forward-compatible code operating in stateless environments that are relying on an exploding universe of servers and emitting event streams to allow for real-time observability and alerts when something goes wrong. When new builds occur, they need to launch rapidly (with the full expectation that some will die equally quickly). Services need to return to full functionality as rapidly as possible. When features don't work, we must have an immediate ability to turn them off programmatically through an API. When new software is released and users update their clients, but then encounter bugs, we must have the ability to execute swift and seamless rollbacks. Old clients and old servers need to be able to communicate with new clients.

And while SRE is assessing and monitoring these activities and laying out strategic responses, the work in all of these areas is completely that of developers. Therefore, while Dev staff are *doing*, SRE is today's definition of *done*.

Float Like a Butterfly...

In addition to all of the considerations already mentioned, a fundamental characteristic must define code in our modern DevOps (and related SRE) era: *lean*. And by this we're talking about saving money. "But what," you may ask, "does code have to do with saving money?"

Well, one illustration might be cloud providers who charge companies for a plethora of discrete services. Some of these costs are directly affected by the code being output by those corporate cloud service subscribers. *Cost reductions can therefore come from the creation and use of innovative developer tools, as well as writing and deploying better code.*

The very nature of a global, we-never-close, software-driven society with a constant desire for newer, better software features and services means that DevOps can't be concerned with only production and deployments. It *must* also be attentive to the bottom line of business itself. And although this may seem to be yet another burden thrown into the mix, think about it the next time the boss says that costs must be cut. Instead of negative, knee-jerk solutions, such as employee layoffs or reductions in salaries and benefits, needed savings may be found in positive, business-profile-enhancing moves like going serverless and moving to the cloud. Then, no one gets fired, and the coffee and donuts in the breakroom are still free!

Being lean not only saves money, but also gives companies the opportunity to improve their marketplace impact. When firms can achieve efficiencies without staff reductions, they can retain optimal levels of team strength. When teams continue to be well compensated and cared for, they'll be more motivated to produce their best possible work. When that output is achieving success, it means customers are grinning. So long as *customers continue to get well-functioning new features quickly as a result of faster deployments*, well…they'll keep coming back for more and spreading the word to others. And *that's* a virtuous cycle that means money in the bank.

Integrity, Authentication, and Availability

Hand in hand, and shoulder to shoulder with any and all DevOps activities is the perpetual question of *security*. Of course, some will choose to address this concern by hiring a chief information security officer. And that's great because there'll always be a go-to person to blame when something goes wrong. A better option might be to actually analyze, *within* a DevOps framework, how individual employees, work teams, and companies as a whole *think* about security and how it can be strengthened.

We talk much more about this in Chapter 10, but for now consider that: breaches, bugs, Structured Query Language (SQL) injections, buffer overflows, and more aren't new. What's different is the increasing speed of their appearance, their rising quantity, and the cleverness with which malicious individuals and entities are able to act. It's not surprising. With more and more code being released, more and more problems will follow, with each type demanding different solutions.

With faster deployments, it becomes ever more critical to be more reactive to risks and threats. The 2018 discovery of the Meltdown and Spectre security vulnerabilities made it clear that some threats are impossible to prevent. We are in a race, and *the only thing to do is to deploy fixes as quickly as possible.*

Fierce Urgency

It should be clear by now that *DevOps is not a plot, but a response to evolutionary pressures*. It's a means to an ends that does the following:

- Delivers better quality
- Produces savings
- Deploys features faster
- Strengthens security

And it doesn't matter who likes it or not, or who came up with the idea first, or even its original intent. What matters is covered in the next section.

The Software Industry Has Fully Embraced DevOps

By now, every company is a DevOps company (*https://oreil.ly/tkSSZ*). So, get on board...because you don't have any other choice.

The DevOps of today, what DevOps has evolved into, is, as stated earlier, an infinity loop. It doesn't mean that groups and departments no longer exist. It doesn't mean that everyone is responsible for their areas of concern along with those of everyone else along this continuum.

It *does* mean that everyone should be working together. It *does* mean that software professionals within a given enterprise must be aware of and taking into reasonable consideration the work that all of their other colleagues are doing. They need to care about the issues their peers are confronting, how those matters can and do impact the work *they* do, the products and services their company offers, and how the *totality* of this affects their firm's marketplace reputation.

This is why *DevOps engineer* is a term that makes no sense because it implies the existence of someone who can comprehensively and competently do (or is, at least, completely versed in) everything that occurs within the DevOps infinity loop. No such person exists. They never will. In fact, even *trying* to be a DevOps engineer is a mistake because it runs entirely counter to what DevOps is, which is eliminating silos where code developers are walled off from QA testers, who are walled off from release personnel, and so on.

DevOps is a coming together of efforts, interests, and feedback in a continuous effort to create, secure, deploy, and perfect code. DevOps is about *collaboration*. And as collaborations are organic, communicative endeavors, well...just as collaboration engineering isn't a thing, neither is DevOps engineering (no matter what any institute or university might promise).

Making It Manifest

Knowing what DevOps is (and isn't) only establishes a concept. The question is, how can it be sensibly and effectively implemented and sustained in software firms far and wide? Best advice? Here goes.

First, you can have DevOps enablers, DevOps evangelists, DevOps consultants and coaches (and I know how Scrum spoiled all those terms for all of us, but there aren't any better ones). That's OK. But DevOps is *not* an engineering discipline. We want site/service reliability engineers, production engineers, infrastructure engineers, QA engineers, and so on. But once a company has a DevOps engineer, the next thing it's almost guaranteed to have is a DevOps department, which will just be another silo that's likely to be nothing more than an existing department that's been rebranded, so it *looks* like the firm is on the DevOps bandwagon.

A DevOps office isn't a sign of progress. Rather, it's simply back to the future. Then, the next thing that will be needed is a way to foster collaborations between Dev and DevOps, which will necessitate the coining of yet another term. How about *DevDevOps*?

Second, DevOps is about nuances and small things. Like cultures (especially corporate cultures), it's about attitudes and relationships. You may not be able to clearly define those cultures, but they exist all the same. DevOps is also not about code, engineering practices, or technical prowess. No tool you can buy, no step-by-step manual, and no home edition board game can help you create DevOps in your organization.

It's about *behaviors* that are encouraged and nurtured within companies. And much of this is simply about how rank-and-file staff are treated, the structure of the firm, and the titles people hold. It's about how often people have an opportunity to get together (especially in nonmeeting settings), where they sit and eat, talk shop and nonshop, tell jokes, etc. It's in these spaces, not within data centers, where cultures form, grow, and change.

Finally, companies should actively seek and invest in T-shaped people (Ж-shaped is even better, as my Russian-speaking readers might suggest). As opposed to I-shaped individuals (who are absolute experts in one area) or generalists (who know a good bit about a lot, but have no mastery of any particular discipline), a T-shaped person has world-class expertise in at least one thing. This is the long vertical line of the "T" that firmly roots their depth of knowledge and experience. The "T" is crossed above by a breadth of accumulated capabilities, know-how, and wisdom in other arenas.

The total package is someone who demonstrates a clear and keen propensity to adapt to circumstances, learn new skills, and meet the challenges of today. In fact, this is a nearly perfect definition of an ideal DevOps staffer. T-shaped personnel allow businesses to work effectively on prioritized workloads, instead of only what companies think their in-house capacities can bear. T-folks can see and are intrigued by the big picture. This makes them terrific collaborators, which, as a result, leads to the construction of empowered teams.

We All Got the Message

The good news is that a decade after ops invented DevOps, they completely understand that it's not only about them. It's about *everybody*. We can see the change with our own eyes. For example, the 2019 "Accelerate: State of DevOps" report (*https://oreil.ly/vICAO*) got more developers to participate in the study than ops or SRE personnel! To find more profound evidence that things have changed, we return full circle to Gene Kim. Also in 2019, the man who helped novelize the ops end of the equation with *The Phoenix Project* released *The Unicorn Project* (IT Revolution). If the earlier book gave short shrift to developers, here our hero is Maxine, her company's *lead developer* (and ultimate savior).

DevOps began with ops, no question about it. But the motivation wasn't the subjugation of developers, nor the supremacy of operations professionals. It was and remains predicated on everyone seeing everyone else, appreciating their value and contributions to an enterprise—not simply out of respect or courtesy, but as personal self-interest and business survival, competitiveness, and growth.

And if you're scared that DevOps is going to overwhelm you in a sea of ops concepts, it's actually most likely to be the other way around. Just look at SRE's definition by Google (*https://sre.google*) (the company that invented the discipline):

> SRE is what you get when you treat operations as if it's a software problem.

So, the ops folks want to be developers now? Welcome. Software problems belong to *all* software professionals *all* the time. We're in the problem-solving business—which means that everyone is a little bit of an SRE, a little bit of a developer, a little bit into operations…because it's all the same thing. They're all just intertwined facets that allow us to devise solutions for the software of today, as well as the individual and societal problems of tomorrow.

## CHAPTER 2

The System of Truth

Stephen Chin

A complex system that works is invariably found to have evolved from a simple system that worked.
    —John Gall (Gall's law)

To have an effective DevOps pipeline, it is important to have a single system of truth to understand what bits and bytes are being deployed into production. Typically, this starts with a source code management system that contains all of the source code that gets compiled and built into the production deployment. By tracing a production deployment back to a specific revision in source control, you can do root cause analysis of bugs, security holes, and performance issues.

Source code management solves several key roles in the software delivery lifecycle:

Collaboration
    Large teams working on a single codebase would constantly get blocked by one another without effective source code management, reducing productivity as the team size grows.

Versioning
    Source code systems let you track versions of the code to identify what is being deployed into production or released to a customer.

History
    By keeping a chronological record of all versions of software as it is developed, it is possible to revert to an older version of the code or identify the specific change that caused a regression.

Attribution

Knowing who made the changes in a particular file allows you to identify owner-ship, assess domain expertise, and assess risk when making changes.

Dependencies

Source code has become the canonical source for other key metadata about the project, like dependencies on other packages.

Quality

A source code management system allows for easy peer review of changes before they are accepted, increasing the overall quality of the software.

Since source code management plays such a critical role in software development, it is important to understand how it works and select a system that best meets the needs of your organization and the desired DevOps workflow.

Three Generations of Source Code Management

Collaboration is a big part of software development, and as you scale with larger teams, the ability to collaborate effectively on a shared codebase often becomes a bottleneck to developer productivity. Also, the complexity of systems tends to increase, so rather than managing a dozen files or a handful of modules, it is common to see thousands of source files that need to be updated en masse to accomplish system-wide changes and refactorings.

To manage the need to collaborate on codebases, *source code management (SCM)* systems were created. The first-generation SCM systems handled collaboration via file locking. Examples of these are SCCS and RCS, which required that you lock files before editing, make your changes, and then release the lock for other folks to contribute. This seemingly eliminated the possibility of two developers making conflicting changes, with two major drawbacks:

- Productivity was still impacted since you had to wait for other developers to fin-ish their changes before editing. In systems with large files, this could effectively limit the concurrency to only one developer at a time.

- This did not solve the problem of conflicts across files. It is still possible for two developers to modify different files with interdependencies and create a buggy or unstable system by introducing conflicting changes.

A substantial improvement was made in the second-generation version control sys-tems, starting with Concurrent Versions System (CVS) created by Dick Grune. CVS was revolutionary in its approach to (or lack of) file locking. Rather than preventing you from changing files, it would allow multiple developers to make their simultane-ous (and possibly conflicting) changes to the same files. This was later resolved via file merging: the conflicting files were analyzed via a difference (diff) algorithm, and any conflicting changes were presented to the user to resolve.

By delaying the resolution of conflicting changes to a check-in, CVS allowed multiple developers to freely modify and refactor a large codebase without becoming blocked on other changes to the same files. This not only increases developer productivity, but also allows for the isolation and testing of large features separately, which can later be merged into an integrated codebase.

The most popular second-generation SCM is currently Apache Subversion, which is designed as a drop-in replacement for CVS. It offers several advantages over CVS, including tracking commits as a single revision, which avoids file-update collisions that can corrupt the CVS repository state.

The third generation of version control is distributed version control systems (DVCSs). In a DVCS, every developer has a copy of the entire repository along with the full history stored locally. Just as in a second-generation version control system, you check out a copy of the repository, make changes, and check it back in. However, to integrate those changes with other developers, you sync your entire repository in a peer-to-peer fashion.

Several early DVCS systems existed, including GNU Arch, Monotone, and Darcs, but DVCS become popularized by Git and Mercurial. Git was developed as a direct response to the Linux team's need for a stable and reliable version control system that could support the scale and requirements for open source operating system development, and it has become the de facto standard for both open source and commercial version control system usage.

DVCSs offer several advantages over server-based version control:

Working entirely offline
Since you have a local copy of the repository, checking code in and out, merging, and managing branches can all be done without a network connection.

No single point of failure
Unlike a server-based SCM, where only one copy of the entire repository with full history exists, a DVCS creates a copy of the repository on every developer's machine, increasing redundancy.

Faster local operations
Since most version control operations are local to the machine, they are much faster and not affected by network speed or server load.

Decentralized control
Since syncing the code involves copying the entire repository, this makes it much easier to fork a codebase, and in the case of open source projects can make it much easier to start an independent effort when the main project has stalled or taken an undesirable direction.

Ease of migration
Converting from most SCM tools into Git is a relatively straightforward operation, and you can retain commit history.

And distributed version control has a few disadvantages, including these:

Slower initial repository sync
The initial sync includes copying the entire repository history, which can be much slower.

Larger storage requirements
Since everyone has a full copy of the repository and all history, very large and/or long-running projects may require a sizable disk requirement.

No ability to lock files
Server-based version control systems offer some support for locking files when a binary file that cannot be merged needs to be edited. With DVCSs locking mechanics cannot be enforced, which means only files that can be merged (for example, text) are suitable for versioning.

Choosing Your Source Control

Hopefully, by now you are convinced that using a modern DVCS is the way to go. It provides the best capabilities for local and remote development of any size team.

Also, of the commonly used version control systems, Git has become the clear winner in adoption. This is shown clearly by looking at the Google Trends analysis of the most commonly used version control systems, as shown in Figure 2-1.

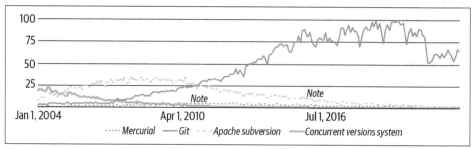

Figure 2-1. Popularity of version control systems from 2004 through 2022 (source: Google Trends (https://oreil.ly/qRxyG))

Git has become the de facto standard in the open source community, which means a wide base of support exists for its usage along with a rich ecosystem. However, sometimes convincing your boss or peers to adopt new technologies is difficult if they have a deep investment in a legacy source control technology.

Here are some reasons you can use to convince your boss to upgrade to Git:

Reliability
> Git is written like a filesystem, including a proper filesystem check tool (`git fsck`) and checksums to ensure data reliability. And given it is a DVCS, you probably have your data also pushed to multiple external repositories, creating several redundant backups of the data.

Performance
> Git is not the first DVCS, but it is extremely performant. It was built from the ground up to support Linux development with extremely large codebases and thousands of developers. Git continues to be actively developed by a large open source community.

Tool support
> There are over 40 frontends for Git and support in just about every major IDE (JetBrains IntelliJ IDEA, Microsoft Visual Studio Code, Eclipse, Apache NetBeans, etc.), so you are unlikely to find a development platform that does not fully support it.

Integrations
> Git has first-class integrations with IDEs, issue trackers, messaging platforms, continuous integration servers, security scanners, code review tools, dependency management, and cloud platforms.

Upgrade tools
> There are migration tools to ease the transition from other version-control systems to Git, such as `git-svn` that supports bidirectional changes from Subversion to Git, or the Team Foundation Version Control (TFVC) repository import tool for Git.

In summary, there is not much to lose by upgrading to Git, and a lot of additional capabilities and integrations to start to take advantage of. Getting started with Git is as simple as downloading a release (*https://oreil.ly/dxgt4*) for your development machine and creating a local repository.

However, the real power comes in collaboration with the rest of your team, and this is most convenient if you have a central repository to push changes to and collaborate with. Several companies offer commercial Git repos that you can self-host or run on their cloud platform. These include AWS CodeCommit, Assembla, Azure DevOps, GitLab, SourceForge, GitHub, RhodeCode, Bitbucket, Gitcolony, and others.

According to data from the JetBrains "State of the Developer Ecosystem 2020" report shown in Figure 2-2, these Git-based source control systems accounted for over 96% of the commercial source control market.

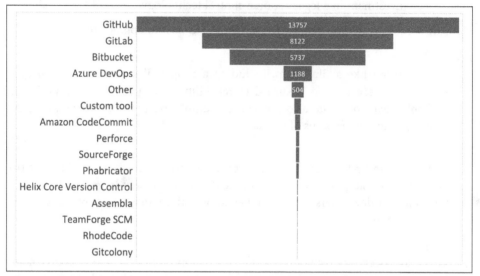

Figure 2-2. Data from the JetBrains "State of the Developer Ecosystem 2020" (https://oreil.ly/e9yJu) report on usage of version control services (source: JetBrains CC BY 4.0 (https://oreil.ly/W5qPM))

All of these version control services offer additional services on top of basic version control, including capabilities like these:

- Collaboration

Code reviews
> Having an efficient system for code reviews is important to maintain code integrity, quality, and standards.

Advanced pull request/merge features
> Many vendors implement advanced features on top of Git that help with multirepository and team workflows for more-efficient change request management.

Workflow automation
> Approvals in a large organization can be both fluid and complicated, so having automation of team and corporate workflows improves efficiency.

Team comments/discussions

Effective team interaction and discussions that can be tied to specific pull requests and code changes help improve communication within and around the team.

Online editing

In-browser IDEs allow for collaboration on source code from anywhere, on almost any device. GitHub even recently released Codespaces (*https://oreil.ly/1PKf4*) to give you a fully functional development environment hosted by GitHub.

- Compliance/security

Tracking

Being able to track the code history is a core feature of any version control system, but often additional compliance checks and reports are required.

Auditing changes

For control and regulatory purposes, auditing the changes to a codebase is often required, so having tools to automate this can be helpful.

Permissions management

Fine-grained roles and permissions allow for restricting access to sensitive files or codebases.

Bill of materials

For auditing purposes, a full list of all software modules and dependencies is often required, and can be generated off the source code.

Security vulnerability scanning

Many common security vulnerabilities can be uncovered by scanning the codebase and looking for common patterns that are used to exploit deployed applications. Using an automated vulnerability scanner on the source code can help identify vulnerabilities early in the development process.

- Integration

Issue tracking

By having tight integration with an issue tracker, you can tie specific change-sets to a software defect, making it easier to identify the version a bug is fixed in and trace any regressions.

CI/CD

Typically, a continuous integration server will be used to build the code checked into source control. A tight integration makes it easier to kick off builds, report back on success and test results, and automate promotion and/or deployment of successful builds.

Binary package repository
> Fetching dependencies from a binary repository and storing build results provides a central place to look for artifacts and to stage deployments.

Messaging integration
> Team collaboration is important to a successful development effort, and making it easy to discuss source files, check-ins, and other source control events simplifies communication with platforms like Slack, Microsoft Teams, Element, etc.

Clients (desktop/IDE)
> A lot of free clients and plug-ins for various IDEs allow you to access your source control system, including open source clients from GitHub, Bitbucket, and others.

When selecting a version control service, it is important to make sure that it fits into the development workflow of your team, integrates with other tools that you already use, and fits into your corporate security policies. Often companies have a version control system that is standardized across the organization, but there may be benefits to adopting a more modern version control system, especially if the corporate standard is not a DVCS like Git.

Making Your First Pull Request

To get a feel for how version control works, we are going to run through a simple exercise to create your first pull request to the official book repository on GitHub. A section of the readme file is dedicated to reader comments, so you can join the rest of the readers in showing your accomplishment in learning modern DevOps best practices!

This exercise doesn't require installing any software or using the command line, so it should be easy and straightforward to accomplish. Finishing this exercise is highly recommended so you understand the basic concepts of distributed version control that we go into more detail on later in the chapter.

To start, you need to navigate to the book repository (*https://oreil.ly/ApzqX*). For this exercise, you need to be logged in so you can create a pull request from the web user interface. If you don't already have a GitHub account, signing up and getting started is easy and free.

The DevOps Tools for Java Developers repository GitHub page is shown in Figure 2-3. The GitHub UI shows the root files and the contents of a special file called *README.md* by default. We are going to make edits to the readme file, which is coded in a visual text language called Markdown.

Since we have only read access to this repository, we are going to create a personal clone of the repository, known as a *fork*, that we can freely edit to make and propose the changes. Once you are logged in to GitHub, you can start this process by clicking the Fork button highlighted in the upper-right corner.

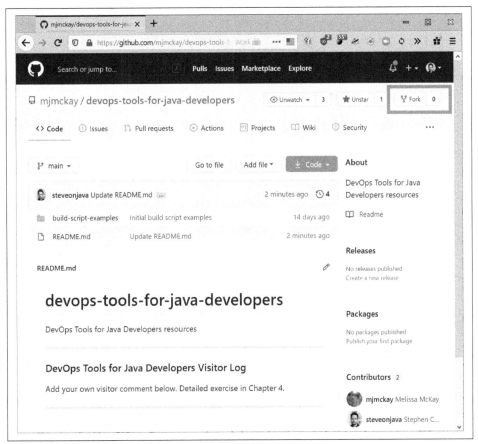

Figure 2-3. The GitHub repository containing this book's samples

Your new fork will get created under your personal account at GitHub. Once your fork is created, complete the following steps to open the web-based text editor:

1. Click the *README.md* file that you want to edit to see the details page.
2. Click the pencil icon on the details page to edit the file.

Once you click the pencil icon, you will see the web-based text editor shown in Figure 2-4. Scroll down to the section with the visitor log, and add your own personal comment to the end to let folks know you completed this exercise.

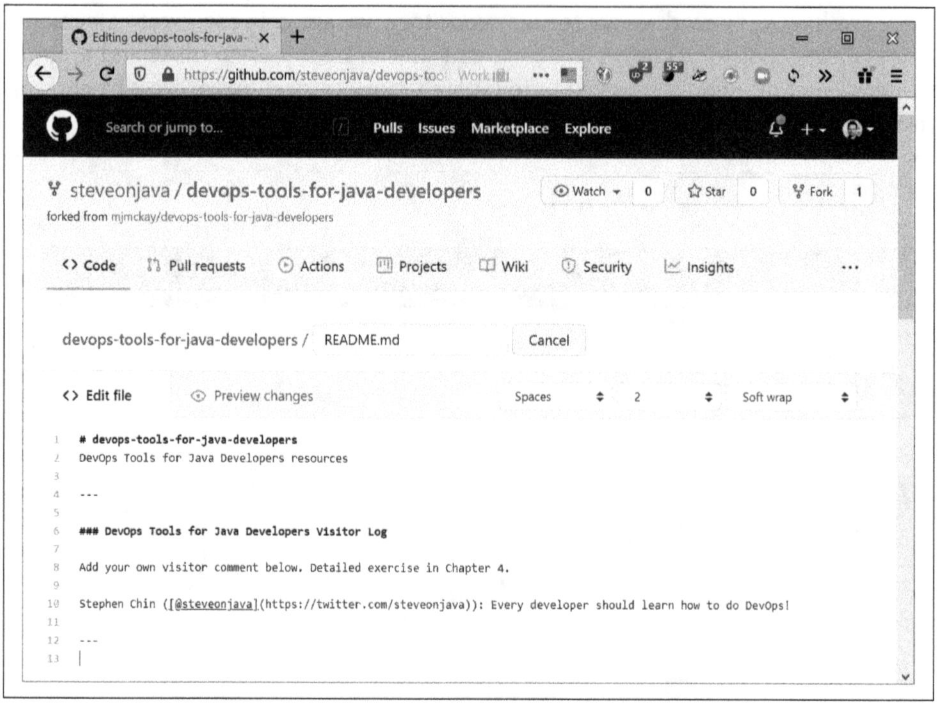

Figure 2-4. The GitHub web-based text editor for making quick changes to files

The recommended format for visitor log entries is as follows:

```
Name (@optional_twitter_handle): Visitor comment
```

If you want to be fancy on the Twitter handle and link to your profile, the Markdown syntax for Twitter links is as follows:

```
@twitterhandle
```

To check your changes, you can click the "Preview changes" tab, which will show the rendered output once it's inserted into the original readme.

When you are satisfied with your changes, scroll down to the code commit section shown in Figure 2-5. Enter a helpful description for the change to explain your updates. Then go ahead and click the "Commit changes" button.

For this example, we will simply commit to the main branch, which is the default. However, if you were working in a shared repository, you would commit your pull request to a feature branch that can be integrated separately.

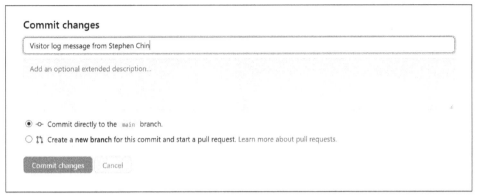

Figure 2-5. Using GitHub UI to commit changes to a repository you have write access to

After you have made a change to your forked repository, you can submit this as a pull request for the original project. This will notify the project maintainers (in this case, the book authors) that a proposed change is waiting for review and let them choose whether to integrate it into the original project.

To do this, go to the "Pull requests" tab in the GitHub user interface. This screen has a button to create a "New pull request" that will present you with a choice of the "base" and "head" repository to be merged, as shown in Figure 2-6.

In this case, since you have only one change, the default repositories should be selected correctly. Simply click the "Create pull request" button, and a new pull request against the original repository will be submitted for review.

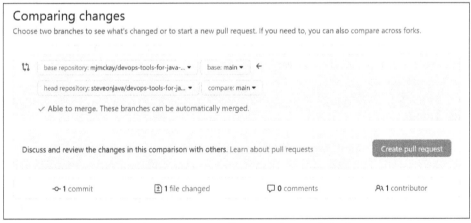

Figure 2-6. User interface for creating a pull request from a forked repository

This completes your submission of a pull request! Now it is up to the original repository owners to review and comment on, or accept/reject the pull request. While you don't have write access to the original repository to see what this looks like, Figure 2-7 shows you what will be presented to the repository owners.

Once the repository owners accept your pull request, your custom visitor log greeting will be added to the official book repository.

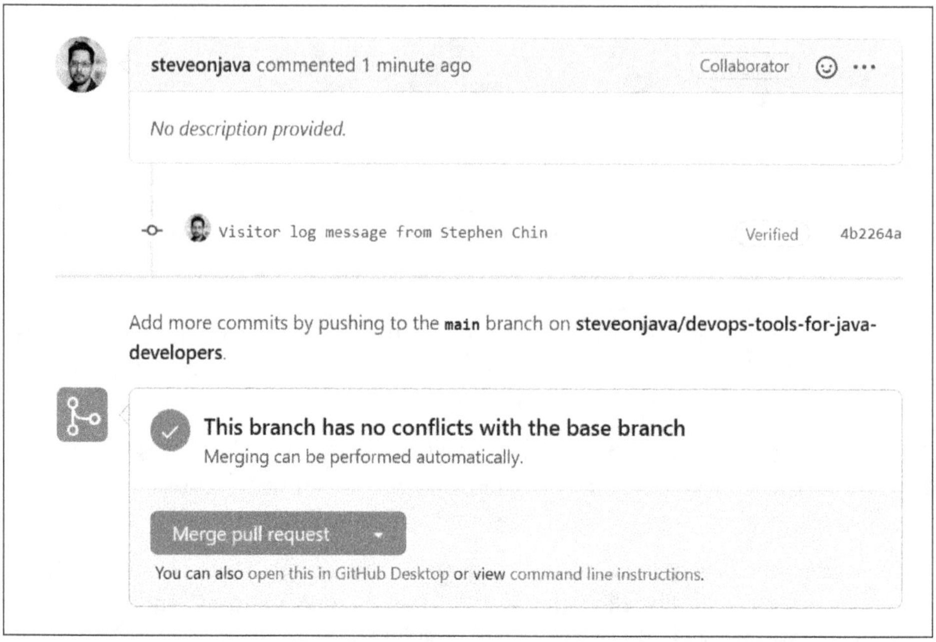

Figure 2-7. The repository owner user interface for merging in the resulting pull request

This workflow is an example of the fork and pull request collaboration model for handling project integration. We will talk a bit more about collaboration patterns and the sort of projects and team structures they are most suitable for in "Git Collaboration Patterns" on page 38.

Git Tools

In the previous section, we showed an entire web-based workflow for Git using the GitHub UI. However, other than code reviews and repository management, most developers spend the majority of their time in one of the client-based user interfaces to Git. The available client interfaces can be broadly split into the following categories:

Command line
An official Git command-line client may already be installed on your system or is easily added.

GUI clients
> The official Git distribution comes with a couple of open source tools that can be used to more easily browse your revision history or to structure a commit. Also, several third-party free and open source Git tools can make working with your repository easier.

Git IDE plug-ins
> Often you need to go no further than your favorite IDE to work with your distributed source control system. Many major IDEs have Git support packaged by default or offer a well-supported plug-in.

Git Command-Line Basics

The Git command line is the most powerful interface to your source control system, allowing for all local and remote options to manage your repository. You can check whether you have the Git command line installed by typing the following on the console:

```
git --version
```

If you have Git installed, the command will return the operating system and version that you are using, similar to this:

```
git version 2.26.2.windows.1
```

However, if you don't have Git installed, here's the easiest way to get it on various platforms:

- Linux distributions:
  - *Debian-based:* `sudo apt install git-all`
  - *RPM-based:* `sudo dnf install git-all`
- macOS
  - Running `git` on macOS 10.9 or later will ask you to install it.
  - Another easy option is to install GitHub Desktop (*https://oreil.ly/0x2A3*), which installs and configures the command-line tools.
- Windows
  - The easiest way is to simply install GitHub Desktop, which installs the command-line tools as well.
  - Another option is Git for Windows (*https://oreil.ly/BioSg*).

Regardless of which approach you use to install Git, you will end up with the same great command-line tools, which are well supported across all desktop platforms.

To start with, it is helpful to understand the basic Git commands. Figure 2-8 shows a typical repository hierarchy with one central repository and three clients who have cloned it locally. Notice that every client has a full copy of the repository as well as a working copy where they can make changes.

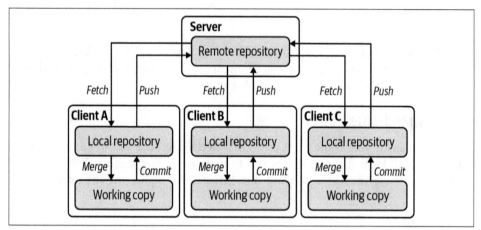

Figure 2-8. A typical central server pattern for distributed version control collaboration

Some of the Git commands that allow you to move data between repositories as well as the working copy are shown. Now let's go through some of the most common commands that are used to manage your repository and collaborate in Git.

- Repository management:

  clone
  > Makes a connected copy of another local or remote repository on the local filesystem. For those coming from a concurrent version control system like CVS or Subversion, this command serves a similar purpose to checkout, but is semantically different in that it creates a full copy of the remote repository. All of the clients in Figure 2-8 would have cloned the central server to begin.

  init
  > Creates a new, empty repository. However, most of the time you will start by cloning an existing repository.

- Changeset management:

  add
  > Adds file revisions to version control, which can be either a new file or modifications to an existing file. This is different from the add command in CVS or Subversion in that it does not *track* the file and needs to be called

every time the file changes. Make sure to call add on all new and modified files before committing.

mv

Renames or moves a file/directory, while also updating the version control record for the next commit. It is similar in use to the mv command in Unix and should be used instead of filesystem commands to keep version control history intact.

restore

Allows you to restore files from the Git index if they are deleted or erroneously modified.

rm

Removes a file or directory, while also updating the version control record for the next commit. It is similar in use to the rm command in Unix and should be used instead of filesystem commands to keep version control history intact.

- History control:

branch

With no arguments, lists all branches in the local repository. It can also be used to create a new branch or delete branches.

commit

Saves changes in the working copy to the local repository. Before running commit, make sure to register all your file changes by calling add, mv, and rm on files that have been added, modified, renamed, or moved. You also need to specify a commit message that can be done on the command line with the -m option; or if omitted, a text editor (such as vi) will be spawned to allow you to enter a message.

merge

Joins changes from the named commits into the current branch. If the merged history is already a descendant of the current branch, a "fast-forward" is used to combine the history sequentially. Otherwise, a merge is created that combines the history; the user is prompted to resolve any conflicts. This command is also used by git pull to integrate changes from the remote repository.

rebase

Replays the commits from your current branch on the upstream branch. This is different from merge in that the result will be a linear history rather than a merge commit, which can make the revision history easier to follow.

The disadvantage is that rebase creates entirely new commits when it moves the history, so if the current branch contains changes that have previously been pushed, you are rewriting history that other clients may depend upon.

reset
: Reverts the HEAD to a previous state, and has several practical uses such as reverting an add or undoing a commit. However, if those changes have been pushed remotely, this can cause problems with the upstream repository. Use with care!

switch
: Switches between branches for the working copy. If you have changes in the working copy, this can result in a three-way merge, so it is often better to commit or stash your changes first. With -c, this command will create a branch and immediately switch to it.

tag
: Allows you to create a tag on a specific commit that is signed by PGP. This uses the default email address's PGP key. Since tags are cryptographically signed and unique, they should not be reused or changed once pushed. Additional options on this command allow for deleting, verifying, and listing tags.

log
: Shows the commit logs in a textual format. It can be used for a quick view of recent changes, and supports advanced options for the history subset shown and formatting of the output. Later in this chapter, we also show how to visually browse the history by using tools like gitk.

- Collaboration:

fetch
: Pulls the history from a remote repository into the local repository, but makes no attempt to merge it with local commits. This is a safe operation that can be performed at any time and repeatedly without causing merge conflicts or affecting the working copy.

pull
: Equivalent to a git fetch followed by git merge FETCH_HEAD. It is convenient for the common workflow of grabbing the latest changes from a remote repository and integrating it with your working copy. However, if you have local changes, pull can cause merge conflicts that you will be forced to resolve. For this reason, it is often safer to fetch first and then decide if a simple merge will suffice.

push

Sends changes to the upstream remote repository from the local repository. Use this after a `commit` to push your changes to the upstream repository so other developers can see your changes.

Now that you have a basic understanding of the Git commands, let's put this knowledge into practice.

Git Command-Line Tutorial

To demonstrate how to use these commands, we will go through a simple example to create a new local repository from scratch. For this exercise, we are assuming you are on a system with a Bash-like command shell. This is the default on most Linux distributions as well as macOS. If you are on Windows, you can do this via Windows PowerShell, which has sufficient aliases to emulate Bash for basic commands.

If this is your first time using Git, it is a good idea to put in your name and email, which will be associated with all of your version control operations. You can do this with the following commands:

```
git config --global user.name "Put Your Name Here"
```

```
git config --global user.email "your@email.address"
```

After configuring your personal information, go to a suitable directory to create your working project. First, create the project folder and initialize the repository:

```
mkdir tutorial
```

```
cd tutorial
```

```
git init
```

This creates the repository and initializes it so you can start tracking revisions of files. Let's create a new file that we can add to revision control:

```
echo "This is a sample file" > sample.txt
```

To add this file to revision control, use the `git add` command as follows:

```
git add sample.txt
```

And you can add this file to version control by using the `git commit` command:

```
git commit sample.txt -m "First git commit!"
```

Congratulations on making your first command-line commit using Git! You can double-check to make sure that your file is being tracked in revision control by using the `git log` command, which should return output similar to the following:

```
commit 0da1bd4423503bba5ebf77db7675c1eb5def3960 (HEAD -> master)
Author: Stephen Chin <steveonjava@gmail.com>
```

```
Date:    Sat Mar 12 04:19:08 2022 -0700

    First git commit!
```

From this, you can see some of the details that Git stores in the repository, including branch information (the default branch is `master`), and revisions by globally unique identifiers (GUIDs). Though you can do a lot more from the command line, it is often easier to use a Git client built for your workflow or IDE integration that is designed for a developer workflow. The next couple of sections talk about these client options.

Git Clients

Several free and open source clients that you can use to work with Git repos more easily are optimized for various different workflows. Most clients do not try to do everything, but specialize in visualizations and functionality for specific workflows.

The default Git installation comes with a couple of handy visual tools that make committing and viewing history easier. These tools are written in Tcl/Tk, are cross-platform, and are easily launched from the command line to supplement the Git command-line interface (CLI).

The first tool, `gitk`, provides an alternative to the command line for navigating, viewing, and searching the Git history of your local repository. The `gitk` user interface displaying the history for the ScalaFX open source project is shown in Figure 2-9.

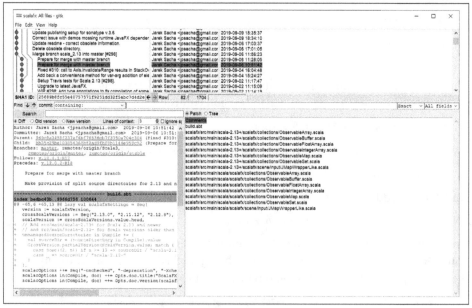

Figure 2-9. The bundled Git history viewer application

The top pane of `gitk` displays the revision history with branching information drawn visually, which can be useful for deciphering complicated branch history. Below this are search filters that can be used to find commits containing specific text. Finally, for the selected changeset, you can see the changed files and a textual diff of the changes, which is also searchable.

The other tool that comes bundled with Git is `git-gui`. Unlike `gitk`, which only shows information about the repository history, `git-gui` allows you to modify the repository by executing many of the Git commands including `commit`, `push`, `branch`, `merge`, and others.

Figure 2-10 shows the `git-gui` user interface for editing the source code repository for this book. On the left side, all of the changes to the working copy are shown, with the unstaged changes on top and the files that will be included in the next commit on the bottom. The details for the selected file are shown on the right side with the full file contents for new files, or a diff for modified files. At the bottom right, buttons are provided for common operations like Rescan, Sign Off, Commit, and Push. Further commands are available in the menu for advanced operations like branching, merging, and remote repository management.

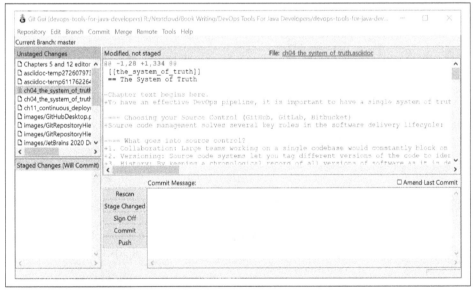

Figure 2-10. The bundled Git collaboration application

`git-gui` is an example of a workflow-driven user interface for Git. It doesn't expose the full set of functionality available on the command line, but is convenient for the commonly used Git workflows.

Another example of a workflow-driven user interface is *GitHub Desktop*. This is the most popular third-party GitHub user interface, and as mentioned earlier, also conveniently comes bundled with the command-line tools so you can use it as an installer for the Git CLI and aforementioned bundled GUIs.

GitHub Desktop is similar to `git-gui`, but is optimized for integration with GitHub's service, and the user interface is designed to make it easy to follow workflows similar to GitHub Flow. The GitHub Desktop user interface editing the source repository for another great book, *The Definitive Guide to Modern Java Clients with JavaFX*, is shown in Figure 2-11.

Figure 2-11. GitHub's open source desktop client

In addition to the same sort of capabilities as `git-gui` to view changes, commit revisions, and pull/push code, GitHub Desktop has a bunch of advanced features that make managing your code much easier:

- Commit attribution
- Syntax highlighted diffs
- Image diff support

- Editor and shell integration
- CI status of pull requests

GitHub Desktop can be used with any Git repo, but has features tailored specifically for use with GitHub-hosted repositories. Here are some other popular Git tools:

Sourcetree (https://www.sourcetreeapp.com)
A free, but proprietary, Git client made by Atlassian. It is a good alternative to GitHub Desktop and has only a slight bias toward Atlassian's Git service, Bitbucket.

GitKraken Client (https://www.gitkraken.com)
A commercial and featureful Git client. It is free for open source developers, but paid for commercial use.

TortoiseGit (https://tortoisegit.org)
A free, GNU Public License (GPL), Git client based on TortoiseSVN. The only downside is that it is Windows only.

Others
A full list of Git GUI clients is maintained on the Git website (*https://oreil.ly/JPi0J*).

Git desktop clients are a great addition to the arsenal of available source control management tools you have available. However, the most useful Git interface may already be at your fingertips, right inside your IDE.

Git IDE Integration

Many integrated development environments (IDEs) include Git support either as a standard feature, or as a well-supported plug-in. Chances are that you need to go no further than your favorite IDE to do basic version control operations like adding, moving, and removing files, committing code, and pushing your changes to an upstream repository.

One of the most popular Java IDEs is JetBrains IntelliJ IDEA. It has a Community Edition that is open source as well as a commercial version with additional features for enterprise developers. The IntelliJ Git support is full featured, with the ability to sync changes from a remote repository, track and commit changes performed in the IDE, and integrate upstream changes. The integrated Commit tab for a Git changeset is shown in Figure 2-12.

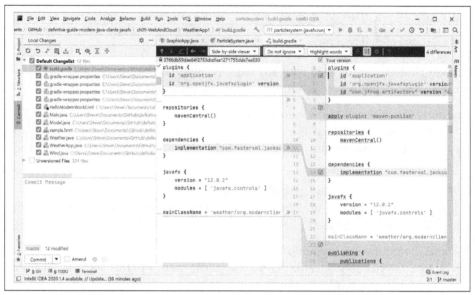

Figure 2-12. IntelliJ Commit tab for managing working copy changes

IntelliJ offers a rich set of features that you can use to customize the Git behavior to your team workflow. For example, if your team prefers a git-flow or GitHub Flow workflow, you can choose to merge on update (more details on Git workflows in the next section). However, if your team wants to keep a linear history as prescribed in OneFlow, you can choose to rebase on update instead. IntelliJ also supports the native credential provider as well as the open source KeePass password manager.

Another IDE that offers great Git support is Eclipse, a fully open source IDE that has strong community support and is run by the Eclipse Foundation. The Eclipse Git support is provided by the EGit project, which is based on JGit, a pure Java implementation of the Git version control system.

Because of the tight integration with the embedded Java implementation of Git, Eclipse has the most full-featured Git support. From the Eclipse user interface, you can accomplish almost everything that you would normally have to do from the command line, including rebasing, cherry-picking, tagging, patching, and more. The rich set of features is obvious from the Preferences dialog, shown in Figure 2-13. This dialog has 12 configuration pages detailing how the Git integration works and is supported by a user guide that is almost a book itself at 161 pages.

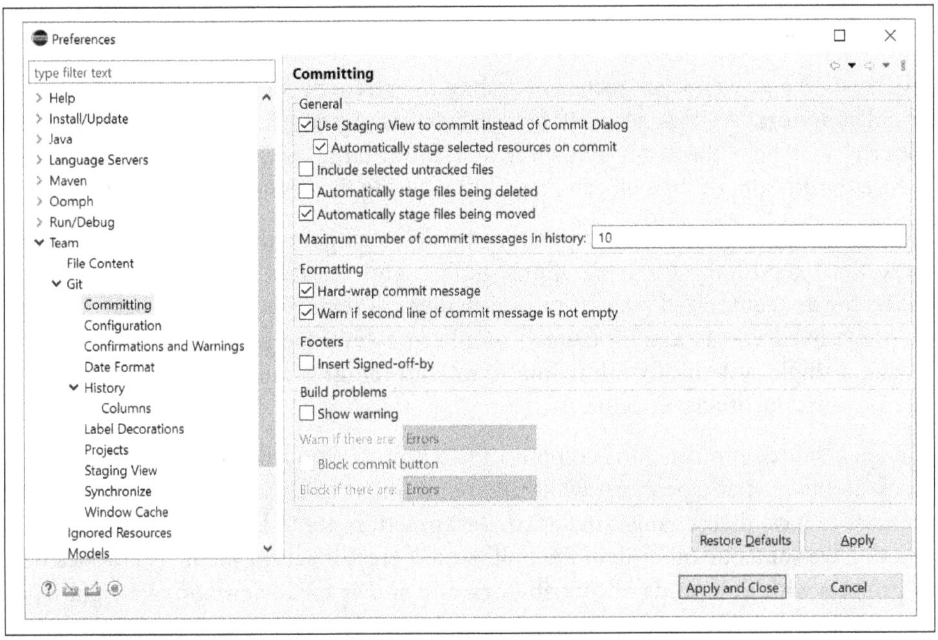

Figure 2-13. Eclipse Preferences dialog for Git configuration

Other Java IDEs that you can expect great Git support from include the following:

NetBeans
Offers a Git plug-in that fully supports workflow from the IDE.

Visual Studio Code
Supports Git along with other version control systems out of the box.

BlueJ
A popular learning IDE built by King's College London also supports Git in its team workflows.

Oracle JDeveloper
While it doesn't support complicated workflows, JDeveloper does have basic support for cloning, committing, and pushing to Git repos.

So far in this chapter, you have added a whole set of new command-line, desktop, and integrated tools to your arsenal to work with Git repos. This range of community- and industry-supported tools means that no matter your operating system, project workflow, or even team preference, you will find full tooling support to be successful with your source control management. The next section goes into more detail on collaboration patterns that are well supported by the full range of Git tools.

Git Collaboration Patterns

DVCSs have a proven track record of scaling to extremely large teams with hundreds of collaborators. At this scale, it is necessary to agree on uniform collaboration patterns that help the team avoid rework, avoid large and unwieldy merges, and reduce the amount of time blocked on administering the version control history.

Most projects follow a central repository model: a single repository is designated as the official repository for integrations, builds, and releases. Even though a DVCS allows for noncentralized peer-to-peer exchanges of revisions, these are best reserved for short-lived efforts among a small number of developers. For any large project, having a single system of truth is important and requires one repository that everyone agrees is the official codeline.

For open source projects, it is common for a limited set of developers to have write access to the central repository, while other committers *fork* the project and issue pull requests to have their changes included. Best practices are to have small pull requests, and to have someone other than the pull request creator accept them. This scales well to projects with thousands of contributors, and allows for review and oversight from a core team when the codebase is not well understood.

However, for most corporate projects, a shared repository with a single master branch is preferred. The same workflow with pull requests can be used to keep a central or release branch clean, but this simplifies the contribution process and encourages more frequent integration, which reduces the size and difficulty of merging in changes. For teams on tight deadlines or following an Agile process with short iterations, this also reduces the risk of last-minute integration failures.

The last best practice employed by most teams is to use branches to work on features, which then get integrated back into the main codeline. Git makes it inexpensive to create short-lived branches, so it is common to create and merge back in a branch for work that takes only a couple of hours. The risk with creating long-lived feature branches is that if they diverge too much from the main trunk of code development, they can become difficult to integrate back in.

Following these general best practices for distributed version control, several collaboration models have emerged. They share a lot of commonalities and primarily diverge in their approach to branching, history management, and integration speed.

git-flow

Git-flow is one of the earliest Git workflows and was inspired by a blog post (*https://oreil.ly/v6aI4*) from Vincent Driessen. It laid the groundwork for later Git collaboration workflows like GitHub Flow; however, git-flow is a more complicated workflow than most projects require and can add additional branch management and integration work.

Key attributes include the following:

Development branches
Branch per feature

Merge strategy
No fast-forward merges

Rebasing history
No rebasing

Release strategy
Separate release branch

In git-flow, there are two long-lived branches: one for development integration, called *develop*, and another for final releases, called *master*. Developers are expected to do all of their coding in feature branches that are named according to the feature they are working on and integrate that with the develop branch once complete. When the develop branch has the features necessary for a release, a new release branch is created that is used to stabilize the codebase with patches and bugfixes.

Once the release branch has stabilized and is ready for release, it is integrated into the master branch and given a release tag. Once on the master, only hotfixes are applied, which are small changes managed on a dedicated branch. These hotfixes also need to be applied back to the develop branch and any other concurrent releases that need the same fix. Figure 2-14 shows a sample diagram for git-flow.

Because of the design decisions on git-flow, it tends to create a complicated merge history. By not taking advantage of fast-forward merges or rebasing, every integration becomes a commit, and the number of concurrent branches can be hard to follow even with visual tools. Also, the complicated rules and branch strategy require team training and are difficult to enforce with tools, often requiring check-ins and integration to be done from the command-line interface.

 Git-flow is best applied to explicitly versioned projects that have multiple releases needing to be maintained in parallel. Usually, this is not the case for web applications, which have only one *latest* version and can be managed with a single release branch.

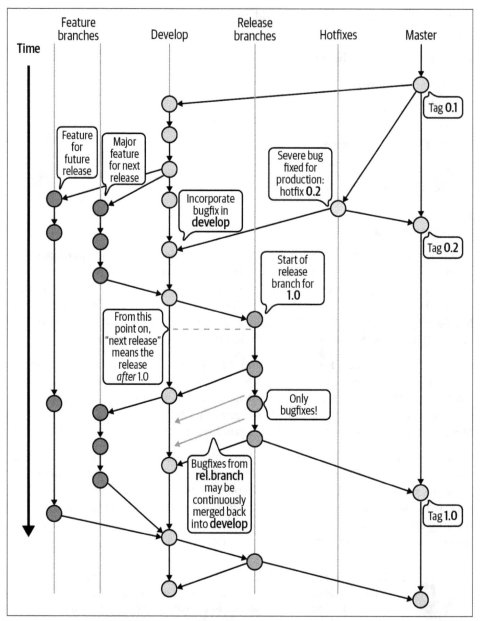

Figure 2-14. Managing branches and integration with git-flow (source: Vincent Driessen, Creative Commons BY-SA) (https://oreil.ly/baH6Z)

If your project is in the sweet spot where git-flow excels, it is a very well-thought-out collaboration model. Otherwise, you may find that a simpler collaboration model will suffice.

GitHub Flow

GitHub Flow is a simplified Git workflow launched in response to the complexity of git-flow by Scott Chacon in another prominent blog (*https://oreil.ly/l7gTx*). GitHub Flow or a close variant has been adopted by most development teams, since it is easier to implement in practice, handles the common case for continuous released web development, and is well supported by tools.

Key attributes include the following:

Development branches
Branch per feature

Merge strategy
No fast-forward merges

Rebasing history
No rebasing

Release strategy
No separate release branches

GitHub Flow takes a simple approach to branch management, using *master* as the main codeline as well as the release branch. Developers do all of their work on short-lived feature branches and integrate them back into the master as soon as their code passes tests and code reviews.

 In general, GitHub Flow makes good use of available tooling by having a straightforward workflow with a simple branching strategy and no use of complicated arguments to enable fast-forward merges or replace merges with rebasing. Developers who are not familiar with the team process or not as familiar with the command-line Git interface therefore find GitHub Flow easy to use.

The GitHub Flow collaboration model works well for server-side and cloud-deployed applications, where the only meaningful version is the latest release. In fact, GitHub Flow recommends that teams continuously deploy to production to avoid feature stacking, in which a single release build has multiple features that increase complexity and make it harder to determine the breaking change. However, for more complicated workflows with multiple concurrent releases, GitHub Flow needs to be modified to accommodate.

GitLab Flow

GitLab Flow is basically an extension of GitHub Flow, as documented on GitLab's website (*https://oreil.ly/P1LzH*). It takes the same core design principles about using a master as a single long-lived branch and doing the majority of development on feature branches. However, it adds a few extensions to support release branches and history cleanup that many teams have adopted as best practices.

Key attributes include the following:

Development branches
Branch per feature

Merge strategy
Open-ended

Rebasing history
Optional

Release strategy
Separate release branches

The key difference between GitHub Flow and GitLab Flow is the addition of release branches. This is recognition that most teams are not practicing continuous deployment at the level GitHub does. Having release branches allows stabilization of code before it gets pushed into production; however, GitLab Flow recommends making patches to the master and then cherry-picking them for release rather than having an extra hotfix branch like git-flow.

The other significant difference is the willingness to edit history using `rebase` and `squash`. By cleaning up the history before committing to master, it is easier to retroactively go back and read the history to discover when key changes or bugs were introduced. However, this involves rewriting the local history and can be dangerous when that history has already been pushed to the central repository.

 GitLab Flow is a modern take on the GitHub Flow philosophy to collaboration workflow, but ultimately your team has to decide on the features and branch strategy based on your project's needs.

OneFlow

OneFlow, another collaboration workflow based on git-flow, was proposed by Adam Ruka and introduced in a detailed blog (*https://oreil.ly/euJ37*). OneFlow makes the same adaptation as GitHub/GitLab Flow in squashing the separate develop branch in favor of feature branches and direct integration on the main branch. However, it keeps the release and hotfix branches that are used in git-flow.

Key attributes include the following:

Development branches
    Branch per feature

Merge strategy
    No fast-forward merges without rebase

Rebasing history
    Rebasing recommended

Release strategy
    Separate release branches

The other big deviation in OneFlow is that it heavily favors modifying history to keep the Git revision history readable. It offers three merge strategies that have varying levels of revision cleanliness and rollback friendliness:

Rebase
    This makes the merge history mostly linear and easy to follow. It has the usual caveat that changesets pushed to the central server should not be rebased and makes it more difficult to roll back changes since they are not captured in a single commit.

merge -no-ff
    This is the same strategy used in git-flow and has the disadvantage that the merge history is largely nonsequential and difficult to follow.

rebase + merge -no-ff
    This is a rebase workaround that tacks on an extra merge integration at the end so it can be rolled back as a unit even though it is still mostly sequential.

 OneFlow is a thoughtful approach to a Git collaboration workflow that is created from the experience of developers on large enterprise projects. It can be seen as a modern variant on git-flow that should serve the needs of projects of any size.

Trunk-Based Development

All of the aforementioned approaches are variants of the feature branch development model; all active development is done on branches that get merged into either the master or a dedicated development branch. They take advantage of the great support Git has for branch management, but if features are not granular enough, they suffer from the typical integration problems that have plagued teams for decades. The longer the feature branch is in active development, the higher the likelihood for merge conflicts with other features and maintenance going on in the master branch (or trunk).

Trunk-based development solves this problem by recommending that all development happen on the main branch with very short integrations that occur anytime that tests are passing, but not necessarily waiting for a full feature to be completed.

Key attributes include the following:

Development branches
    Optional, but no long-lived branches

Merge strategy
    Only if using development branches

Rebasing history
    Rebasing recommended

Release strategy
    Separate release branches

Paul Hammant, a strong advocate for trunk-based development, has set up a full website (*https://oreil.ly/HFo0J*) and written a book on the topic. While this is not a new approach to collaboration on source control management systems, it is a proven approach to Agile development in large teams and works equally well on classic central SCMs like CVS and Subversion, and modern DVCSs like Git.

Summary

Good source control systems and practices lay the foundation for a solid DevOps approach to building, releasing, and deploying code quickly. In this chapter, we discussed the history of source control systems and explained why the world has moved to embrace distributed version control.

This consolidation has built a rich ecosystem of source control servers, developer tools, and commercial integrations. Finally, through the adoption of distributed version control by DevOps thought leaders, best practices and collaboration workflows have been established that you can follow to help make your team successful with adopting a modern SCM.

In the next few chapters, we will drill into systems that connect to your source control management system, including continuous integration, package management, and security scanning, that allow you to rapidly deploy to traditional or cloud native environments. You are on the way to building a comprehensive DevOps platform that will support whatever workflow you need to meet your quality and deployment objectives.

## CHAPTER 3

An Introduction to Containers

Melissa McKay

Any fool can know. The point is to understand.
—Albert Einstein

If you know the why, you can live any how.
—Friedrich Nietzsche

At the time of this writing, the use of containers in production and other environments is growing exponentially, and best practices around containerizing applications are still being discussed and defined. As we home in on efficiency improvements and consider specific use cases, techniques and patterns have evolved that come highly recommended by the blogosphere and professional practitioners through experience. And as expected, a fair share of patterns and common uses have evolved, as well as antipatterns that I hope this chapter will help you recognize and avoid.

My own trial-and-error introduction to containers felt like stirring up a hornet's nest (oh, the stings!). I was undeniably unprepared. Containerization on the surface is deceptively simple. Knowing what I know now about how to develop and deploy with containers, especially within the Java ecosystem, I hope to pass this knowledge on in a way that will help prevent similar pain for you. This chapter outlines the essential concepts you will need to successfully containerize your applications and discusses *why* you would even want to do such a thing.

Chapter 4 discusses the bigger picture of microservices, but here we will start with learning about one of the basic building blocks of microservice deployments that you will no doubt encounter if you haven't already: the container. Note that the concept of microservices, an architectural concern, *does not imply the use of containers*; rather, it's the concern of *deploying* these services, especially in a cloud native environment, that usually begins the conversation around containerization.

Let's start with considering *why* we would use a container. The best way to do that is to back up and get some context on how we got here to begin with. Patience is a virtue. If you persevere, going through this history lesson will also naturally lead you to a clearer understanding of *what* a container actually is.

Understanding the Problem

I'm certain I'm not alone in experiencing the company of an "elephant in the room." Despite the looming frame, deafening noise, and potential for dangerous consequences when ignored, this elephant-sized subject is just allowed to roam, unchallenged. I've witnessed it. I'm guilty of it. I've even had the distinct pleasure of *being* said elephant.

In the context of containerization, I'm going to make the argument that we need to address *two* elephants in the room—in the form of two questions: *What is a container?* and *Why would we use a container?* Those sound simple enough. How could anyone miss these basic starting points?

Perhaps it's because the microservice movement tends to lead into discussions about deploying containers more now than ever, and we're suffering from the fear of missing out. Maybe it's because a container implementation is expected by default with the exceedingly popular Kubernetes ride, and "our K8s cluster" is the cool new phrase to include in our conversations. It might even just be that we are suffering such an onslaught of new technologies and tools in the DevOps ecosystem that, as a developer (a Java developer, no less), if we stop to ask questions, we fear getting left behind. Whatever the reasons may be, before we can even get into the details of how to build and use containers, these *what* and *why* questions must be addressed.

I'm deeply grateful for the incredible colleagues and mentors I've had the privilege of working with over the years. I frequently recall, from the formative years of my career, sage advice that has become a mantra of mine. It's simple; always begin and then proceed working on any project with a constant, repeating question in mind: *What is the problem you are trying to solve?* The success of your solution will be measured by how well it meets this requirement—that it indeed solves the original problem.

Carefully consider whether you are solving the right problem to begin with. Be especially vigilant to reject problem statements that are actually implementation instructions in disguise, like this one: *Improve the performance of your application by breaking it into containerized microservices.* You will be better served by a problem statement like this: *To decrease the time it takes for customers to complete their objectives, improve the performance of the application by 5%.* Note that the latter statement includes a tangible metric to gauge success and is not restricted to a microservices implementation.

This same principle applies to your day-to-day choices in what tools you use, what frameworks and languages you choose to code within, how you choose to design a system, and even how you package and deploy your software to production. What problem are you solving with the choices you've made? And how do you know if you've chosen the best tool for the job? One way is to understand the problem the particular tool under review is intended to solve. And the best way to do that is to look at its history. This practice should be in place for every tool you pick up to use. I guarantee that you will make better decisions knowing its history, and you will benefit from skirting known pitfalls or, at the very least, have some justification for accepting any disadvantages and moving forward anyway.

My plan is not to completely bore you with historical details, but you should know some basic information and important milestones before jumping into containerizing every bit of code put in front of you. By understanding more about the original problem and the solutions that have come out of it, you'll be able to intelligently explain why you are choosing to deploy with containers.

I don't want to go all the way back to the Big Bang, but I'm going to go back more than 50 years, mostly to make the point that virtualization and containerization are not new. In fact, this concept has been worked on and improved for more than half a century. I've picked out some points to highlight that will bring us up to speed quickly. This is not intended to be a deep technical manual on any of the topics mentioned—rather, just enough material to wrap your mind around the progress that has been made over time and how we've ended up where we are today.

Let's begin.

The History of Containers

In the 1960s and '70s, computing resources were in general exceptionally limited and expensive (by today's standards). It took a long time for processes to complete (again, by today's standards), and it was common for a computer to be dedicated for a long period of time to a single task for a single user. Efforts were begun to improve the sharing of compute resources and address the bottlenecks and inefficiency brought by these limitations. But just being able to share resources was not enough. A need arose for a method of sharing resources without getting in each other's way or having one person inadvertently cause an entire system to crash for everyone. Both hardware and software that advanced virtualization technology started to trickle in. One development in software is chroot, which is where we'll begin.

In 1979, during the development of the seventh edition of Unix, chroot was developed and then in 1982 was added to the Berkeley Software Distribution (BSD). This system command changed the apparent root directory for a process and its children, which resulted in a limited view of the filesystem in order to provide an environment for testing a different distribution, for example. Although a step in the right direction, chroot was just a start on the path to providing the isolation of applications required from us today. In 2000, FreeBSD expanded the concept and introduced the more sophisticated jail command and utility in FreeBSD 4.0. Its features (improved in the later 5.1 and 7.2 releases) help further isolate filesystems, users, and networks, and include the ability to assign an IP address to each jail.

In 2004, Solaris containers and zones brought us ahead even further by giving an application full user, process, and filesystem space and access to system hardware. Google jumped in with its *process containers* in 2006, later renamed *cgroups*, which centered around isolating and limiting the resource usage of a process. In 2008, *cgroups* were merged into the Linux kernel, which, along with Linux namespaces, led to IBM's development of Linux Containers (LXC).

Now things get even more interesting. Docker became open source in 2013. That same year, Google offered its Let Me Contain That For You (lmctfy) open source project, which gave applications the ability to create and manage their own subcontainers. And from there, we saw the use of containers explode—Docker containers specifically. Initially, Docker used LXC as its default execution environment, but in 2014 Docker chose to swap out its use of the LXC toolset for launching containers with *libcontainer*, a native solution written in Go. Soon after, the lmctfy project ceased active development with the intention of joining forces and migrating the core concepts to the libcontainer project.

A lot more happened during this period of time. I'm intentionally skipping over additional details about other projects, organizations, and specifications that were developed because I want to get to a specific event in 2015. This event is especially important because it will give you some insight into some of the activity and motivations behind shifts in the market, especially concerning Docker.

On June 22, 2015, the establishment of the Open Container Initiative (OCI) (*https://oreil.ly/Vsr6U*) was announced. This is an organization under the Linux Foundation (*https://oreil.ly/J5ioU*) with the goal of creating open standards for container runtimes and image specification. Docker is a heavy contributor, but Docker's announcement of this new organization listed participants including Apcera, Amazon Web Services (AWS), Cisco, CoreOS, EMC, Fujitsu, Google, Goldman Sachs, HP, Huawei Technologies, IBM, Intel, Joyent, Pivotal Software, the Linux Foundation, Mesosphere, Microsoft, Rancher Labs, Red Hat, and VMware. Clearly, the development of containers and the ecosystem around them has reached a significant point to glean this much attention, and has evolved to where establishing some common ground will be beneficial to all parties involved.

When the formation of the OCI was announced, Docker also announced its intention to donate its base container format and runtime, runC. In quick succession, *runC* became the reference implementation for the OCI Runtime Specification (*https://oreil.ly/lLia7*), and the Docker v2 Schema 2 image format, donated in April 2016, became the basis for the OCI Image Format Specification (*https://oreil.ly/mmPu4*). Version 1.0 of these specifications (*https://oreil.ly/y6QwF*) were both released in July 2017.

 runC is a repackage of libcontainer, which meets the requirements of the OCI runtime specification. In fact, as of this writing, the source code for runC (*https://oreil.ly/hbUaP*) contains a directory called *libcontainer*.

In tandem with developments in the container ecosystem, orchestration of these systems was also under rapid development. On July 21, 2015, one month after the OCI was established, Google released Kubernetes v1.0. Along with this release, the Cloud Native Computing Foundation (CNCF) (*https://www.cncf.io*) was established in partnership with Google and the Linux Foundation. Another important step taken by Google and released with v1.5 of Kubernetes in December 2016 was the development of the Container Runtime Interface (CRI), which created the level of abstraction needed to allow the Kubernetes machine daemon, *kubelet*, to support alternative low-level container runtimes. In March 2017, Docker, also a member of the CNCF, contributed its CRI-compatible runtime *containerd* that it had developed in order to integrate runC into Docker v1.11.

In February 2021, Docker donated yet another reference implementation to the CNCF. This contribution was centered around the distribution of images (pushing and pulling container images). Three months later, in May 2021, the OCI released version 1.0 of the OCI Distribution Spec (*https://oreil.ly/JfGvb*) based on the Docker Registry HTTP API V2 protocol.

Today, the use of containers and orchestration systems like Kubernetes is typical fare for cloud native deployments. Containers are an important factor in keeping deployments flexible among a variety of hosts and play a huge role in scaling distributed applications. Cloud providers including AWS, Google Cloud, Microsoft Azure, and others are continuously bulking up their offerings using shared infrastructure and pay-per-use storage.

Congratulations for getting through that bit of history! In a few paragraphs, we spanned more than 50 years of development and advancement. You were introduced to a lot of the projects that have evolved into our solutions as well as some of the common terms used in the context of containers and their deployment. You've also learned how much Docker has contributed to the state of containers today—which makes this a perfect time to get a solid understanding of the container ecosystem, the technical details behind containers, and the implementation components that come into play.

But wait! Before we dive into that, let's discuss that second elephant. You learned a lot about *what* happened, but *why* did the industry shift in this way?

Why Containers?

Knowing what containers are and how to describe them is not enough. To talk intelligently about them, you should have some understanding of *why* they are used. What are the advantages of using containers? Some of this may seem obvious, given what you now know about containers and their history, but it's worth going in depth before jumping into the fray. Project changes and any introduction of a new tech stack should always be intentional with a thoughtful cost-benefit analysis. Following the crowd is not a good enough reason in and of itself.

Your first question is likely along the lines of *why are containers a developer's concern?* —a valid question, indeed. If containers are simply a method of deployment, it seems that this should be in the wheelhouse of operations. It is here that we approach a blurry line between development and operations, an argument for a DevOps mindset. Packaging your app into a container involves more thought and foresight from the developer's perspective than you may initially think. After you've learned some of the best practices and some of the problems encountered by others' experience, you will find yourself considering the packaging *while* developing your application. Certain aspects of the process will drive the decisions you make about how your application or service uses memory, how it uses the filesystem, how you plug in observability hooks, how you allow for different configurations, and how you communicate with other services (such as databases). These are just a few examples. Ultimately, it will depend on how your team is organized, but on a DevOps team, I would expect that as a developer, knowing how to build and maintain container images and to understand the container environment will be valuable.

I recently had the opportunity to be part of a panel discussion for the Cloud and DevOps international track at The Developer's Conference titled "Cloud Efficiency and Simplicity: What Will the Future Bring?" As part of this discussion, we talked about the current state of technologies available and where we would expect more simplification. I introduced the following question/analogy to the discussion: *How many of us would be driving cars today if we were expected to build our own?* We are still in very early stages of so many technologies in this area. The market is ripe for manufacturers of full-featured products that allow our software and services to take full advantage of the scalability, availability, and resilience that the cloud has to offer, packaged in a way that reduces complexity. However, we are still in the middle of designing the individual pieces and parts that would be used to build something like this.

Containers are a huge step in this direction, providing a useful level of abstraction between the packaging of an application and the infrastructure where it will be deployed. I anticipate a time when developers will no longer need to be involved in the details at the level of containers, but for now, *we should be*. At the very least, we should have a seat at the table to make sure that development concerns are addressed moving forward. To that end, and to satisfy any remaining doubts about why you should even broach the subject of containers, let's learn more.

Think about all it takes to package, deploy, and run your Java application. To begin development, you install a particular version of the Java Development Kit (JDK) to your development machine. Then you might install a dependency manager such as Apache Maven or Gradle to pull in all of the needed third-party libraries you choose to use in your app and package it up into a WAR or a JAR file. At this point, it might be ready to deploy... *somewhere*.

And here the problems begin. What is installed on the production server—what version of the Java runtime, what application server (for example, JBoss, Apache Tomcat, WildFly)? Are other processes running on the production server that might interfere with your application's performance? Does your application require root access for any reason, and is your application user set up appropriately with the correct permissions? Does your app require access to external services like a database or APIs for alive or well checks? Before any of these questions can be answered, do you even have access to a dedicated production server to begin with, or do you need to begin the process of requesting one to be provisioned for your application? And then what happens when your application is strained with heavy activity—are you able to scale quickly and automatically, or must you begin the provisioning process all over again?

Given these issues, it's easy to see why virtualization using virtual machines (VMs) became such an attractive option. VMs provide more flexibility when it comes to isolating application processes, and the ability to snapshot a VM can provide consistency in deployments. However, VM images are large and not easy to move around because they include an entire OS, which contributes to their overall bulk.

More than a few times when first introducing fellow developers to containers, I've gotten the response, "Oh! So a container is like a VM?" While it's convenient to think of *containers* as analogous to VMs, an important distinction exists. VMs (VMware vSphere, Microsoft Hyper-V, and others) are an abstraction of the hardware, emulating a complete server. In a sense, the entire operating system is included in a VM. VMs are managed by a software layer called a *hypervisor*, which divides and allocates the host's resources to the VMs as required.

Containers, on the other hand, are not as heavy as a traditional VM. Rather than include an entire OS, a Linux container, for example, can be thought of as a Linux distribution that shares the host operating system. As shown in Figure 3-1, VMs and containers are different levels of abstraction, as is the Java Virtual Machine (JVM).

Where does the JVM fit in all of this? It gets confusing when terms like *virtual machine* are overloaded. The JVM is a completely different abstraction altogether and is a *process* virtual machine as opposed to a *system* virtual machine. Its primary concern is to provide the Java Runtime Environment (or JRE, the implementation of the JVM) for a Java application. The JVM virtualizes the host's processor(s) for the purpose of executing Java bytecode.

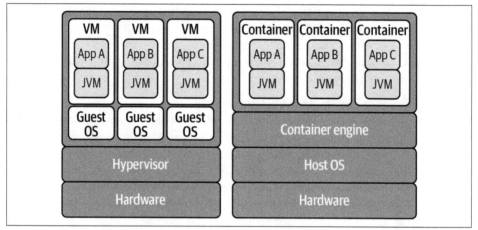

Figure 3-1. VMs versus containers

Containers are a lightweight solution that promises to solve most of the issues around application consistency, process isolation, and OS-level dependencies. This method of packaging a service or application can utilize caching mechanisms that drastically reduce the time it takes to get an application deployed and up and running. Rather than having to wait for custom provisioning and setup, containers can be deployed to existing infrastructure—whether that's an available dedicated server, an existing VM on premises in a private data center, or cloud resources.

Even if you choose not to utilize containers in production, you are well advised to consider a couple of other use cases around development and test environments.

A big challenge in onboarding a new developer to a team is the time spent setting up their local development environment. It is generally understood that it's going to take some time to get a developer to the point where they can contribute their first bug fix or improvement. While some companies dictate the development tools (consistency is often believed to improve support efforts and therefore efficiency), developers have more choices today than ever. I'm of the opinion that forcing a specific toolset on developers when they are already accustomed to something different actually has the opposite effect. Frankly, in many cases, it simply just isn't necessary anymore—especially now that we can utilize containers.

Containers help keep the runtime environment consistent, and when configured correctly, can easily be launched in dev, test, or production modes. The risk of your service or application behaving differently in these environments because of a missing dependency is greatly reduced since the environment is shipped along with your application in a container image.

This portability improves a developer's ability to sanity-test changes in a local environment as well as the ability to deploy the same version of the code that's in production in order to reproduce a bug. Integration testing with containers also comes with the added benefit of being able to reproduce as close as possible a production environment. For example, instead of using an in-memory database for integration tests, you can now launch containers that match the version of the database used in production. Using a project like TestContainers for this purpose will prevent irregularities in behavior due to slightly different SQL syntax or other differences between database software versions. Using containers in this way improves efficiency by circumventing the complications of installing new software or multiple versions of the same software to your local machine.

If we've learned anything about containers thus far, it is that they are likely here to stay in one form or another. This section began with an illustration of the exponential increase in container usage over the last several years, and the toolsets being continuously developed and improved around the container ecosystem have gained a solid foothold in both development and operations processes. Apart from a huge, and as of yet unknown, advancement in a completely different direction (remember, containers have over 50 years of history behind them), you are well advised to learn about the container ecosystem and how to exploit this technology to your full advantage.

Intro to Container Anatomy

My first experience with containers as a developer was via a project, developed by a third-party contractor, that my team was now responsible to further develop and maintain. Aside from bringing the initial codebase into our internal GitHub organization, a lot of setup needed to happen to establish our internal DevOps environment around the project—setting up our continuous integration and deployment (CI/CD) pipeline as well as our development and test environments, and, of course, our deployment process.

I compare this experience to clearing my desk (even more so after days of neglect). I'm about to reveal entirely too much about my personal habits here, but it's worth doing to make this point. The most time-consuming bit of clearing my desk is a stack of papers and mail that invariably grows to the point of falling over. It's terribly convenient to rush into the house with these items and, because of other urgent tasks on my mind, set them down on the kitchen counter…frequently on top of an existing stack of papers, with the promise that I'll get to it later. The problem is, I never know what's going to be in there. The stack could contain bills that need to be paid, important papers that need filing, or invites or letters that need responding to and thought put toward scheduling on our family calendar. I often dread the amount of time I anticipate it will take to get through it, which only leads to a larger stack of neglected correspondence.

For the project my team was responsible for, my first step was to metaphorically clear the desk. The Dockerfile that I found in the source code was the equivalent of tackling that dreaded stack of papers. Although getting through it and learning the concepts was necessary, I felt like I was getting derailed from the task at hand. Learning a new technology when starting a new project sometimes doesn't get the amount of time it should be allotted during project planning, even though it adds variables and inherent risk to the project timeline. This does *not* mean that new technology should never be introduced. Developers absolutely need to learn new things as the industry grows and changes, but it's best to mitigate risk by either limiting the amount of new tech introduced to a project or being up-front about the variability of the timeline.

 A *Dockerfile* is a text file that contains instructions providing the blueprint for your container. This file is typically named *Dockerfile*, and although originally specific to Docker, because of its wide use, other image-building tools support using Dockerfiles to build a container image (such as Buildah, kaniko, and BuildKit).

The information available here is not meant to be a regurgitation of documentation that's already out there (for example, the online Docker getting started guide (*https:// oreil.ly/Tez72*) is exceptional). Instead, I hope to peel this onion in a way that will orient you on the basics and give you immediate value and enough detail to better estimate what it's going to take to get your own desk cleared and ready for business. You now have quite a bit of information under your belt about containers and how they came to be. This next section covers the terminology and functionality that you will be exposed to as a developer.

Key Container and Image Terminology

The world of containers has its own lexicon, and you will encounter the following terms frequently:

Container
> The encapsulation of an application and all of its required dependencies and system resources running within an isolated "space" on a host machine. Containers share the host machine's operating system and kernel, but utilize low-level features that allow isolation between processes running inside the container and other processes on the same host. Containers enable the portability of an

application or service between computing environments without the risk of changes in behavior because of differing dependency sets.

Container image

An immutable, executable binary that provides all the dependencies and configuration required for creating a container. It encompasses all the environment configuration and explicitly defines all the resources to which a container will have access after it is launched. Images can be thought of as a snapshot of a complete filesystem stored as an archive that can be unpacked and run within the context of a collection of root filesystem changes.

Base image

Images can inherit from other images, and many are built from an initial set of dependencies and configurations that come from a base image. Commonly used base images can describe a base operating system and/or include a specific package or set of dependencies. A base image is not based on any other image and uses the command `scratch` as the first line of the image's Dockerfile.

An image that is based on another will specify the image it inherits from, also known as a *parent image*, in the first line of the Dockerfile. A parent image is not required to be a base image.

Image ID

When an image is built, it is assigned a unique ID in the form of a SHA-256 hash calculated from the contents of the image metadata configuration file.

Image digest

A unique ID in the form of a SHA-256 hash calculated from the contents of an image manifest file.

Image manifest

A JSON file that contains metadata about a container image. It contains the image digests of the image metadata configuration file and all of the image layers.

Image layer

Images are composed of image layers. Image layers are intermediate images that are generated from each command specified in a Dockerfile. As the commands are executed during a build, a corresponding layer is created that consists of the changes made from the previous layer. Beginning with a base layer, subsequent layers are stacked sequentially, and each layer consists of a delta of changes from the previous layer.

Image tag

An alias used to point to a specific image binary within an image repository. The tag can be set to any text but is generally used to indicate a specific version of a named image. A tag is unique to an image binary; however, an image binary can have multiple tags. This capability is commonly used along with semantic versioning to tag the latest minor and/or patch version as the latest major version available.

Be aware that image tags are not always consistently used across all projects and aren't immutable, meaning that a tag can potentially be moved from one binary to another intentionally—or even by mistake. Today's tagged 3.2.1 version of an image pulled from a public container registry is not guaranteed to be an identical binary to tomorrow's 3.2.1 version of that image.

Image repository (image name)
Stores all the versions of an image, making them available for distribution. The name of an image repository is usually referred to as the *image name*.

Container registry
A library of container images that stores collections of image repositories. Often you may hear the terms *Docker registry* and *container registry* used interchangeably; however, be aware that a container registry might not support all image formats specific to both Docker and OCI images.

Docker Architecture and the Container Runtime

Just like Kleenex is a brand of tissue, Docker is a *brand* of container. The Docker company developed an entire technology stack around containerization. So even though the terms *Docker container* and *Docker image* have been somewhat genericized, when you install something like Docker Desktop to your development machine, you are getting more than just the ability to run containers. You're getting an entire container platform that makes building, running, and managing them easy and convenient for developers.

It is important to understand that installing Docker is not required for building container images or running containers. It is simply a widely used and convenient tool for doing so. In much the same way that you can package a Java project without using Maven or Gradle, you can build a container image without using Docker or a Dockerfile. My advice to a developer new to containers would be to take advantage of the toolset Docker provides and then experiment with other options or methods to get a good feel for a comparison. Even if you choose to utilize other tools instead of or in addition to Docker, a lot of time and effort was spent on engineering a good developer experience, and this alone scores big points for including Docker Desktop in your development environment.

With Docker, you get an isolated environment in which a user/application can operate, sharing the host system's OS/kernel without interfering with the operation of another isolated environment on the same system (a container). Docker enables you to do the following:

- Define a container (an image format)
- Build an image of a container
- Manage container images
- Distribute/share container images
- Create a container environment
- Launch/run a container (a container runtime)
- Manage the lifecycle of container instances

The container landscape contains much more than Docker, but many of the container toolset alternatives focus on a subset of these items. Beginning with learning how Docker operates is helpful in understanding and evaluating these alternatives.

A lot of pictures and diagrams are readily available that describe the Docker architecture. An image search online will most likely result in a version of Figure 3-2. This diagram does a fairly good job of showing how Docker works on your development machine—the Docker CLI is the interface available to you to send commands to the Docker daemon to build images, retrieve requested images from an external registry (by default, this is Docker Hub), manage these images in local storage, and then use these images to launch and run containers on your machine.

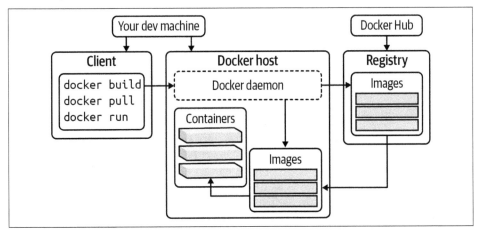

Figure 3-2. Docker architecture

One of the more confusing concepts when first introduced to this landscape is the focus on one aspect of the Docker ecosystem: the *container runtime*. To reiterate, this is just one part of the entire tech stack Docker offers, but because orchestration frameworks like Kubernetes require this portion of functionality to launch and run containers, it is often spoken of as a separate entity from Docker (and in the case of alternative container runtimes, it is).

The topic of container runtimes deserves this section all to itself, because it can be one of the most confusing aspects to someone new to the world of containers. Even more confusing is that container runtimes fall into two different categories, low-level or high-level, depending on what features are implemented. And just to keep you on your toes, some overlap can occur in that feature set.

This is a good spot to present a visual on how container runtimes fit together with what you've learned earlier about the OCI and projects like containerd and runC. Figure 3-3 illustrates the relationship between older and newer versions of Docker, high-level and low-level runtimes, and where Kubernetes fits in.

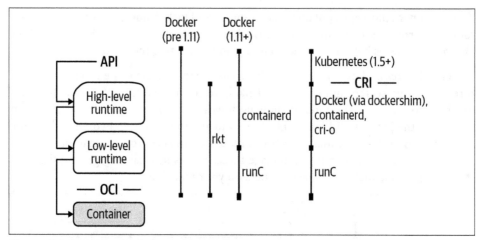

Figure 3-3. Runtimes in the container ecosystem

 One of the best explanations I've come across that really gets into the details of container runtimes along with a historical perspective is a blog series (*https://oreil.ly/Y2Fow*) composed by Ian Lewis, a developer advocate on the Google Cloud Platform Team.

Prior to version 1.11 (released in 2016), Docker could be described as a monolithic application that wrapped up the entire feature set required of a runtime, plus other management tools. Docker did quite a bit of reorganizing its codebase over the last several years, developing abstractions and pulling out discrete functionality. The runC project that was contributed by Docker to the OCI came out of this effort. This was the first and, for some time, the *only* implementation of a low-level container runtime that implemented the OCI Runtime Specification.

Other runtimes are out there, and as of this writing this is an active space, so be sure to reference the current list maintained by the OCI (*https://oreil.ly/Vro14*) for the most up-to-date information. Notable low-level runtime projects include *crun*, an implementation in C led by Red Hat; and *railcar*, an implementation in Rust led by Oracle, although this project is now archived.

The Status of CoreOS rkt

CoreOS was acquired by Red Hat at the beginning of 2018. Prior to that, *rkt* (a CoreOS initiative) had been accepted to the CNCF as an incubating project and looked to be a promising competitor to Docker's containerd project. However, since the CoreOS acquisition, the development of the project went dormant. In mid-2019, rkt was archived by the CNCF, and in February 2020, the project was ended.

It is still possible to use rkt containers, as the code is still available on GitHub (*https:// oreil.ly/GqSMj*), but all maintenance and development activity has come to a stop.

Developing a specification is a challenging feat, and collaboration on the OCI Runtime Specification wasn't any less challenging. Figuring out the boundaries—what *should* and what *should not* be included in the specification—took time before the release of version 1.0. It's clear, however, that just implementing the OCI Runtime Specification isn't enough to drive adoption of an implementation. Additional features are needed to make a low-level runtime usable for developers since we are concerned with much more than just the launching and running of a container.

This leads us to higher-level runtimes like *containerd* and *cri-o*, the two primary players as of this writing that include solutions for many of the concerns around container orchestration, including image management and distribution. Both of these runtimes implement the CRI (which eases the path to a Kubernetes deployment) and delegate low-level container activities to OCI-compliant low-level runtimes (for example, runC).

Kubernetes Deprecation of the Docker Container Runtime

Kubernetes announced that in release 1.20, support for the Docker runtime would be deprecated and removed in a future release (as of this writing, removal is slated for release 1.24). Here's information directly from the 1.20 changelog (*https://oreil.ly/ W7h1N*):

> Docker support in the kubelet is now deprecated and will be removed in a future release. The kubelet uses a module called "dockershim," which implements CRI support for Docker, and it has seen maintenance issues in the Kubernetes community. We encourage you to evaluate moving to a container runtime that is a full-fledged implementation of CRI (v1alpha1 or v1 compliant) as they become available.

What does this mean? Is Docker no longer a viable toolset for Kubernetes deployments? Does this mean you can no longer use Docker Desktop or that you should invest any more time in learning Docker? I'm so glad you asked. Let's pull this apart into the related deployment and development concerns.

Kubernetes is an orchestration framework that manages the deployment and scaling of containers based on a given configuration. To accomplish this, a node agent called *kubelet* runs on each node and manages the configured containers—which means that kubelet must communicate with a container runtime.

The difficulty started when Kubernetes was challenged to support alternative container runtimes in addition to the Docker runtime. Kubernetes supported Docker as a runtime via the *dockershim* module. Remember, Docker is an entire tech stack that includes more than just the runtime. The dockershim module was how CRI support was implemented for the Docker runtime, but since Docker successfully pulled out containerd as a CRI-compatible runtime (and now even Docker itself uses containerd), it no longer makes sense to keep this custom implementation for Docker.

Even though Kubernetes has made changes in favor of supporting multiple container runtimes, Docker images that you build can still be used in Kubernetes cluster. It is still worth learning Docker.

Docker on Your Machine

The second most important thing to understand about containers is that they are not magic. Containers utilize a combination of existing Linux features (as covered at the beginning of this chapter). Container implementations vary in the details, but a container image, in a sense, is simply a tarball of a complete filesystem, and a running container is a Linux process that is constrained to provide a level of isolation from other processes running on a host. The implementation of a Docker container, for example, primarily involves these three ingredients:

- Namespaces
- cgroups
- A union filesystem

But what does a container look like on your local filesystem? First, let's figure out where Docker is storing things on our development machine. Then let's take a look at a real Docker image pulled from Docker Hub.

After installing Docker Desktop, running the command `docker info` from a terminal will provide you with detailed information about your installation. This output includes information about where your images and containers are stored with the label `Docker Root Dir`. The following example output (truncated for brevity) indicates that the Docker root directory is */var/lib/docker*:

```
$ docker info
Client:
 Context:    default
 Debug Mode: false
 Plugins:
  app: Docker App (Docker Inc., v0.9.1-beta3)
  buildx: Build with BuildKit (Docker Inc., v0.5.1-docker)
  compose: Docker Compose (Docker Inc., 2.0.0-beta.1)
  scan: Docker Scan (Docker Inc., v0.8.0)

Server:
 Containers: 5
  Running: 0
  Paused: 0
  Stopped: 5
 Images: 62
 Server Version: 20.10.6
 Storage Driver: overlay2
 …
 Docker Root Dir: /var/lib/docker
 …
```

This result is from an existing Docker Desktop (version 3.3.3) installation on macOS Big Sur. A quick listing of *var/lib/docker* shows the following:

```
$ ls /var/lib/docker
ls: /var/lib/docker: No such file or directory
```

According to the previous output, 5 stopped containers and 62 images are on this system, so how is it that this directory doesn't exist? Is the output incorrect? You can check another place for the image and container storage location, as shown in Figure 3-4, a screenshot of the Preferences section available in the Mac version of the Docker Desktop UI.

However, this location is completely different. A reasonable explanation for this exists, and note that depending on your operating system, your installation may be slightly different. The reason this matters at all is that Docker Desktop for Mac requires a Linux environment to run Linux containers, and to that end, a minimal Linux virtual machine is instantiated during installation. This means that the Docker root directory referred to in the earlier output is actually referencing a directory within this Linux VM.

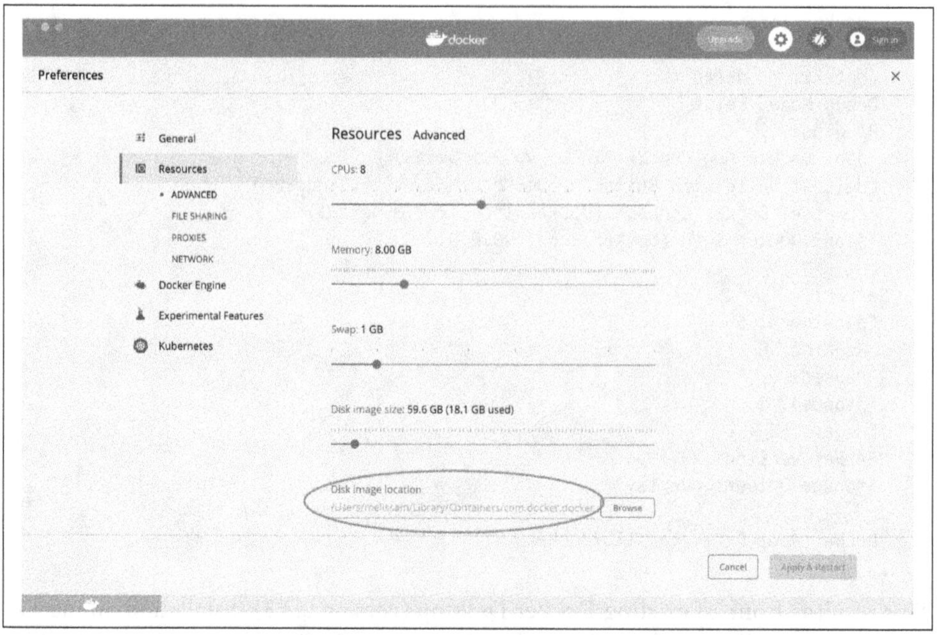

Figure 3-4. Docker Desktop Preferences

But wait…what if you're on Windows? Because containers are sharing the host's operating system, Windows-based containers require a Windows environment to run, and Linux-based containers require a Linux environment. Docker Desktop (version 3.3.3) is a marked improvement from earlier versions (a.k.a Docker Toolbox) in that no additional supporting software is required to run Linux-based containers. In the old days, to run Docker on a Mac, you would need to install something like VirtualBox and boot2docker to get everything up and functioning as expected. Today, Docker Desktop handles the necessary virtualization behind the scenes. Docker Desktop also supports Windows containers via Hyper-V on Windows 10 and Linux containers on Windows 10 via Windows Subsystem for Linux 2 (WSL 2). To run Windows containers on macOS, however, VirtualBox is still required.

Now that you know we need to access the Linux virtual machine to get to this Docker root directory, let's pull a Docker image by using the command **docker pull *IMAGE NAME*** and see what it looks like on the filesystem:

```
$ docker pull openjdk
Using default tag: latest
latest: Pulling from library/openjdk
5a581c13a8b9: Pull complete
26cd02acd9c2: Pull complete
66727af51578: Pull complete
Digest: sha256:05eee0694a2ecfc3e94d29d420bd8703fa9dcc64755962e267fd5dfc22f23664
```

```
Status: Downloaded newer image for openjdk:latest
docker.io/library/openjdk:latest
```

The command **docker images** lists all of the images stored locally. You can see from its output that two versions of the *openjdk* image are stored. The one we pulled in the previous command brought in the image with the tag latest. This is the default behavior, but we could have specified a specific *openjdk* image version like this: **docker pull openjdk:11-jre**:

```
$ docker images
REPOSITORY          TAG             IMAGE ID          CREATED         SIZE
...
openjdk             latest          de085dce79ff      10 days ago     467MB
openjdk             11-jre          b2552539e2dd      4 weeks ago     301MB
...
```

You can learn more details about the latest *openjdk* image by running the **docker inspect** command using the *image ID*:

```
$ docker inspect de085dce79ff
[
    {
        "Id": "sha256:de085dce79ff...",
        "RepoTags": [
            "openjdk:latest"
        ],
...
        "Architecture": "amd64",
        "Os": "linux",
        "Size": 467137618,
        "VirtualSize": 467137618,
        "GraphDriver": {
            "Data": {
                "LowerDir": "/var/lib/docker/overlay2/581137...ca8c47/diff:/var
                /lib/docker/overlay2/7f7929...8f8cb4/diff",
                "MergedDir": "/var/lib/docker/overlay2/693641...940d82/merged",
                "UpperDir": "/var/lib/docker/overlay2/693641...940d82/diff",
                "WorkDir": "/var/lib/docker/overlay2/693641...940d82/work"
            },
            "Name": "overlay2"
        },
        "RootFS": {
            "Type": "layers",
            "Layers": [
                "sha256:1a3adb4bd0a7...",
                "sha256:046fa1e6609c...",
                "sha256:a8a84740beab..."
            ]
        },
...
```

The docker inspect command spits out a ton of interesting information. But what I want to highlight here is the GraphDriver section, which contains the paths to the directories where all the layers that belong to this image live.

Docker images are composed of layers that correspond to instructions in the Docker-file that was used to build the image originally. These layers translate into directories and can be shared across images in order to save space.

Note the LowerDir, MergedDir, and UpperDir sections. The LowerDir section contains all the directories, or layers, that were used to build the original image. These are *read-only*. The *UpperDir* directory contains all the content that has been modified while the container is running. If modifications are needed for a read-only layer in *LowerDir*, then that layer is copied into the *UpperDir* where it can be written to. This is called a *copy-on-write* operation.

It's important to remember that the data in *UpperDir* is ephemeral data that lives only as long as the container lives. In fact, if you have data that you intend to keep, you should utilize the volume features of Docker and mount a location that will stick around even after the container dies. For example, a database-driven application running in a container will likely utilize a volume mounted to the container for the database data.

Lastly, the MergedDir section is kind of like a virtual directory that combines every-thing from *LowerDir* and *Upper Dir*. The way the Union File System works is that any edited layers that were copied into *UpperDir* will overlay layers in *LowerDir*.

 Notice all the references to directories within */var/lib/docker*, the Docker root directory. If you monitor the size of this directory, you will notice that the more images and containers you create and run, the storage space required for this directory will increase substan-tially over time. Consider mounting a dedicated drive, and make sure that you are cleaning up unused images and containers regu-larly. Also, make sure that containerized apps aren't continuously producing unmanaged data files or other artifacts. For example, utilize log shipping and or log rotation to manage logs generated by your container and its running processes.

Any number of containers can be launched using the same image. Each container will be created with the image blueprint and will run independently. In the context of Java, think of a container image as a Java class, and a container as a Java object instantiated from that class.

Containers can be stopped and later restarted without being re-created. To list con-tainers on your system, use the docker ps -a command. Note that the -a flag will display both stopped containers as well as containers currently running:

```
$ docker ps -a
CONTAINER ID   IMAGE     COMMAND     STATUS                      NAMES
9668ba978683   openjdk   "tail -f"   Up 19 seconds               vibrant_jang
582ad818a57b   openjdk   "jshell"    Exited (0) 14 minutes ago   zealous_wilson
```

If you navigate to the Docker root directory, you will see a subdirectory named *containers*. Within this directory, you will find additional subdirectories named after the *container ID* of each container on your system. Stopped containers will retain their state and data in these directories so that they can be restarted if needed. When a container is removed using the `docker rm CONTAINER NAME`, its correlated directory will be deleted.

Remember to regularly remove unused containers from your systems (*remove*, not just stop). I personally witnessed a scenario with this part of the deployment process missing. Every time new images were released, the old containers were stopped and new containers were launched based on the new images. This was an oversight that quickly used up hard drive space and eventually prevented new deployments. The following Docker command is useful to clean up unused containers in bulk:

```
docker container prune
```

```
docker-desktop:~# ls /var/lib/docker/
builder      containers  overlay2   swarm   volumes
buildkit     image       plugins    tmp
containerd   network     runtimes   trust
```

```
docker-desktop:~# ls /var/lib/docker/containers/
9668ba978683b37445defc292198bbc7958da593c6bb3cef6d7f8272bbae1490
582ad818a57b8d125903201e1bcc7693714f51a505747e4219c45b1e237e15cb
```

If you are using Mac for development, remember that your containers are running in a tiny VM that you will need to first access before you can see the Docker root directory contents. For example, on a Mac, you can access and navigate this directory by interactively running a container in privileged mode that has *nsenter* installed (you may need to run this with `sudo`):

```
docker run -it --privileged --pid=host debian \
nsenter -t 1 -m -u -n -i sh
```

Later versions of Windows (10+) now have the capability of running Linux containers natively using Windows Subsystem for Linux (WSL). The default Docker root directory for Windows 11 Home can be found here in File Explorer:

*\\wsl.localhost\docker-desktop-data\version-pack-data\
community\docker*

Basic Tagging and Image Version Management

After working with images awhile, you will see that identifying them and versioning them are a bit different from the way you version your Java software. Working with build tools like Maven has gotten most Java developers accustomed to standard semantic versioning and always specifying dependency versions (or at least accepting of the version Maven chooses to pull within a particular dependency tree). These guardrails are a little more relaxed in other package managers like npm, where a dependency version can be specified as a range in order to allow for ease and flexibility in updating dependencies.

Image versioning can become a stumbling block if not well understood. No guard-rails exist (at least not the kind that Java developers are used to). Flexibility in tagging an image is preferred over any enforcement of good practices. However, just because you *can*, doesn't mean you *should*, and just as with proper versioning of Java libraries and packages, it is best to start out of the gate with a naming and versioning scheme that makes sense and follows an accepted pattern.

Container image names and versions follow a specific format, including multiple components that you rarely see in complete form in examples and tutorials. Most example code and Dockerfiles you find when scouring the internet identify images in an abbreviated format.

It is easiest to visualize image management as a directory structure, where the name of an image (such as *openjdk*) is a directory containing all the versions available for this image. Images are usually identified by a *name* and a version, known as a *tag*. But these two components are composed of subcomponents that have an assumed default value if not specified, and often, even a tag is omitted in commands. For example, the simplest command for pulling the *openjdk* Docker image might take the following form:

```
docker pull openjdk
```

What is this command actually giving us? Aren't there several versions of the *openjdk* image that you could use? Indeed, yes, and if you are concerned with having repeatable builds, you will immediately spot this ambiguity as a potential problem.

The first step is to include the image tag in this command, which represents a version. The following command implies that I would be pulling version 11 of the *openjdk* image:

```
docker pull openjdk:11
```

So what was I pulling previously, if not 11? A special tag called latest is implied by default if a tag is not specified. This tag is intended to point to the latest version of the image available, but that might not always be the case. At any point, a tag can be updated to point to a different version of an image, and in some cases, you might find that the tag latest has not been set to point to anything at all.

It is easy to stumble over the nomenclature as well, notably *tag*, which can mean something different in different contexts. The term *tag* can mean a specific version, or it can also mean the full *image tag*, which includes all the components of identification together, including the image *name*.

Here's the complete format of a Docker image tag with all possible components:

```
[ registry [ :port ] / ] name [ :tag ]
```

The only required component is the image *name*, also known as the *image repository*. If *tag* is not specified, then *latest* is assumed. If the registry is not specified, Docker Hub is the default registry. The following command is an example of how to reference an image on a registry other than Docker Hub:

```
docker pull artifactory-prod.jfrog.io/openjdk:11
```

Image and Container Layers

To build efficient containers, having a thorough understanding of layers is essential. The details behind how you build the source of your containers—your container *images*—greatly impact their size and performance, and some approaches have security implications, making this concept even more important to master.

Basically, Docker images are built by establishing a base layer and then subsequently making small changes until you arrive at your desired final state. Each layer represents a set of changes including, but not limited to, the creation of users and related permissions, modifications to configuration or application settings, and updates to existing packages or adding/removing packages. These changes all amount to additions, modifications, or the removal of sets of files in the resulting filesystem. Layers are stacked on top of each other, each one being a delta of the changes from the previous layer, and each one identified by a SHA-256 hash digest of its contents. As discussed in "Docker on Your Machine" on page 62, these layers are stored within the root Docker directory.

Visualizing layers

One good way to really visualize layers is to use the command-line tool dive, available on GitHub (*https://oreil.ly/M2ZBZ*). Figure 3-5 shows a screenshot of the tool in action using the official latest *openjdk* image pulled from Docker Hub. The left pane displays details about the three layers that compose the *openjdk* image. The right pane highlights the changes each layer applies to the filesystem of the image.

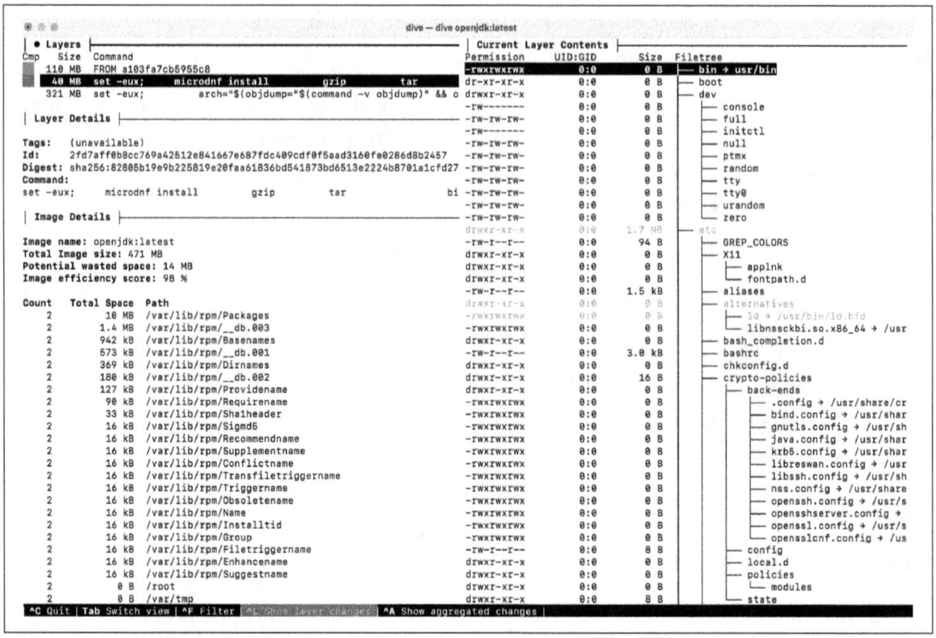

Figure 3-5. `dive` with openjdk

The `dive` tool is useful in showing you what the filesystem would look like if you were to launch a container based on the *openjdk* image. As you move through each subsequent layer, you can see the changes made to the initial filesystem. The most important part to convey here is that subsequent layers may obfuscate parts of the filesystem of the previous layer (in the case of any moves or deletions of files), but the original layer still exists in its original form.

Leveraging layer cache

Utilizing image layers speeds up image requests, builds, and pushes. It's a clever way to decrease the amount of storage required for images. This strategy allows for identical image layers to be shared across multiple images, and reduces the amount of time and bandwidth needed for pulling or pushing images that are already cached locally or stored in the registry.

If you're using Docker, your system will keep an internal cache of all the images you've either requested from external registries or built yourself. When new images are pushed and pulled, comparisons of each of the image layers are made between your local cache and the registry, and decisions are made about whether to push or pull individual layers, increasing efficiency.

Anyone who has ever struggled with their internal Maven repository (haven't we all at some point?), or with any caching mechanism for that matter, is very aware that the efficiency and performance improvements internal cache provides also come with caveats. Sometimes what you have stored in cache is *not* what you intended to use. Using stale cache can easily happen in active development and local testing if you aren't mindful of how and when your local image cache is used.

For example, the commands docker run openjdk and docker pull openjdk behave differently where cache is concerned. The former searches for the specified image in your local cache with the tag latest. If the image exists, the search will be considered satisfied, and a new container based on the cached image will be launched. The latter command will go a step further and update the *openjdk* image on your system if an update exists in the remote registry it was retrieved from.

Another common mistake is assuming a command in a Dockerfile will run again when an image is rebuilt. This is common with RUN commands such as RUN apt-get update. If this line in the Dockerfile doesn't change at all, as it would if you were to specify package names along with specific versions, then the initial layer built with this command will live in your cache. It will not get built again. This is not a bug, but a feature of the cache to speed up build processes. If a layer is determined to be already built, the layer will not be built again.

In an attempt to avoid stale cache, you might be tempted to combine commands on one line (producing one layer) in a Dockerfile in order for changes to be more easily recognized and acted on more frequently. The problem with this approach is that by squashing too much into a single layer, you lose the benefit of the cache altogether.

 As a developer, be conscientious regarding your local cache. And beyond local development, consider how your continuous integration, build servers, and automated integration testing is using cache. Ensuring that all systems are consistent in this way will help keep you from chasing unexplained and intermittent failures.

Best Image Build Practices and Container Gotchas

After some time spent building and playing with images, you're going to discover that you can shoot yourself in the foot in a lot of places in even the most basic build process. The following is a set of practices to keep in mind as you start on your image-building journey. You will discover more, but these are the most important.

Respect the Docker Context and .dockerignore File

You don't want to have certain things in your production Docker image—things like your development environment configuration, keys, your *.git* directory, or other sensitive hidden directories. When you run the command to build a Docker image, you provide the *context*, or the location of files you want to make available to the build process.

The following is a contrived Dockerfile example:

```
FROM ubuntu

WORKDIR /myapp

COPY . /myapp

EXPOSE 8080

ENTRYPOINT ["start.sh"]
```

See the COPY instruction? Depending on what you sent in as the context, this could be problematic. It could be copying *everything* from your working directory into the Docker image you build, which will end up in any container launched from this image.

Make sure to use a *.dockerignore* file to exclude files from the context that you don't want showing up unintentionally. You can use it to avoid accidentally adding any user-specific files or secrets that you might have stored locally. In fact, you can greatly reduce the size of the context (and the time it takes to build) by excluding anything the build doesn't require access to:

```
# Ignore these files in my project
**/*.md
!README.md
passwords.txt
.git
logs/
*/temp
**/test/
```

The *.dockerignore* matching format follows Go's filepath.Match rules (*https://oreil.ly/sCjIv*).

Use Trusted Base Images

Whether you choose to use images that include OpenJDK, Oracle JDK, GraalVM, or other images that include a web server or a database, make sure you are using trusted images as parent images, or creating your own from scratch.

Docker Hub proclaims to be the world's largest library for publicly available container images, with over 100,000 images from software vendors, open source projects, and the community. *Not all of these images should be trusted to use as base images.*

Docker Hub includes a set of curated images labeled "Docker Official Images" that are suitable for use as base images (note that distribution of these requires an agreement with Docker). These details are from the online Docker docs on official images (*https://oreil.ly/TO8Po*):

> Docker, Inc. sponsors a dedicated team that is responsible for reviewing and publishing all content in the Docker Official Images. This team works in collaboration with upstream software maintainers, security experts, and the broader Docker community.

As important as understanding what Java dependencies are brought into your project and the depth of your dependency tree, so is understanding what your base image is bringing in under that one little FROM line at the top of your Dockerfile. The inheritance structure of Dockerfiles can easily obfuscate how much your base image is dragging along with it in the form of additional libraries and packages you don't need or possibly even malevolent content.

Specify Package Versions and Keep Up with Updates

Given the caveats discussed earlier about caching on top of the desire to maintain repeatable builds, specify versions in your Dockerfile just as you would in your Java project. Avoid broken builds and unexpected behavior from new versions or unexpected updates.

That said, it's easy to get complacent with updating versions if they never force you to look at them because of a failed build or test. Regularly audit your project for needed updates and make these updates intentional. This should be part of your regular project planning. I advise that this activity be separate from any other feature development or bug fixing in order to eliminate unrelated moving parts in your development lifecycle.

Keep Your Images Small

It is easy for images to become very large, very fast. Monitor size increases in your automated builds and set up notifications for unusual size changes. Gluttonous disk storage packages can easily sneak in via updates to a base image or be unintentionally included in a COPY statement.

Utilize multistage builds to keep your images small. A multistage build can be set up by creating a Dockerfile that uses multiple FROM statements, which begin a build stage with a different base image. By using multistage builds, you can avoid including things like build tools or package managers that are not needed (and really should not be included) in a production image. For example, the following Dockerfile shows a two-stage build. The first uses a base image that includes Maven. After the Maven build is complete, the required JAR file is copied to the second stage, which uses an image that does *not* include Maven:

```
##################
# First build stage
##################

FROM maven:3.8.4-openjdk-11-slim as build

COPY .mvn .mvn
COPY mvnw .
COPY pom.xml .
COPY src src

RUN ./mvnw package

####################
# Second build stage
##################

FROM openjdk:11-jre-slim-buster

COPY --from=build target/my-project-1.0.jar .

EXPOSE 8080

ENTRYPOINT ["java", "-jar", "my-project-1.0.jar"]
```

This is also a good way to implement the use of a custom *distroless* image, an image that has been stripped of everything (including a shell) but the absolute essentials for running your application.

Beware of External Resources

I have often seen requests to external resources within Dockerfiles in the form of wget commands for installation of proprietary software or even external requests for shell scripts that perform a custom installation. These terrify me. More than general suspicion and paranoia are involved here. Even if the external resource is trusted, the more you relinquish control to parts of your build to external parties, the more likely you are to suffer build failures that are out of your control to fix.

The first response I often get when making this observation is this: "There's nothing to worry about because once you've built your image, it's cached or stored within a base image, and you won't have to ever make the request again."

This is absolutely true. Once you have your base image stored, or your image layer cached, you're good to go. But the first time a new build node (with zero cache) is put into play, or even when a new developer joins your team, building that image might fail. When you need to build a new version of the base image, your build might fail. Why? Because time and time again, external managers of resources will move them, restrict access to them, or simply *dispose of them*.

Protect Your Secrets

I include this because in addition to not moving secrets into your image in the first place, don't think that using a command in a Dockerfile to remove them from a base image or any other previous layer is good enough. I've seen this before as a hack to "fix" a base layer that couldn't be rebuilt right away.

Now that you know how layering works, you know that a subsequent layer deleting items does not actually remove them from the underlying layer. You can't see them if you were to exec into a running container based on that image, but they are still there. They exist on the system the image is stored on, they exist anywhere a container based on that image is launched, and they also exist in the image registry you've chosen for long-term storage. This is close to the equivalent of checking your passwords into source control. Do not put secrets into images to begin with.

Know Your Outputs

Numerous factors can cause a container to continuously grow while it's running. One of the most common is not dealing with log files appropriately. Ensure that your application is logging to a volume where you can implement a log-rotating solution. Given the ephemeral nature of containers, it doesn't make sense to keep logs that you would use for troubleshooting or for compliance stored within the container (on the Docker host).

Summary

Much of this chapter was about exploring Docker. And this is an excellent place to start. Once you are comfortable with images and containers, you can branch out to other tools available in the ecosystem. Depending on the operating system and build utilities you've chosen for your project, tools such as Buildah (*https://buildah.io*), Podman (*https://podman.io*), or Bazel (*https://bazel.build*) might work well for you. You might also choose to use a Maven plug-in such as Jib (*https://oreil.ly/pwGsw*) to build your container image.

One word of caution: whichever tool you choose, understand how your images and containers are built so you don't suffer the consequences of bulky and/or insecure images and containers when you are ready to deploy.

## CHAPTER 4

Dissecting the Monolith

Ixchel Ruiz

The ultimate goal should be to improve the quality of human life through digital innovation.
—Pony Ma Huateng

Throughout history, humans have been obsessed with deconstructing ideas and concepts into simple or composite parts. It is by combining analysis and synthesis that we can achieve a higher level of understanding.

Aristotle called analytics "the resolution of every compound into those things out of which the synthesis is made. For analysis is the converse of synthesis. *Synthesis* is the road from the principles to those things that derive from the principles, and analysis is the return from the end to the principles."

Software development follows a similar approach: analyze a system into its composite parts, identifying inputs, desired outputs, and detail functions. During the analytic process of software development, we have realized that non-business-specific functionality is always required to process inputs and to communicate or persist outputs. This makes it obvious that we could benefit from reusable, well-defined, context-bound, atomic functionality that can be shared, consumed, or interconnected to simplify building software.

Allowing developers to focus primarily on implementing business logic to fulfill purposes—like meeting well-defined needs of a client/business, meeting a perceived need of some set of potential users, or using the functionality for personal needs (to automate tasks)—has been a long-held desire. Too much time is wasted every day reinventing one of the most reinvented wheels: reliable boilerplate code.

The microservices pattern has gained notoriety and momentum in recent years because the promised benefits are outstanding. Avoiding known antipatterns, adopting best practices, and understanding core concepts and definitions are paramount in achieving the benefits of this architectural pattern while reducing the drawbacks of adopting it. This chapter covers antipatterns and contains code examples of microservices written with popular microservice frameworks such as Spring Boot, Micronaut, Quarkus, and Helidon.

Traditionally a monolithic architecture delivers or deploys single units or systems, addressing all requirements from a single source application, and two concepts can be identified: the *monolith application* and the *monolithic architecture*.

A *monolith application* has *only one* deployed instance, responsible for performing all steps needed for a specific function. One characteristic of such an application is a unique interface point of execution.

A *monolithic architecture* refers to an application for which all requirements are addressed from a single source and all parts are delivered as one unit. Components may have been designed to restrict interaction with external clients in order to explicitly limit access of *private* functionality. Components in the monolith may be interconnected or interdependent rather than loosely coupled. In other words, from the outside or user perspective, there is little knowledge of the definitions, interfaces, data, and services of other separate components.

Granularity is the aggregation level exposed by a component to other external cooperating or collaborating parts of software. The level of granularity in software depends on several factors, such as the level of confidentiality that must be maintained within a series of components and not be exposed or available to other consumers.

Modern software architectures are increasingly focused on delivering functionality by bundling or combining software components from different sources, resulting in or emphasizing a finer granularity in level of detail. The functionality exposed then to different components, customers, or consumers is greater than in a monolithic application.

To qualify how independent or interchangeable a module is, we should look closely at the following characteristics:

- Number of dependencies
- Strength of these dependencies
- Stability of the modules it depends on

Any high score assigned to the previous characteristics should trigger a second review of the modeling and definition of the module.

Cloud Computing

Cloud computing has several definitions. Peter Mell and Tim Grance define it as a model for enabling ubiquitous, convenient, on-demand network access to a shared pool of configurable computing resources (such as networks, servers, storage, applications, and services) that can be rapidly provisioned and released with minimal management effort or service provider interaction.

In recent years, cloud computing has increased considerably. For example, cloud infrastructure services spending increased 32% to $39.9 billion in the last quarter of 2020. Total expenditure was more than $3 billion higher than the previous quarter and nearly $10 billion more than Q4 2019, according to Canalys data (*https://oreil.ly/uZdZa*).

Several providers exist, but the market share is not evenly distributed. The three leading service providers are Amazon Web Services (AWS), Microsoft Azure, and Google Cloud. AWS is the leading cloud service provider, accounting for 31% of total spending in Q4 2020. Azure's growth rate accelerated, up by 50%, with a share close to 20%, whereas Google Cloud accounts for a 7% share of the total market.

Utilization of cloud computing services has been lagging. Cinar Kilcioglu and Aadharsh Kannan reported in 2017 in "Proceedings of the 26th International World Wide Web Conference" that usage of cloud resources in data centers shows a substantial gap between the resources that cloud customers allocate and pay for (leasing VMs), and actual resource utilization (CPU, memory, and so on). Perhaps customers are just leaving their VMs on but not actually using them.

Cloud services are divided into categories used for different types of computing:

Software as a service (SaaS)
> The client can use the provider's applications running on a cloud infrastructure. The applications are accessible from various client devices through either a thin client interface, such as a web browser, or a program interface. The client does not manage or control the underlying cloud infrastructure, including network, servers, operating systems, storage, or even individual application capabilities, with the possible exception of limited user-specific application configuration settings.

Platform as a service (PaaS)
> The client can deploy onto the cloud infrastructure client-made or acquired applications created using programming languages, libraries, services, and tools supported by the provider. The consumer does not manage or control the underlying cloud infrastructure, including network, servers, operating systems, or storage, but does have control over the deployed applications and possibly configuration settings for the application-hosting environment.

Infrastructure as a service (IaaS)
> The client is able to provision processing, storage, networks, and other funda-mental computing resources. They can deploy and run arbitrary software, which can *include operating systems and applications*. The client does not manage or control the underlying cloud infrastructure but has control over operating sys-tems, storage, and deployed applications—and possibly limited control of select networking components.

Microservices

The term *microservice* is not a recent one. Peter Rodgers introduced the term *micro-web services* in 2005 while championing the idea of *software as micro-web-services*. *Microservice_architecture*—an evolution of service-oriented architecture (SOA)—arranges an application as a collection of relatively lightweight modular services. Technically, microservices is a specialization of an implementation approach for SOA.

Microservices are small and loosely coupled components. In contrast to monoliths, they can be deployed, scaled, and tested independently, and they have a single respon-sibility, bounded by context, and are autonomous and decentralized. They are usually built around business capabilities, are easy to understand, and may be developed using different technology stacks.

How small should a microservice be? It should be *micro* enough to allow small, self-contained, and rigidly enforced atoms of functionality that can coexist, evolve, or replace the previous ones according to business needs.

Each component or service has little or no knowledge of the definitions of other sepa-rate components, and all interaction with a service is via its API, which encapsulates its implementation details. The messaging between these microservices uses simple protocols and usually is not data intensive.

Antipatterns

The microservice pattern results in significant complexity and is not ideal in all situations. The system is made up of many parts that work independently, and its very nature makes it harder to predict how it will perform in the real world.

This increased complexity is mainly due to the (potentially) thousands of microser-vices running asynchronously in the distributed computer network. Keep in mind that programs that are difficult to understand are also difficult to write, modify, test, and measure. All these concerns will increase the time teams need to spend on understanding, discussing, tracking, and testing interfaces and message formats.

Several books, articles, and papers are available on this particular topic. I recommend a visit to Microservices.io (*https://microservices.io*), Mark Richards's report *Microservices AntiPatterns and Pitfalls* (*https://oreil.ly/KpzyW*) (O'Reilly), and "On the Definition of Microservice Bad Smells" by Davide Taibi and Valentina Lenarduzz (published in *IEEE Software* in 2018).

Some of the most common antipatterns include the following:

API versioning (static contract pitfall)
APIs need to be semantically versioned to allow services to know whether they are communicating with the right version of the service or whether they need to adapt their communication to a new contract.

Inappropriate service privacy interdependency
The microservice requires private data from other services instead of dealing with its own data, a problem that usually is related to a modeling-the-data issue. One solution to consider is merging the microservices.

Multipurpose megaservice
Several business functions are implemented in the same service.

Logging
Errors and microservice information are hidden inside each microservice container. The adoption of a distributed logging system should be a priority as issues are found in all stages of the software lifecycle.

Complex interservice or circular dependencies
A *circular service relationship* is defined as a relationship between two or more services that are interdependent. Circular dependencies can harm the ability of services to scale or deploy independently, as well as violate the acyclic dependencies principle (ADP).

Missing API gateway
When microservices communicate directly with each other, or when the service consumers communicate directly with each microservice, complexity increases and maintenance decreases in the system. The best practice in this case is to use an API gateway.

An *API gateway* receives all API calls from clients and then directs them to the appropriate microservice by request routing, composition, and protocol translation. The gateway usually handles the request by calling multiple microservices and aggregating the results to determine the best route. It is also able to translate between web protocols and web-friendly protocols for internal use.

An application may use an API gateway to provide a single endpoint for mobile customers to query all product data with a single request. The API gateway consolidates various services, such as product information and reviews, and combines and exposes the results.

The API gateway is the gatekeeper for applications to access data, business logic, or functions (RESTful APIs or WebSocket APIs) that allow real-time two-way communication applications. The API gateway typically handles all the tasks involved in accepting and processing up to hundreds of thousands of concurrent API calls, including traffic management, cross-origin resource sharing (CORS) support, authorization and access control, choking, management, and API version control.

Sharing too much

A thin line lies between sharing enough functionality to not repeat yourself and creating a tangled mess of dependencies that prevents service changes from being separated. If an overshared service needs to be changed, evaluating proposed changes in the interfaces will eventually lead to an organizational task involving more development teams.

At some point, the choice of redundancy or library extraction into a new shared service that related microservices can install and develop independently of each other needs to be analyzed.

DevOps and Microservices

Microservices fit perfectly into the DevOps ideal of utilizing small teams to create functional changes to the enterprise's services one step at a time—the idea of breaking large problems into smaller pieces and tackling them systematically. To reduce the friction between development, testing, and deployment of smaller independent services, a series of continuous delivery pipelines to maintain a steady flow of these stages has to be present.

DevOps is a key factor in the success of this architectural style, providing the necessary organizational changes to minimize coordination between teams responsible for each component and to remove barriers to effective, reciprocal interaction between development and operations teams.

 I strongly dissuade any team from adopting the microservices pattern without a robust CI/CD infrastructure in place or without a widespread understanding of the basic concepts of pipelines.

Microservice Frameworks

The JVM ecosystem is vast and provides plenty of alternatives for a particular use case. Dozens of microservice frameworks and libraries are available, to the point that it can be tricky to pick a winner among candidates.

That said, certain candidate frameworks have gained popularity for several reasons: developer experience, time to market, extensibility, resource (CPU, memory) consumption, startup speed, failure recovery, documentation, third-party integrations, and more. These frameworks—Spring Boot, Micronaut, Quarkus, and Helidon—are covered in the following sections. Take into account that some of the instructions may require additional tweaks based on newer versions, as some of these technologies evolve quite rapidly. I strongly recommend reviewing the documentation of each framework.

Additionally, these examples require Java 11 as a minimum, and trying out Native Image also requires an installation of GraalVM. There are many ways to get these versions installed in your environment. I recommend using SDKMAN! (*https:// sdkman.io*) to install and manage them. For brevity, I concentrate on production code alone—a single framework could fill a whole book! It goes without saying that you should take care of tests as well. The goal for each example is to build a trivial "Hello World" REST service that can take an optional name parameter and reply with a greeting.

If you have not worked with GraalVM before, it's an umbrella project for a handful of technologies that enable the following features:

- A just-in-time (JIT) compiler written in Java, which compiles code on the fly, transforming interpreted code into executable code. The Java platform has had a handful of JITs, most written using a combination of C and C++. Graal happens to be the most modern one, written in Java.

- A virtual machine named *Substrate VM* that's capable of running hosted languages such as Python, JavaScript, and R on top of the JVM in such a way that the hosted language benefits from tighter integration with JVM capabilities and features.

- Native Image, a utility that relies on ahead-of-time (AOT) compilation, which transforms bytecode into machine-executable code. The resulting transformation produces a platform-specific binary executable.

All four candidate frameworks covered here provide support for GraalVM in one way or another, chiefly relying on GraalVM Native Image to produce platform-specific binaries with the goal of reducing deployment size and memory consumption. Be aware that there's a trade-off between using the Java mode and the GraalVM Native

Image mode. The latter can produce binaries with a smaller memory footprint and faster startup time but requires longer compilation time; long-running Java code will eventually become more optimized (that's one of the key features of the JVM), whereas native binaries cannot be optimized while running. Development experience also varies, as you may need to use additional tools for debugging, monitoring, measuring, and so forth.

Spring Boot

Spring Boot is perhaps the most well-known among the four candidates, as it builds on top of the legacy laid out by the Spring Framework. If developer surveys are to be taken at face value, more than 60% of Java developers have some sort of experience interacting with Spring-related projects, making Spring Boot the most popular choice.

The Spring way lets you assemble applications (or microservices, in our case) by composing existing components, customizing their configuration, and promising low-cost code ownership, as your custom logic is supposedly smaller in size than what the framework brings to the table, and for most organizations that's true. The trick is to find an existing component that can be tweaked and configured before writing your own. The Spring Boot team makes a point of adding as many useful integrations as needed, from database drivers to monitoring services, logging, journaling, batch processing, report generation, and more.

The typical way to bootstrap a Spring Boot project is by browsing to the Spring Initializr (*https://start.spring.io*), selecting the features you require in your application, and clicking the Generate button. This action creates a ZIP file that you can download to your local environment to get started. In Figure 4-1, I've selected the Web and Spring Native features. The first feature adds components that let you expose data via REST APIs; the second enhances the build with an extra packaging mechanism that can create Native Images with Graal.

Unpacking the ZIP file and running the `./mvnw verify` command at the root directory of the project ensures a sound starting point. You'll notice the command will download a set of dependencies if you've not built a Spring Boot application before on your target environment. This is normal Apache Maven behavior. These dependencies won't be downloaded again the next time you invoke a Maven command—unless dependency versions are updated in the *pom.xml* file.

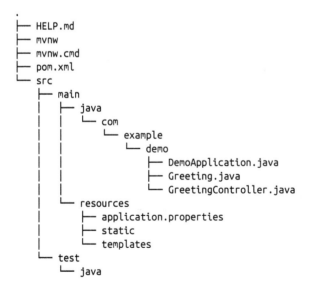

Figure 4-1. Spring Initializr

The project structure should look like this:

```
.
├── HELP.md
├── mvnw
├── mvnw.cmd
├── pom.xml
└── src
    ├── main
    │   ├── java
    │   │   └── com
    │   │       └── example
    │   │           └── demo
    │   │               ├── DemoApplication.java
    │   │               ├── Greeting.java
    │   │               └── GreetingController.java
    │   └── resources
    │       ├── application.properties
    │       ├── static
    │       └── templates
    └── test
        └── java
```

Our current task requires two additional sources that were not created by the Spring Initializr website: *Greeting.java* and *GreetingController.java*. These two files can be created using your text editor or IDE of choice. The first, *Greeting.java*, defines a data object that will be used to render content as JavaScript Object Notation (JSON), a typical format used to expose data via REST. Additional formats are also supported, but JSON support comes out of the box without any additional dependencies required. This file should look like this:

```java
package com.example.demo;

public class Greeting {
    private final String content;

    public Greeting(String content) {
        this.content = content;
    }

    public String getContent() {
        return content;
    }
}
```

There's nothing special about this data holder except that it's immutable; depending on your use case, you might want to switch to a mutable implementation, but for now this will suffice. Next is the REST endpoint itself, defined as a GET call on a */greeting* path. Spring Boot prefers the *controller* stereotype for this kind of component, no doubt harkening back to the days when Spring MVC (yes, that's model-view-controller) was the preferred option to create web applications. Feel free to use a different filename, but the component annotation must remain untouched:

```java
package com.example.demo;

import org.springframework.web.bind.annotation.GetMapping;
import org.springframework.web.bind.annotation.RequestParam;
import org.springframework.web.bind.annotation.RestController;

@RestController
public class GreetingController {
    private static final String template = "Hello, %s!";

    @GetMapping("/greeting")
    public Greeting greeting(@RequestParam(value = "name",
        defaultValue = "World") String name) {
        return new Greeting(String.format(template, name));
    }
}
```

The controller may take a `name` parameter as input and will use the value `World` when this parameter is not supplied. Notice that the return type of the mapped method is a plain Java type; it's the data type we just defined in the previous step. Spring Boot will automatically marshal data from and to JSON based on the annotations applied to the controller and its methods, as well as sensible defaults put in place. If we leave the code as is, the return value of the `greeting()` method will be automatically transformed into a JSON payload. This is the power of Spring Boot's developer experience, relying on defaults and predefined configuration that may be tweaked as needed.

You can run the application by either invoking the `/.mvnw spring-boot:run` command, which runs the application as part of the build process, or by generating the application JAR and running it manually—that is, `./mvnw package` followed by `java -jar target/demo-0.0.1.SNAPSHOT.jar`. Either way, an embedded web server will be started listening on port 8080; the */greeting* path will be mapped to an instance of *GreetingController*. All that's left is to issue a couple of queries, such as the following:

```
// using the default name parameter
$ curl http://localhost:8080/greeting
{"content":"Hello, World!"}

// using an explicit value for the name parameter
$ curl http://localhost:8080/greeting?name=Microservices
{"content":"Hello, Microservices!"}
```

Take note of the output generated by the application while running. On my local environment, it shows (on average) that the JVM takes 1.6 seconds to start up, while the application takes 600 milliseconds to initialize. The size of the generated JAR is roughly 17 MB. You may also want to take notes on the CPU and memory consumption of this trivial application. For some time now, it's been suggested that the use of GraalVM Native Image can reduce startup time and binary size. Let's see how we can make that happen with Spring Boot.

Remember how we selected the Spring Native feature when the project was created? Unfortunately, by version 2.5.0 the generated project does not include all required instructions in the *pom.xml* file. We must make a few tweaks. To begin with, the JAR created by `spring-boot-maven-plugin` requires a classifier; otherwise, the resulting Native Image may not be properly created. That's because the application JAR already contains all dependencies inside a Spring Boot—specific path that's not handled by `native-image-maven-plugin`, which we also have to configure. The updated *pom.xml* file should look like this:

```xml
<?xml version="1.0" encoding="UTF-8"?>
<project xmlns="http://maven.apache.org/POM/4.0.0"
    xmlns:xsi="http://www.w3.org/2001/XMLSchema-instance"
    xsi:schemaLocation="http://maven.apache.org/POM/4.0.0
    https://maven.apache.org/xsd/maven-4.0.0.xsd">
    <modelVersion>4.0.0</modelVersion>
    <parent>
        <groupId>org.springframework.boot</groupId>
        <artifactId>spring-boot-starter-parent</artifactId>
        <version>2.5.0</version>
    </parent>
    <groupId>com.example</groupId>
    <artifactId>demo</artifactId>
    <version>0.0.1-SNAPSHOT</version>
    <name>demo</name>
    <description>Demo project for Spring Boot</description>
    <properties>
        <java.version>11</java.version>
        <spring-native.version>0.10.0-SNAPSHOT</spring-native.version>
    </properties>
    <dependencies>
        <dependency>
            <groupId>org.springframework.boot</groupId>
            <artifactId>spring-boot-starter-web</artifactId>
        </dependency>
        <dependency>
            <groupId>org.springframework.experimental</groupId>
            <artifactId>spring-native</artifactId>
            <version>${spring-native.version}</version>
        </dependency>
        <dependency>
            <groupId>org.springframework.boot</groupId>
            <artifactId>spring-boot-starter-test</artifactId>
            <scope>test</scope>
        </dependency>
    </dependencies>

    <build>
        <plugins>
            <plugin>
                <groupId>org.springframework.boot</groupId>
                <artifactId>spring-boot-maven-plugin</artifactId>
                <configuration>
                    <classifier>exec</classifier>
                </configuration>
            </plugin>
            <plugin>
                <groupId>org.springframework.experimental</groupId>
                <artifactId>spring-aot-maven-plugin</artifactId>
                <version>${spring-native.version}</version>
                <executions>
                    <execution>
```

```xml
                    <id>test-generate</id>
                    <goals>
                        <goal>test-generate</goal>
                    </goals>
                </execution>
                <execution>
                    <id>generate</id>
                    <goals>
                        <goal>generate</goal>
                    </goals>
                </execution>
            </executions>
        </plugin>
    </plugins>
</build>
<repositories>
    <repository>
        <id>spring-release</id>
        <name>Spring release</name>
        <url>https://repo.spring.io/release</url>
    </repository>
</repositories>
<pluginRepositories>
    <pluginRepository>
        <id>spring-release</id>
        <name>Spring release</name>
        <url>https://repo.spring.io/release</url>
    </pluginRepository>
</pluginRepositories>

<profiles>
    <profile>
        <id>native-image</id>
        <build>
            <plugins>
                <plugin>
                    <groupId>org.graalvm.nativeimage</groupId>
                    <artifactId>native-image-maven-plugin</artifactId>
                    <version>21.1.0</version>
                    <configuration>
                        <mainClass>
                            com.example.demo.DemoApplication
                        </mainClass>
                    </configuration>
                    <executions>
                        <execution>
                            <goals>
                                <goal>native-image</goal>
                            </goals>
                            <phase>package</phase>
                        </execution>
                    </executions>
```

```
            </plugin>
          </plugins>
        </build>
      </profile>
    </profiles>
  </project>
```

One more step before we can give it a try: make sure to have a version of GraalVM installed as your current JDK. The selected version should closely match the version of `native-image-maven-plugin` found in the *pom.xml* file. The `native-image` executable must also be installed in your system; you can do that by invoking `gu install native-image`. The `gu` command is provided by the GraalVM installation.

With all settings in place, we can generate a native executable by invoking `./mvnw -Pnative-image package`. You'll notice a flurry of text going through the screen as new dependencies may be downloaded, and perhaps a few warnings related to missing classes—that's normal. The build also takes longer than usual, and here lies the trade-off of this packaging solution: we are increasing development time to speed up execution time at production. Once the command finishes, you'll notice a new file *com.example.demo.demoapplication* inside the *target* directory. This is the native executable. Go ahead and run it.

Did you notice how fast the startup was? On my environment, I get on average a startup time of 0.06 seconds, while the application takes 30 milliseconds to initialize itself. You may recall these numbers were 1.6 seconds and 600 milliseconds when running in Java mode. That's a serious speed boost! Now have a look at the size of the executable; in my case, it's around 78 MB. Oh well, looks like some things have grown for the worse—or have they? This executable is a single binary that provides everything needed to run the application, whereas the JAR we used earlier requires a Java runtime to run. The size of a Java runtime is typically in the 200 MB range and is composed of multiple files and directories. Of course, smaller Java runtimes may be created with jlink (*https://oreil.ly/agfRB*), in which case that adds another step during the build process. There's no free lunch.

Let's stop with Spring Boot for now, keeping in mind that there's a whole lot more to it than what has been shown here. On to the next framework.

Micronaut

Micronaut began life in 2017 as a reimagination of the Grails framework but with a modern look. Grails is one of the few successful "clones" of the Ruby on Rails (RoR) framework, leveraging the Groovy programming language. Grails made quite the splash for a few years, until the rise of Spring Boot took it out of the spotlight, prompting the Grails team to find alternatives, which resulted in Micronaut. On the surface, Micronaut provides a similar user experience to Spring Boot, as it also allows developers to compose applications based on existing components and sensible defaults.

One of Micronaut's key differentiators is the use of compile-time dependency injection for assembling the application, as opposed to runtime dependency injection, which is the preferred way of assembling applications with Spring Boot so far. This seemingly trivial change lets Micronaut exchange a bit of development time for a speed boost at runtime as the application spends less time bootstrapping itself; this can also lead to less memory consumption and less reliance on Java reflection, which historically has been slower than direct method invocations.

There are a handful of ways to bootstrap a Micronaut project, but the preferred one is to browse to Micronaut Launch (*https://oreil.ly/QAdrG*) and select the settings and features you'd like to see added to the project. The default application type defines the minimum settings to build a REST-based application such as the one we'll go through in a few minutes. Once satisfied with your selection, click the Generate Project button, as shown in Figure 4-2, which results in a ZIP file that can be downloaded to your local development environment.

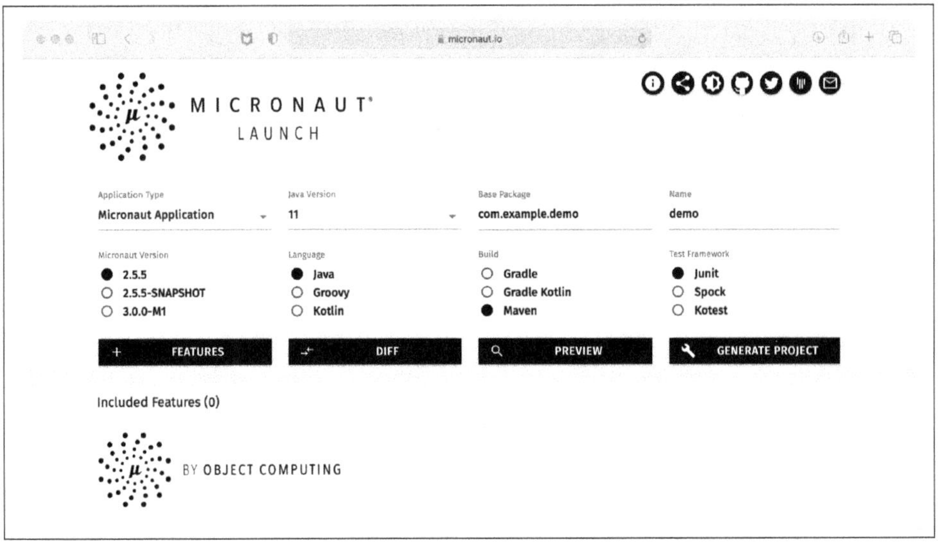

Figure 4-2. Micronaut Launch

Similarly as we did for Spring boot, unpacking the ZIP file and running the `./mvnw verify` command at the root directory of the project ensures a sound starting point. This command invocation will download plug-ins and dependencies as needed; the build should succeed after a few seconds if everything goes right. The project structure should look like the following one after adding a pair of additional source files:

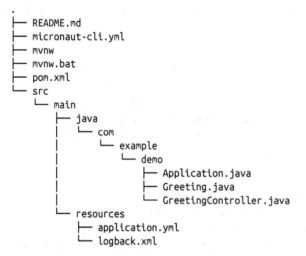

```
.
├── README.md
├── micronaut-cli.yml
├── mvnw
├── mvnw.bat
├── pom.xml
└── src
    └── main
        ├── java
        │   └── com
        │       └── example
        │           └── demo
        │               ├── Application.java
        │               ├── Greeting.java
        │               └── GreetingController.java
        └── resources
            ├── application.yml
            └── logback.xml
```

The *Application.java* source file defines the entry point, which we'll leave untouched for now as there's no need to make any updates. Similarly, we'll leave the *application.yml* resource file unchanged as well; this resource supplies configuration properties that don't require changes at this point.

We need two additional source files: the data object defined by *Greeting.java*, whose responsibility is to contain a message sent back to the consumer, and the actual REST endpoint defined by *GreetingController.java*. The controller stereotype goes all the way back to the conventions laid out by Grails, also followed by pretty much every RoR clone. You can certainly change the filename to anything that suits your domain, though you must leave the @Controller annotation in place. The source for the data object should look like this:

```
package com.example.demo;

import io.micronaut.core.annotation.Introspected;

@Introspected
public class Greeting {
    private final String content;

    public Greeting(String content) {
        this.content = content;
    }

    public String getContent() {
        return content;
    }
}
```

Once more we rely on an immutable design for this class. Note the use of the `@Introspected` annotation, which signals Micronaut to inspect the type at compile time and include it as part of the dependency-injection procedure. Usually, the annotation can be left out, as Micronaut will figure out that the class is required. But its use is paramount when it comes to generating the native executable with GraalVM Native Image; otherwise, the executable won't be complete. The second file should look like this:

```
package com.example.demo;

import io.micronaut.http.annotation.Controller;
import io.micronaut.http.annotation.Get;
import io.micronaut.http.annotation.QueryValue;

@Controller("/")
public class GreetingController {
    private static final String template = "Hello, %s!";

    @Get(uri = "/greeting")
    public Greeting greeting(@QueryValue(value = "name",
        defaultValue = "World") String name) {
        return new Greeting(String.format(template, name));
    }
}
```

We can appreciate that the controller defines a single endpoint mapped to `/greeting`, takes an optional parameter named `name`, and returns an instance of the data object. By default, Micronaut will marshal the return value as JSON, so no extra configuration is required to make it happen. Running the application can be done in a couple of ways. You can either invoke `./mvnw mn:run`, which runs the application as part of the build process, or invoke `./mvnw package`, which creates a *demo-0.1.jar* in the *target* directory that can be launched in the conventional way—that is, with `java -jar target/demo-0.1.jar`. Invoking a couple of queries to the REST endpoint may result in output similar to this:

```
// using the default name parameter
$ curl http://localhost:8080/greeting
{"content":"Hello, World!"}

// using an explicit value for the name parameter
$ curl http://localhost:8080/greeting?name=Microservices
{"content":"Hello, Microservices!"}
```

Either command launches the application quite quickly. On my local environment, the application is ready to process requests by 500 milliseconds on average, or three times the speed of Spring Boot for equivalent behavior. The size of the JAR file is also a bit smaller, at 14 MB in total. As impressive as these numbers may be, we can get a speed boost if the application were to be transformed using GraalVM Native Image into a native executable. Fortunately for us, the Micronaut way is friendlier with this kind of setup, resulting in everything we require already configured in the generated project. That's it. No need to update the build file with additional settings—it's all there.

You do require an installation of GraalVM and its `native-image` executable, though, as we did before. Creating a native executable is as simple as invoking `./mvnw -Dpackaging=native-image package`, and after a few minutes we should get an executable named `demo` (as a matter of fact, it's the project's `artifactId` if you were wondering) inside the *target* directory. Launching the application with the native executable results in a 20–millisecond startup time on average, which is a one-third gain in speed compared to Spring Boot. The executable size is 60 MB, which correlates to the reduced size of the JAR file.

Let's stop exploring Micronaut and move to the next framework: Quarkus.

Quarkus

Although *Quarkus* was announced in early 2019, work on it began much earlier. Quarkus has a lot of similarities with the two candidates we've seen so far. It offers great development experience based on components, convention over configuration, and productivity tools. Even more, Quarkus decided to also use compile-time dependency injection like Micronaut, allowing it to reap the same benefits, such as smaller binaries, faster startup, and less runtime magic. At the same time, Quarkus adds its own flavor and distinctiveness, and perhaps most important for some developers, Quarkus relies more on standards than the other two candidates. Quarkus implements the MicroProfile specifications, which are standards that come from JakartaEE (previously known as JavaEE), and additional standards developed under the MicroProfile project umbrella.

You can get started with Quarkus by browsing to the Quarkus Configure Your Application page (*https://code.quarkus.io*) to configure values and download a ZIP file. This page is loaded with plenty of goodies, including many extensions to choose from to configure specific integrations such as databases, REST capabilities, monitoring, and more. The RESTEasy Jackson extension must be selected, allowing Quarkus to seamlessly marshal values to and from JSON. Clicking the "Generate your application" button should prompt you to save a ZIP file into your local system, the contents of which should look similar to this:

```
.
├── README.md
├── mvnw
├── mvnw.cmd
├── pom.xml
└── src
    ├── main
    │   ├── docker
    │   │   ├── Dockerfile.jvm
    │   │   ├── Dockerfile.legacy-jar
    │   │   ├── Dockerfile.native
    │   │   └── Dockerfile.native-distroless
    │   ├── java
    │   │   └── com
    │   │       └── example
    │   │           └── demo
    │   │               ├── Greeting.java
    │   │               └── GreetingResource.java
    │   └── resources
    │       ├── META-INF
    │       │   └── resources
    │       │       └── index.html
    │       └── application.properties
    └── test
        └── java
```

We can appreciate that Quarkus adds Docker configuration files out of the box,
as it was designed to tackle microservice architectures in the cloud via containers
and Kubernetes. But as time has passed, its range has grown wider by supporting
additional application types and architectures. The *GreetingResource.java* file is also
created by default, and it's a typical Jakarta RESTful Web Services (JAX-RS) resource.
We'll have to make some adjustments to that resource to enable it to handle the
Greeting.java data object. Here's the source for that:

```
package com.example.demo;

public class Greeting {
    private final String content;

    public Greeting(String content) {
        this.content = content;
    }

    public String getContent() {
        return content;
    }
}
```

The code is pretty much identical to what we've seen before in this chapter. There's
nothing new or surprising about this immutable data object. Now, in the case of the
JAX-RS resource, things will look similar yet different, as the behavior we seek is the

same as before, though the way we instruct the framework to perform its magic is via JAX-RS annotations. Thus the code looks like this:

```java
package com.example.demo;

import javax.ws.rs.DefaultValue;
import javax.ws.rs.GET;
import javax.ws.rs.Path;
import javax.ws.rs.QueryParam;

@Path("/greeting")
public class GreetingResource {
    private static final String template = "Hello, %s!";

    @GET
    public Greeting greeting(@QueryParam("name")
        @DefaultValue("World") String name) {
        return new Greeting(String.format(template, name));
    }
}
```

If you're familiar with JAX-RS, this code should be no surprise to you. But if you're not familiar with the JAX-RS annotations, what we do here is mark the resource with the REST path we'd like to react to; we also indicate that the greeting() method will handle a GET call, and that its name parameter has a default value. Nothing more needs to be done to instruct Quarkus to marshal the return value into JSON, as that will happen by default.

Running the application can be done in a couple of ways as well, using the developer mode as part of the build. This is one of the features that has a unique Quarkus flavor, as it lets you run the application and pick up any changes you made automatically without having to manually restart the application. You can activate this mode by invoking /.mvnw compile quarkus:dev. If you make any changes to the source files, you'll notice that the build will automatically recompile and load the application.

You may also run the application using the java interpreter as we've seen before, which results in a command such as java -jar target/quarkus-app/quarkus-run.jar. Note that we're using a different JAR, although the *demo-1.0.0-SNAPSHOT.jar* does exist in the *target* directory; the reason to do it this way is that Quarkus applies custom logic to speed up the boot process even in the Java mode.

Running the application should result in startup times with 600 milliseconds on average, which is pretty close to what Micronaut does. Also, the size of the full application is in the 13 MB range. Sending a couple of GET requests to the application without and with a name parameter results in output similar to the following:

```
// using the default name parameter
$ curl http://localhost:8080/greeting
{"content":"Hello, World!"}
```

```
// using an explicit value for the name parameter
$ curl http://localhost:8080/greeting?name=Microservices
{"content":"Hello, Microservices!"}
```

It should be no surprise that Quarkus also supports generating native executables via GraalVM Native Image, given that it targets cloud environments where small binary size is recommended. Because of this, Quarkus comes with batteries included, just like Micronaut, and generates everything you need from the get-go. There's no need to update the build configuration to get started with native executables. As with the other examples, you must ensure that the current JDK points to a GraalVM distribution and that the `native-image` executable is found in your path. Once this step has been cleared, all that's left is to package the application as a native executable by invoking `./mvnw -Pnative package`. This activates the `native` profile, which instructs the Quarkus build tools to generate the native executable.

After a couple of minutes, the build should have produced an executable named *demo-1.0.0-SNAPSHOT-runner* inside the *target* directory. Running this executable shows that the application starts up in 15 milliseconds on average. The size of the executable is close to 47 MB, which makes Quarkus the framework that yields the fastest startup and smallest executable size so far when compared to previous candidate frameworks.

We're done with Quarkus for the time being, leaving us with the fourth candidate framework: Helidon.

Helidon

Last but not least, *Helidon* is a framework specifically crafted for building microservices with two flavors: SE and MP. The MP flavor stands for *MicroProfile* and lets you build applications by harnessing the power of standards; this flavor is a full implementation of the MicroProfile specifications. The SE flavor, on the other hand, does not implement MicroProfile, yet delivers similar functionality using a different set of APIs. Pick a flavor based on the APIs you'd like to interact with and your preference for standards; either way, Helidon gets the job done.

Given that Helidon implements MicroProfile, we can use yet another site to bootstrap a Helidon project. The MicroProfile Starter site (*https://oreil.ly/3U7RG*) (Figure 4-3) can be used to create projects for all supported implementations of the MicroProfile specification by versions.

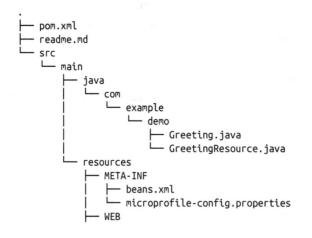

Figure 4-3. MicroProfile Starter

Browse to the site, select which MP version you're interested in, choose the MP implementation (in our case, Helidon), and perhaps customize some of the available features. Then click the Download button to download a ZIP file containing the generated project. The ZIP file contains a project structure similar to the following, except of course I've already updated the sources with the two files required to make the application work as we want it:

```
.
├── pom.xml
├── readme.md
└── src
    └── main
        ├── java
        │   └── com
        │       └── example
        │           └── demo
        │               ├── Greeting.java
        │               └── GreetingResource.java
        └── resources
            ├── META-INF
            │   ├── beans.xml
            │   └── microprofile-config.properties
            ├── WEB
```

```
|   └── index.html
├── logging.properties
└── privateKey.pem
```

As it happens, the source files *Greeting.java* and *GreetingResource.java* are identical to the sources we saw in the Quarkus example. How is that possible? First because the code is definitely trivial, but also (and more important) because both frameworks rely on the power of standards. As a matter of fact, the *Greeting.java* file is pretty much identical across all frameworks—except for Micronaut, which requires an additional annotation, but only if you're interested in generating native executables; otherwise, it's 100% identical. If you decided to jump ahead to this section before browsing the others, here's what the *Greeting.java* file looks like:

```
package com.example.demo;

import io.helidon.common.Reflected;

@Reflected
public class Greeting {
    private final String content;

    public Greeting(String content) {
        this.content = content;
    }

    public String getContent() {
        return content;
    }
}
```

It's just a regular immutable data object with a single accessor. The *Greeting Resource.java* file, which defines the REST mappings needed for the application, follows:

```
package com.example.demo;

import javax.ws.rs.DefaultValue;
import javax.ws.rs.GET;
import javax.ws.rs.Path;
import javax.ws.rs.QueryParam;

@Path("/greeting")
public class GreetingResource {
    private static final String template = "Hello, %s!";

    @GET
    public Greeting greeting(@QueryParam("name")
        @DefaultValue("World") String name) {
        return new Greeting(String.format(template, name));
    }
}
```

We can appreciate the use of JAX-RS annotations, as we can see there's no need for Helidon-specific APIs at this point. The preferred way to run a Helidon application is to package the binaries and run them with the `java` interpreter. That is, we lose a bit of build tool integration (for now), yet we can still use the command line to perform iterative development. Thus invoking `mvn package` followed by `java -jar/demo.jar` compiles, packages, and runs the application with an embedded web server listening on port 8080. We can send a couple of queries to it, such as this one:

```
// using the default name parameter
$ curl http://localhost:8080/greeting
{"content":"Hello, World!"}

// using an explicit value for the name parameter
$ curl http://localhost:8080/greeting?name=Microservices
{"content":"Hello, Microservices!"}
```

If you look at the output where the application process is running, you'll see that the application starts with 2.3 seconds on average, which makes it the slowest candidate we have seen so far, while the binaries' size is close to 15 MB, putting it in the middle of all measurements. But as the adage goes, you can't judge a book by its cover. Helidon provides more features out of the box automatically configured, which would account for the extra startup time and the larger deployment size.

If startup speed and deployment size were issues, you could reconfigure the build to remove those features that may not be needed, as well as switch to native executable mode. Fortunately, the Helidon team has embraced GraalVM Native Image as well, and every Helidon project, bootstrapped as we've done ourselves, comes with the required configuration to create native binaries. There's no need to tweak the *pom.xml* file if you follow the conventions. Execute the `mvn -Pnative-image package` command, and you'll find a binary executable named *demo* inside the *target* directory. This executable weighs about 94 MB, the largest so far, while its startup time is 50 milliseconds on average, in the same range as the previous frameworks.

Up to now, we've caught a glimpse of what each framework has to offer, from base features to build tool integration. As a reminder, there are several reasons to pick one candidate framework over another. I encourage you to write down a matrix for each relevant feature/aspect that affects your development requirements and assess each one of those items with every candidate.

Serverless

This chapter began by looking at monolithic applications and architectures, usually pieced together by components and tiers clumped together into a single, cohesive unit. Changes or updates to a particular piece require updating and deploying the whole. Failure at one particular place could bring down the whole as well. Then we moved on to microservices. Breaking the monolith into smaller chunks that can be updated and deployed individually and independently of one another should take care of the previously mentioned issues, but microservices bring a host of other issues.

Before, it was enough to run the monolith inside an application server hosted on big iron, with a handful of replicas and a load balancer for good measure. This setup has scalability issues. With the microservices approach, we can grow or collapse the mesh of services depending on the load. That boosts elasticity, but now we have to coordinate multiple instances and provision runtime environments, load balancers become a must, API gateways are needed, network latency rears its ugly head, and did I mention distributed tracing? Yes, those are a lot of things to be aware of and manage. But what if you didn't have to? What if someone else took care of the infrastructure, monitoring, and other "minutiae" required to run applications at scale? This is where the serverless approach comes in: where you concentrate on the business logic at hand and let the serverless provider deal with everything else.

While distilling a component into smaller pieces, one thought should come to mind: "What's the smallest reusable piece of code I can turn this component into?" If your answer is a Java class with a handful of methods and perhaps a couple of injected collaborators/services, you're close, but you're not there yet. The smallest piece of reusable code is, as a matter of fact, a single method. Picture a microservice defined as a single class that performs the following steps:

1. Reads the input arguments and transforms them into a consumable format as required by the next step
2. Performs the actual behavior required by the service, such as issuing a query to a database, indexing, or logging
3. Transforms the processed data into an output format

Now, each of these steps may be organized in separate methods. You may soon realize that some of these methods are reusable as is or parameterized. A typical way to solve this would be to provide a common *super type* among microservices. This creates a strong dependency among types, and for some use cases, that's all right. But for others, updates to the common code have to happen as soon as possible, in a versioned fashion, without disrupting currently running code, so I'm afraid we may need an alternative.

With this scenario in mind, if the common code were to be provided instead as a set of methods that can be invoked independently of one another, with their inputs and outputs composed in such a way that you establish a pipeline of data transformations, then we arrive at what are now known as *functions*. Offerings such as *function as a service* (FaaS) are a common subject among serverless providers.

In summary, FaaS is a fancy way to say that you compose applications based on the smallest deployment unit possible and let the provider figure out all the infrastructure details for you. In the following sections, we'll build and deploy a simple function to the cloud.

Setting Up

Nowadays every major cloud provider has an FaaS offering at your disposal, with add-ons that hook into other tools for monitoring, logging, disaster recovery, and more; just pick the one that meets your needs. For the sake of this chapter, we'll pick AWS Lambda, which was, after all, the originator of the FaaS idea. We'll also pick Quarkus as the implementation framework, as it's the one that currently provides the smallest deployment size. Be aware that the configuration shown here may need some tweaks or might be totally outdated; always review the latest versions of the tools required to build and run the code. We'll use Quarkus 1.13.7 for now.

Setting up a function with Quarkus and AWS Lambda requires having an AWS account (*https://aws.amazon.com*), the AWS CLI (*https://oreil.ly/0dYrb*) installed on your system, and the AWS Serverless Application Model (SAM) CLI (*https://oreil.ly/h7gdD*) if you'd like to run local tests.

Once you have that covered, the next step is to bootstrap the project, for which we would be inclined to use Quarkus (*https://code.quarkus.io*) as before except that a function project requires a different setup. So it's better to switch to using a Maven archetype:

```
mvn archetype:generate \
    -DarchetypeGroupId=io.quarkus \
    -DarchetypeArtifactId=quarkus-amazon-lambda-archetype \
    -DarchetypeVersion=1.13.7.Final
```

Invoking this command in interactive mode will ask you a few questions, such as the group, artifact, version (GAV) coordinates for the project, and the base package. For this demo, let's go with these:

- `groupId`: com.example.demo
- `artifactId`: demo
- `version`: 1.0-SNAPSHOT (the default)
- `package`: com.example.demo (same as `groupId`)

This results in a project structure suitable to build, test, and deploy a Quarkus project as a function deployable to AWS Lambda. The archetype creates build files for both Maven and Gradle, but we don't need the latter for now; it also creates three function classes, but we need only one. Our aim is to have a file structure similar to this one:

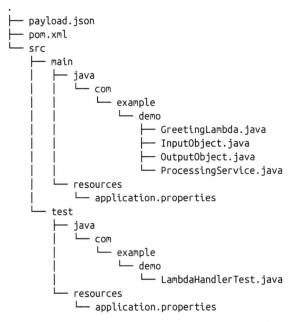

```
.
├── payload.json
├── pom.xml
└── src
    ├── main
    │   ├── java
    │   │   └── com
    │   │       └── example
    │   │           └── demo
    │   │               ├── GreetingLambda.java
    │   │               ├── InputObject.java
    │   │               ├── OutputObject.java
    │   │               └── ProcessingService.java
    │   └── resources
    │       └── application.properties
    └── test
        ├── java
        │   └── com
        │       └── example
        │           └── demo
        │               └── LambdaHandlerTest.java
        └── resources
            └── application.properties
```

The gist of the function is to capture inputs with the InputObject type, process them with the ProcessingService type, and then transform the results into another type (OutputObject). The GreetingLambda type puts everything together. Let's have a look at both input and output types first—after all, they are simple types that are concerned with only containing data, with no logic whatsoever:

```java
package com.example.demo;

public class InputObject {
    private String name;
    private String greeting;

    public String getName() {
        return name;
    }

    public void setName(String name) {
        this.name = name;
    }

    public String getGreeting() {
        return greeting;
    }

    public void setGreeting(String greeting) {
        this.greeting = greeting;
    }
}
```

The lambda expects two input values: a greeting and a name. We'll see how they get transformed by the processing service in a moment:

```
package com.example.demo;

public class OutputObject {
    private String result;
    private String requestId;

    public String getResult() {
        return result;
    }

    public void setResult(String result) {
        this.result = result;
    }

    public String getRequestId() {
        return requestId;
    }

    public void setRequestId(String requestId) {
        this.requestId = requestId;
    }
}
```

The output object holds the transformed data and a reference to the requestID. We'll use this field to show how we can get data from the running context.

All right, the processing service is next; this class is responsible for transforming the inputs into outputs. In our case, it concatenates both input values into a single string, as shown here:

```
package com.example.demo;

import javax.enterprise.context.ApplicationScoped;

@ApplicationScoped
public class ProcessingService {
    public OutputObject process(InputObject input) {
        OutputObject output = new OutputObject();
        output.setResult(input.getGreeting() + " " + input.getName());
        return output;
    }
}
```

What's left is to have a look at GreetingLambda, the type used to assemble the function itself. This class requires implementing a known interface supplied by Quarkus, whose dependency should be already configured in the *pom.xml* file created with the archetype. This interface is parameterized with input and output types. Luckily, we have those already. Every lambda must have a unique name and may access its running context, as shown next:

```
package com.example.demo;

import com.amazonaws.services.lambda.runtime.Context;
import com.amazonaws.services.lambda.runtime.RequestHandler;

import javax.inject.Inject;
import javax.inject.Named;

@Named("greeting")
public class GreetingLambda
    implements RequestHandler<InputObject, OutputObject> {
    @Inject
    ProcessingService service;

    @Override
    public OutputObject handleRequest(InputObject input, Context context) {
        OutputObject output = service.process(input);
        output.setRequestId(context.getAwsRequestId());
        return output;
    }
}
```

All the pieces fall into place. The lambda defines input and output types and invokes the data processiong service. For the purpose of demonstration, this example shows the use of dependency injection, but you could reduce the code by moving the behavior of `ProcessingService` into `GreetingLambda`. We can quickly verify the code by running local tests with `mvn test`, or if you prefer `mvn verify`, as that will also package the function.

Note that additional files are placed in the *target* directory when the function is packaged, specifically a script named *manage.sh*, which relies on the AWS CLI tool to create, update, and delete the function at the target destination associated with your AWS account. Additional files are required to support these operations:

function.zip
> The deployment file containing the binary bits

sam.jvm.yaml
> Local test with AWS SAM CLI (Java mode)

sam.native.yaml
> Local test with AWS SAM CLI (native mode)

The next step requires you to have an *execution role* configured, for which it's best to refer to the AWS Lambda Developer Guide (*https://oreil.ly/97ACL*) in case the procedure has been updated. The guide shows you how to get the AWS CLI configured (if you have not done so already) and create an execution role that must be added as an environment variable to your running shell. For example:

```
LAMBDA_ROLE_ARN="arn:aws:iam::1234567890:role/lambda-ex"
```

In this case, 1234567890 stands for your AWS account ID, and lambda-ex is the name of the role of your choosing. We can proceed with executing the function, for which we have two modes (Java, native) and two execution environments (local, production); let's tackle the Java mode first for both environments and then follow it up with native mode.

Running the function on a local environment requires the use of a Docker daemon, which by now should be commonplace in a developer's toolbox; we also require using the AWS SAM CLI to drive the execution. Remember the set of additional files found inside the *target* directory? We'll use the *sam.jvm.yaml* file alongside another file that was created by the archetype when the project was bootstrapped, called *payload.json*. Located at the root of the directory, its contents should look like this:

```
{
  "name": "Bill",
  "greeting": "hello"
}
```

This file defines values for the inputs accepted by the function. Given that the function is already packaged, we just have to invoke it, like so:

```
$ sam local invoke --template target/sam.jvm.yaml --event payload.json
Invoking io.quarkus.amazon.lambda.runtime.QuarkusStreamHandler::handleRequest
(java11)
Decompressing /work/demo/target/function.zip
Skip pulling image and use local one:
amazon/aws-sam-cli-emulation-image-java11:rapid-1.24.1.

Mounting /private/var/folders/p_/3h19jd792gq0zr1ckqn9jb0m0000gn/T/tmppesjj0c8 as
/var/task:ro,delegated inside runtime container
START RequestId: 0b8cf3de-6d0a-4e72-bf36-232af46145fa Version: $LATEST

 --/ _ \/ / / / _ | / _ \/ //_/ / / / _/
 -/ /_/ / /_/ / __ |/ , _/ ,< / /_/ /\ \
--_____/_/ |_/_/|_/_/|_|\____/___/
[io.quarkus] (main) quarkus-lambda 1.0-SNAPSHOT on
JVM (powered by Quarkus 1.13.7.Final) started in 2.680s.
[io.quarkus] (main) Profile prod activated.
[io.quarkus] (main) Installed features: [amazon-lambda, cdi]
END RequestId: 0b8cf3de-6d0a-4e72-bf36-232af46145fa
REPORT RequestId: 0b8cf3de-6d0a-4e72-bf36-232af46145fa  Init Duration: 1.79 ms
Duration: 3262.01 ms Billed Duration: 3300 ms
Memory Size: 256 MB    Max Memory Used: 256 MB
{"result":"hello Bill","requestId":"0b8cf3de-6d0a-4e72-bf36-232af46145fa"}
```

The command will pull a Docker image suitable for running the function. Take note of the reported values, which may differ depending on your setup. On my local environment, this function would cost me 3.3 seconds, and 256 MB for its execution. This can give you an idea of how much you'll be billed when running your system as a set of functions. However, local is not the same as production, so let's deploy the function to the real deal. We'll use the *manage.sh* script to accomplish this feat, by invoking the following commands:

```
$ sh target/manage.sh create
$ sh target/manage.sh invoke
Invoking function
++ aws lambda invoke response.txt --cli-binary-format raw-in-base64-out
++ --function-name QuarkusLambda --payload file://payload.json
++ --log-type Tail --query LogResult
++ --output text base64 --decode
START RequestId: df8d19ad-1e94-4bce-a54c-93b8c09361c7 Version: $LATEST
END RequestId: df8d19ad-1e94-4bce-a54c-93b8c09361c7
REPORT RequestId: df8d19ad-1e94-4bce-a54c-93b8c09361c7  Duration: 273.47 ms
Billed Duration: 274 ms Memory Size: 256 MB
Max Memory Used: 123 MB Init Duration: 1635.69 ms
{"result":"hello Bill","requestId":"df8d19ad-1e94-4bce-a54c-93b8c09361c7"}
```

As you can see, the billed duration and memory usage decreased, which is good for our wallet, although the init duration went up to 1.6, which would delay the response, increasing the total execution time across the system. Let's see how these numbers change when we switch from Java mode to native mode. As you may recall, Quarkus lets you package projects as native executables out of the box, but remember that Lambda requires Linux executables, so if you happen to be running on a non-Linux environment, you'll need to tweak the packaging command. Here's what needs to be done:

```
# for linux
$ mvn -Pnative package

# for non-linux
$ mvn package -Pnative -Dquarkus.native.container-build=true \
  -Dquarkus.native.container-runtime=docker
```

The second command invokes the build inside a Docker container and places the generated executable on your system at the expected location, whereas the first command executes the build as is. With the native executable now in place, we can execute the new function both in local and production environments. Let's see the local environment first:

```
$ sam local invoke --template target/sam.native.yaml --event payload.json
Invoking not.used.in.provided.runtime (provided)
Decompressing /work/demo/target/function.zip
Skip pulling image and use local one:
amazon/aws-sam-cli-emulation-image-provided:rapid-1.24.1.
```

```
Mounting /private/var/folders/p_/3h19jd792gq0zr1ckqn9jb0m0000gn/T/tmp1zgzkuhy as
/var/task:ro,delegated inside runtime container
START RequestId: 27531d6c-461b-45e6-92d3-644db6ec8df4 Version: $LATEST
 __ ___ __  ____  __ ___ __ ___  ____
--/ __ \/ / / / _ | / / _ \/ //_/ / / / __/
-/ /_/ / /_/ / __ |/ / , _/ ,< / /_/ /\ \
--_____/_/ |_/_/|_/_/|_|\____/___/
[io.quarkus] (main) quarkus-lambda 1.0-SNAPSHOT native
(powered by Quarkus 1.13.7.Final) started in 0.115s.
[io.quarkus] (main) Profile prod activated.
[io.quarkus] (main) Installed features: [amazon-lambda, cdi]
END RequestId: 27531d6c-461b-45e6-92d3-644db6ec8df4
REPORT RequestId: 27531d6c-461b-45e6-92d3-644db6ec8df4  Init Duration: 0.13 ms
Duration: 218.76 ms     Billed Duration: 300 ms Memory Size: 128 MB
Max Memory Used: 128 MB
{"result":"hello Bill","requestId":"27531d6c-461b-45e6-92d3-644db6ec8df4"}
```

The billed duration decreased by one order of magnitude, going from 3300 ms to just 300 ms, and the used memory was halved; this looks promising compared to its Java counterpart. Will we get better numbers when running on production? Let's look:

```
$ sh target/manage.sh native create
$ sh target/manage.sh native invoke
Invoking function
++ aws lambda invoke response.txt --cli-binary-format raw-in-base64-out
++ --function-name QuarkusLambdaNative
++ --payload file://payload.json --log-type Tail --query LogResult --output text
++ base64 --decode
START RequestId: 19575cd3-3220-405b-afa0-76aa52e7a8b5 Version: $LATEST
END RequestId: 19575cd3-3220-405b-afa0-76aa52e7a8b5
REPORT RequestId: 19575cd3-3220-405b-afa0-76aa52e7a8b5  Duration: 2.55 ms
Billed Duration: 187 ms Memory Size: 256 MB     Max Memory Used: 54 MB
Init Duration: 183.91 ms
{"result":"hello Bill","requestId":"19575cd3-3220-405b-afa0-76aa52e7a8b5"}
```

The total billed duration results in 30% speedup, and the memory usage is less than half of that before; but the real winner is the initialization time, which takes roughly 10% of the previous time. Running your function in native mode results in faster startup and better numbers across the board.

Now it's up to you to decide the combination of options that will give you the best results. Sometimes staying in Java mode is good enough even for production, or going native all the way may give you the edge. Whichever way it may be, measurements are key—don't guess!

Summary

We covered a lot of ground in this chapter, starting with a traditional monolith, breaking it into smaller parts with reusable components that can be deployed independently, known as microservices, and going all the way to the smallest deployment unit possible: a function. Trade-offs occur along the way, as microservice architectures are inherently more complex, composed as they are of more moving parts. Network latency becomes a real issue and must be tackled accordingly. Other aspects such as data transactions become more complex as their span may cross service boundaries, depending on the case. The use of Java and native executable mode yields different results and requires to be customized setup, each with its own pros and cons. My recommendation, dear reader, is to evaluate, measure, and then select a combination; keep tabs on numbers and service level agreements (SLAs), because you may need to reevaluate decisions along the road and make adjustments.

Table 4-1 summarizes the measurements obtained by running the sample application on both Java and native image modes, on my local environment and remote, for each one of the candidate frameworks. The size columns show the deployment unit size, while the time columns depict the time from startup up to the first request.

Table 4-1. Measurement summary

Framework	Java - size	Java - time	Native - size	Native - time
Spring Boot	17 MB	2200 ms	78 MB	90 ms
Micronaut	14 MB	500 ms	60 MB	20 ms
Quarkus	13 MB	600 ms	47 MB	13 ms
Helidon	15 MB	2300 ms	94 MB	50 ms

As a reminder, you are encouraged to take your own measurements. Changes to the hosting environment, JVM version and settings, framework version, network conditions, and other environment characteristics will yield different results. The numbers shown should be taken with a grain of salt, never as authoritative values.

## CHAPTER 5

Continuous Integration

Melissa McKay

Always make new mistakes.
—Esther Dyson

Back in Chapter 2, you learned the value of source control and a common code repository. After you have organized and settled on your source control solution, you need to take a few more steps to reach an end result where your users can bask in the perfect user experience of your delivered software.

Think about the process that you would take as an individual developer to progress your software through the entire software development lifecycle. After determining the acceptance criteria for a particular feature or bug fix for your software, you would proceed with adding the actual lines of code along with the related unit tests to the codebase. Then, you would compile and run all of the unit tests to ensure that your new code works as you expect (or at least as defined by your unit tests) and doesn't break known existing functionality. After you find that all tests pass, you would build and package your application and verify functionality in the form of integration tests in a quality assurance (QA) environment. Finally, happy with the green light from your well-oiled and maintained test suites, you would deliver and/or deploy your software to a production environment.

If you have any development experience at all, you know as well as I do that software rarely falls into place so neatly. Strict implementation of the ideal workflow described is too simplistic when you begin working on a larger project with a team of developers. Multiple complications are introduced that can gum up the gears of the software delivery lifecycle and throw your schedule into a lurch. This chapter discusses how continuous integration and the related best practices and toolsets will help you steer clear of or mitigate the most common hurdles and headaches that software development projects often encounter on the path to delivery.

Adopt Continuous Integration

Continuous integration (CI) is most commonly described as frequently integrating code changes from multiple contributors into the main source code repository of a project. In practice, this definition by itself is a little vague. Exactly how often is *frequently*? What does integrating actually mean in this context? Is it enough just to coordinate pushing code changes to the source code repository? And most important, what problem does this process solve—for what benefit(s) should you adopt this practice?

The concept of CI has been around now for quite some time. According to Martin Fowler (*https://oreil.ly/3sYHE*), the term *continuous integration* originated with Kent Beck's Extreme Programming development process, as one of its original 12 practices. In the DevOps community, the term itself is now as common as butter on toast. But the way it is implemented may vary from team to team and project to project. The benefits are hit-or-miss if there isn't a thorough understanding of the original intent or if best practices are abandoned.

It's interesting to see how our understanding of CI has changed over time. The way we talk about it now is much different from when it was initially introduced by Beck to address the issues of concurrent development. The problems we have today are more about keeping regular and frequent builds efficient while minimizing bugs, whereas initially, CI and the proliferation of build tools that spun out from it was more about getting a project to build *at all* after development was complete. Instead of trying to assemble a project only *after* all the coding has been completed by the team, CI required a change in mindset—to regularly build *during* development.

Today, CI is meant to identify bugs and compatibility issues as quickly as possible in the development cycle through regular and frequent builds. The basic premise of CI is that if developers integrate changes often, bugs can be found sooner in the process, and less time is spent hunting down when and where a problem was introduced. The longer a bug goes undiscovered, the greater the potential for it to become entrenched in the surrounding codebase.

It is much easier from a development perspective to find, catch, and fix bugs closer to when they are introduced rather than extract them from layers of code that have already moved to later stages of the delivery pipeline. Bugs that evade discovery until the latest acceptance phases, and especially those that escape all the way to release, directly translate to more money spent to fix and less time spent on new features. In the case of fixing a bug in production, in many instances, there is now a requirement to patch existing deployments in addition to including and documenting the fix in a new version. This inherently reduces the time the team has available to spend on the development of new features.

It's important to understand that implementing a CI solution does *not* equate to software that never has any bugs. It would be foolish to use such a definitive measure to determine whether the implementation of CI is worthy. A more valuable metric might be the number of bugs or compatibility issues that were caught by CI. In much the same way that a vaccine is never 100% effective in a large population, CI is simply another level of protection to filter the most obvious bugs from a release. By itself, CI will never replace the well-known benefits of software development best practices that are in the purview of the initial design and development steps. It will, however, provide a better safety net for software as it is repeatedly handled and massaged by multiple developers over time. Martin Fowler puts it this way: "Continuous integration doesn't get rid of bugs, but it does make them dramatically easier to find and remove."

My first experience with CI was during an internship at a small company that adopted the software development methodology of Extreme Programming (XP), of which CI is an important aspect. We did not have an incredibly fancy system using all of the latest and greatest DevOps tools. What we did have was a common code repository, and a single build server located in a small closet in the office.

Unbeknownst to me when I first joined the development team, a speaker was set up on the build server that would erupt in the sound of emergency sirens if a fresh checkout from source control resulted in the failure of a build or any automated tests. We were a relatively young team, so this part of our CI was mostly in jest, but guess who learned *remarkably* quickly not to push code to the main repository without first verifying that the project built successfully and passed unit tests?

To this day, I feel exceptionally fortunate to have been exposed to this practice in this way. The simplicity of it underscored the most important aspects of CI. I want to call out three by-products of this simple setup:

Code integration was regular and rarely complicated
> My team had agreed to follow XP practices, which encourage integration as often as every few hours (*https://oreil.ly/0A7P9*). More important than a specific time interval was the amount of code requiring integration at any given point. When planning and breaking down actual development work, we focused our efforts on creating small, completable tasks, always beginning with the simplest thing that can possibly work (*https://oreil.ly/Scb94*). By *completable*, I mean after the development task was complete, it could be integrated into the main code repository and the result would be expected to build successfully and pass all unit tests. This practice of organizing code updates in as small a package as possible made regular and frequent integration to the main source code repository a normal and unremarkable activity. Rarely was significant time spent on large integration efforts.

Build and test failures were relatively easy to troubleshoot
> Because the project was built and automated tests were run at regular intervals, it was readily apparent where to start troubleshooting any failures. A relatively small amount of code would have been touched since the latest successful build, and if the problem couldn't immediately be identified and resolved, we would start with reverting the latest merge and work backward as needed to restore a clean build.

Bugs and compatibility issues introduced by integration and caught by the CI system were fixed immediately
> The loud sound of the siren let *everyone* on the team know that a problem needed to be addressed, a problem that could not be ignored. Because our CI system halted progress whenever a build or test failure occurred, everyone was on board to figure out what was wrong and what to do to fix the problem. Team communication, coordination, and cooperation were all in top shape because no one would be able to move forward until the issue was resolved. A majority of the time, the offending code could be identified simply by analyzing the most recent merge, and the responsibility to fix was assigned to that developer or pair of developers. At times, a discussion with the entire team was necessary because of a compatibility issue around multiple recent merges, as changes in one part of the system negatively affected another seemingly unrelated part. These instances required our team to reevaluate the code changes being made holistically and then decide together the best plan of action.

These three factors were key to the success of our CI solution. You might have discerned that all three imply the prerequisites of a healthy codebase and a healthy development team. Without these, the initial implementation of a CI solution will undoubtedly be more difficult. However, implementing a CI solution will in turn have a positive impact on the codebase, and taking the first steps will provide a measure of benefit that will be well worth the effort.

It is true there is much more to an effective CI solution than simple coordination of code contribution to a shared repository and following a mandate to integrate at an agreed-upon frequency. The following sections will walk you through the essentials of a complete, practicable CI solution that will help unburden and accelerate the software development process.

Declaratively Script Your Build

Regardless of the state of your project—whether it's greenfield, legacy, a small individual library, or a large multimodule project—your first task in implementing a CI solution should be to *script your build*. Having a consistent and repeatable process that you can automate will help avoid the frustration of buggy build permutations due to the mismanagement of dependencies, forgetting to include needed resources when creating the distributable package, or unintentionally neglecting build steps, among other pitfalls.

You will reap a tremendous amount of time savings from scripting your build. Your project *build lifecycle* (all of the discrete steps required to build your project) can easily grow more complicated over time, especially as you consume more and more dependencies, include various resources, add modules, and add tests. You may also need to build your project differently depending on the intended deployment environment. For example, you might need to enable debugging capabilities in a development or QA environment, but disable debugging in a build intended for release to production as well as prevent test classes from being included in the distributable package. Manually performing all of the required steps involved in building a Java project, including consideration for configuration differences per environment, is a hotbed for human error. The first time you neglect a step like building an updated dependency and consequently must repeat a build of a huge multimodule project to correct your mistake, you will appreciate the value of a build script.

Whatever tool or framework you choose for scripting your build, take care to use a *declarative* approach rather than *imperative*. Here's a quick reminder of the meaning of these terms:

Imperative
    Defining an exact procedure with implementation details

Declarative
    Defining an action without implementation details

In other words, keep your build script focused on *what* you need to do rather than *how* to do it. This will help keep your script understandable, maintainable, testable, and scalable by encouraging reuse on other projects or modules. To accomplish this, you may need to establish or conform to a known convention, or write plug-ins or other external code referenced from your build script that provides the implementation details. Some build tools are more apt to foster a declarative approach than others. This usually comes with the cost of conforming to a convention versus flexibility.

The Java ecosystem has several well-established build tools available, so I would be surprised if you are currently manually compiling your project with `javac` and packaging your class files into a JAR or other package type. You likely already have some sort of build process and script established, but in the unlikely scenario that you do not, you are starting a brand-new Java project, or you are looking to improve an existing script to utilize best practices, this section summarizes a few of the most common build tools/frameworks available in the Java ecosystem and what they provide you out of the box.

First, it is important to map out your build process, to determine what you need from your build script in order to gain the most benefit. To build a Java project, at the bare minimum you need to specify the following:

Java version
   The version of Java required to compile the project

Source directory path
   The directory that includes all of the source code for the project

Destination directory path
   The directory where compiled class files are expected to be placed

Names, locations, and versions of needed dependencies
   The metadata necessary to locate and gather any dependencies required by your project

With this information, you should be able to execute a minimal build process with the following steps:

1. Collect any needed dependencies.
2. Compile the code.
3. Run tests.
4. Package your application.

The best way to show how to massage your build process into a build script is by example. The following examples demonstrate the use of three of the most common build tools to script the minimal build process described for a simple Hello World Java application. In no way do these examples explore all of the functionality available in these tools. They are simply meant as a crash course to help you either begin to understand your existing build script or write your first build script to benefit from a full CI solution.

In evaluating a build tool, bear in mind the actual process your project requires to complete a build. Your project may require scripting additional steps that are not shown here, and one build tool may be more suited than another to accomplish this. It is important that the tool you choose helps you programmatically define and accelerate the build process your project requires rather than arbitrarily force you to modify your process to fit the requirements of the tool. That said, when you learn the capabilities of a tool, reflect on your process and be mindful of changes that would benefit your team. This is most important with established projects. Changes to the process, however well-intentioned, can be painful for a development team. They should be made only intentionally, with a clear understanding of the reason for the change and, of course, a clear benefit.

Build with Apache Ant

Apache Ant is an open source project released under an Apache License by the Apache Software Foundation. According to the Apache Ant documentation (*https://ant.apache.org*), the name is an acronym for Another Neat Tool and was initially part of the Tomcat codebase, written by James Duncan Davidson for the purpose of building Tomcat. Its first initial release was in 2000.

Apache Ant is a build tool written in Java that provides a way to describe a build process as declarative steps within an XML file. This is the first build tool that I was exposed to in my Java career, and although Ant has heavy competition today, it is still an active project and widely used often in combination with other tools.

Key Ant Terminology

You will encounter the following terms when working with Apache Ant:

Ant task
> A small unit of work, such as deleting a directory or copying a file. Under the covers, Ant tasks map to Java objects, which contain the implementation details for the task. Many built-in tasks are available in Ant as well as the ability to create custom tasks.

Ant target
> Ant tasks are grouped into Ant targets. An Ant target is invoked by Ant directly. For example, for a target named *compile*, you would run the command `ant compile`. Ant targets can be configured to depend on each other in order to control the order of execution.

 Some Ant build files can grow to be quite large. In the same directory as *build.xml*, you can run the following command to get a list of available targets:

```
ant -projecthelp
```

Ant build file
> An XML file used to configure all of the Ant tasks and targets utilized by a project. By default, this file is named *build.xml* and is found at the root of the project directory.

Example 5-1 is a simple Ant build file I created and executed with Ant 1.10.8.

Example 5-1. Ant build script (build.xml)

```xml
<project name="my-app" basedir="." default="package"> ❶

    <property name="version" value="1.0-SNAPSHOT"/> ❷
    <property name="finalName" value="${ant.project.name}-${version}"/>
    <property name="src.dir" value="src/main/java"/>
    <property name="build.dir" value="target"/>
    <property name="output.dir" value="${build.dir}/classes"/>
    <property name="test.src.dir" value="src/test/java"/>
    <property name="test.output.dir" value="${build.dir}/test-classes"/>
    <property name="lib.dir" value="lib"/>

    <path id="classpath"> ❸
        <fileset dir="${lib.dir}" includes="**/*.jar"/>
    </path>

    <target name="clean">
        <delete dir="${build.dir}"/>
    </target>

    <target name="compile" depends="clean"> ❹
        <mkdir dir="${output.dir}"/>
        <javac srcdir="${src.dir}"
               destdir="${output.dir}"
               target="11" source="11"
               classpathref="classpath"
               includeantruntime="false"/>
    </target>

    <target name="compile-test">
        <mkdir dir="${test.output.dir}"/>
        <javac srcdir="${test.src.dir}"
               destdir="${test.output.dir}"
               target="11" source="11"
               classpathref="classpath"
               includeantruntime="false"/>
    </target>

    <target name="test" depends="compile-test"> ❺
        <junit printsummary="yes" fork="true">
            <classpath>
                <path refid="classpath"/>
                <pathelement location="${output.dir}"/>
                <pathelement location="${test.output.dir}"/>
            </classpath>

            <batchtest>
                <fileset dir="${test.src.dir}" includes="**/*Test.java"/>
            </batchtest>
        </junit>
    </target>
```

```
<target name="package" depends="compile,test"> ❻
    <mkdir dir="${build.dir}"/>
    <jar jarfile="${build.dir}/${finalName}.jar"
        basedir="${output.dir}"/>
</target>

</project>
```

❶ The value of the `default` attribute of the project can be set to the name of a
    default target to run when Ant is invoked without a target. For this project, the
    command `ant` without any arguments will run the *package* target.

❷ Property elements are hardcoded, immutable values that may be used more than
    once in the rest of the build script. Using them helps with both readability and
    maintainability.

❸ This path element is how I chose to manage the location of needed dependencies
    for this project. In this case, both the *junit* and *hamcrest-core* JARs are manually
    placed in the directory configured here. This technique implies that dependen-
    cies would be checked into source control along with the project. Although it
    was simple to do for this example, this is not a recommended practice. Chapter 6
    discusses package management in detail.

❹ The `compile` target is responsible for the compilation of the source code (this
    project specifies Java 11) and placement of the resulting class files in the config-
    ured location. This target depends on the *clean* target, meaning the clean target
    will be run first, to ensure that compiled class files are fresh and not left over
    from an old build.

❺ The `test` target configures the JUnit Ant task that will run all of the available unit
    tests and print the results to the screen.

❻ The `package` target will assemble and place a final JAR file in the configured
    location.

Executing the one-line command `ant package` will take our Java project, compile it,
run unit tests, and then assemble a JAR file for us. Ant is flexible, rich in functionality,
and satisfies our goal of scripting a minimal build. The XML configuration file is a
clean, straightforward way of documenting the project's build lifecycle. By itself, Ant
is lacking in the way of dependency management. However, tools like Apache Ivy
(*https://oreil.ly/7t5v5*) have been developed to extend this functionality to Ant.

Build with Apache Maven

According to the Apache Maven Project documentation (*https://oreil.ly/CziRT*), *maven* is a Yiddish word meaning *accumulator of knowledge*. Like Apache Ant, Maven is also an open source project of the Apache Software Foundation. It began as an improvement to the Jakarta turbine project build that was utilizing varied configurations of Ant for each subproject. Its first official release was in 2004.

Like Apache Ant, Maven uses an XML document, (a POM file) to describe and manage Java projects. This document records information about the project, including a unique identifier for the project, the required compiler version, configuration property values, and metadata on all required dependencies and their versions. One of the most powerful features of Maven is its dependency management and the ability to use repositories to share dependencies with other projects.

Maven relies heavily on convention in order to provide a uniform method of managing and documenting a project that can easily scale across all projects using Maven. A project is expected to be laid out on the filesystem in a specific way. To keep the script declarative, customized implementations require building custom plug-ins. Although it can be extensively customized to override expected defaults, Maven works out of the box with little configuration if you conform to the expected project structure.

Key Maven Terminology

You will encounter the following terms when working with Maven:

Lifecycle phase
> A discrete step in a project's build lifecycle. Maven defines a list of default phases that are executed sequentially during a build. The default phases are *validate*, *compile*, *test*, *package*, *verify*, *install*, and *deploy*. Two other Maven lifecycles consist of phases that handle cleaning and documentation for the project. Invoking Maven with a lifecycle phase will execute all of the lifecycle phases in order, up to and including the given lifecycle phase.

Maven goal
> Handles the implementation details of the execution of a lifecycle phase. A goal can be configured to be associated with multiple lifecycle phases.

Maven plug-in
> A collection of common Maven goals with a common purpose. Goals are provided by plug-ins to be executed in the lifecycle phase they are bound to.

POM file
> The Maven *Project Object Model*, or POM, is implemented as an XML configuration file that includes the configuration for all of the Maven lifecycle phases, goals, and plug-ins required for the project's build lifecycle. The name of this

---

file is *pom.xml* and is found at the root of a project. In multimodule projects, a POM file at the root of the project is potentially a *parent* POM that provides inherited configuration to POMs that specify the parent POM. All project POM files extend Maven's *Super POM*, which is provided by the Maven installation itself and includes default configuration.

Example 5-2 is a simple POM file I configured for my Java 11 environment using Maven 3.6.3.

Example 5-2. Maven POM file (pom.xml)

```xml
<?xml version="1.0" encoding="UTF-8"?>

<project xmlns="http://maven.apache.org/POM/4.0.0"
         xmlns:xsi="http://www.w3.org/2001/XMLSchema-instance"
         xsi:schemaLocation=
             "http://maven.apache.org/POM/4.0.0
             http://maven.apache.org/xsd/maven-4.0.0.xsd">
  <modelVersion>4.0.0</modelVersion>

  <groupId>com.mycompany.app</groupId> ❶
  <artifactId>my-app</artifactId>
  <version>1.0-SNAPSHOT</version>

  <name>my-app</name>
  <!-- FIXME change it to the project's website -->
  <url>http://www.example.com</url>

  <properties> ❷
    <project.build.sourceEncoding>UTF-8</project.build.sourceEncoding>
    <maven.compiler.release>11</maven.compiler.release>
  </properties>

  <dependencies> ❸
    <dependency>
      <groupId>junit</groupId>
      <artifactId>junit</artifactId>
      <version>4.11</version>
      <scope>test</scope>
    </dependency>
  </dependencies>

  <build> ❹
    <pluginManagement>
      <plugins>
        <plugin> ❺
          <artifactId>maven-compiler-plugin</artifactId>
          <version>3.8.0</version>
        </plugin>
```

```
      </plugins>
    </pluginManagement>
  </build>
</project>
```

❶ Every project is uniquely identified by its configured `groupId`, `artifactId`, and
    `version`.

❷ Properties are hardcoded values that can potentially be used in multiple places in
    the POM file. They can be either custom properties or built-in properties used by
    plug-ins or goals.

❸ In the `dependencies` block, all direct dependencies of the project are identified.
    This project relies on JUnit to run the unit tests, so the *junit* dependency is
    specified here. JUnit has a dependency itself on *hamcrest-core*, but Maven is
    smart enough to figure that out without having to include it here. By default,
    Maven will pull these dependencies from Maven Central.

❹ The `build` block is where plug-ins are configured. Unless there is configuration
    you want to override, this block isn't required.

❺ Default plug-in bindings exist for all of the lifecycle phases, but in this case,
    I wanted to configure `maven-compiler-plugin` to use Java version 11 rather
    than the default. The property that controls this for the plug-in is `maven`
    `.compiler.release` in the `properties` block. This configuration could have
    been put in the `plugins` block, but it makes sense to move it to the `properties`
    block for better visibility toward the top of the file. This property replaces
    `maven.compiler.source` and `maven.compiler.target` that is usually seen when
    using older versions of Java.

 It is a good idea to lock down all of your Maven plug-in versions
to avoid using Maven defaults. Specifically, pay special attention to
Maven instructions for configuring your build script when using
older versions of Maven and Java versions 9 or greater. The default
plug-in versions of your Maven installation might not be compatible with later versions of Java.

Because of the strong reliance on convention, this Maven build script is quite brief.
With this small POM file, I am able to execute `mvn package` to compile, run tests,
and assemble a JAR file, all utilizing default settings. If you spend any time with
Maven, you will quickly realize that it is much more than just a build tool and is
chock-full of powerful features. For someone new to Maven, its potential complexity
can be overwhelming. Also, customization through creating a new Maven plug-in is

daunting when the customization is minor. At the time of this writing, the Apache Maven Project (*https://oreil.ly/CziRT*) documentation contains excellent resources, including a Maven in 5 Minutes (*https://oreil.ly/dkxa6*) guide. I highly recommend starting with these resources if you are unfamiliar with Maven.

Although the Apache Maven Ant Plugin (*https://oreil.ly/DOg5K*) is no longer maintained, it is possible to generate an Ant build file from a Maven POM file. Doing this will help you appreciate everything you get out of the box with Maven's convention and defaults! In the same directory as your *pom.xml* file, invoke the Maven plug-in with the command `mvn ant:ant`.

Build with Gradle

Gradle is an open source build tool under the Apache 2.0 license. Hans Dockter, the founder of Gradle, explained in the Gradle Forums (*https://oreil.ly/1mEwy*) that his original idea was to call the project Cradle with a C. He ultimately decided on the name Gradle with a G since it used Apache Groovy for the domain-specific language (DSL). Gradle 1.0 was released in 2012, so in comparison to Apache Ant and Apache Maven, Gradle is the new kid on the block.

One of the biggest differences between Gradle and Maven and Ant is that the Gradle build script is not XML based. Instead, Gradle build scripts can be written with either a Groovy or Kotlin DSL. Like Maven, Gradle also utilizes convention, but is more flexible compared to Maven. The Gradle documentation (*https://oreil.ly/Vvhch*) touts the flexibility of the tool and includes instructions on how to easily customize your build.

Gradle has extensive online documentation on migrating Maven builds to Gradle (*https://oreil.ly/RqR1s*). You can generate a Gradle build file from an existing Maven POM.

Key Gradle Terminology

You will encounter the following terms when working with Gradle:

Domain-specific language (DSL)
  Gradle scripts use a DSL specific to Gradle. With the Gradle DSL, you can write a Gradle script using either Kotlin or Groovy language features. The Gradle Build Language Reference (*https://oreil.ly/Q6bQH*) documents the Gradle DSL.

Gradle task
> A discrete step in your build lifecycle that can include implementations of units of work like copying files, inputs that the implementation uses, and outputs that the implementation affects. Tasks can specify dependencies on other tasks to control the order of execution. Your project build will consist of multiple tasks that a Gradle build will configure and then execute in the appropriate order.

Gradle lifecycle tasks
> Common tasks provided by Gradle's Base plug-in, including *clean*, *check*, *assemble*, and *build*. Other plug-ins can apply the Base plug-in for access to these tasks.

Gradle plug-in
> A collection of Gradle tasks and the mechanism for adding extensions to existing functionality, features, conventions, configuration, and other customizations to your build.

Gradle build phase
> Gradle build phases are not to be confused with Maven phases. A Gradle build will move through three fixed build phases: *initialization*, *configuration*, and *execution*.

Example 5-3 is a simple Gradle build file that I generated from the content of Example 5-2 in the previous section.

Example 5-3. Gradle build script (build.gradle)

```
/*
 * This file was generated by the Gradle 'init' task.
 */

plugins {
    id 'java'  ❶
    id 'maven-publish'
}

repositories {  ❷
    mavenLocal()
    maven {
        url = uri('https://repo.maven.apache.org/maven2')
    }
}

dependencies {
    testImplementation 'junit:junit:4.11'  ❸
}

group = 'com.mycompany.app'
version = '1.0-SNAPSHOT'
```

```
description = 'my-app'
sourceCompatibility = '11' ❹

publishing {
    publications {
        maven(MavenPublication) {
            from(components.java)
        }
    }
}

tasks.withType(JavaCompile) { ❺
    options.encoding = 'UTF-8'
}
```

❶ Gradle plug-ins are applied by adding their *plug-in ID* to the plugins block.
The java plug-in is a Gradle Core plug-in that provides compilation, testing,
packaging, and other functionality for Java projects.

❷ Repositories for dependencies are provided in the repositories block. Dependencies are resolved using these settings.

❸ Gradle handles dependencies similarly to Maven. The JUnit dependency is
required for our unit tests, so it is included in the dependencies block.

❹ The sourceCompatibility configuration setting is provided by the java plug-in
and maps to the source option of javac. There is also a targetCompatibility
configuration setting. Its default value is the value of sourceCompatibility, so
there was no reason to add it to the build script.

❺ The flexibility of Gradle allows me to add explicit encoding for the Java compiler.
A task provided by the java plug-in, called compileJava, is of the type Java
Compiler. This code block sets the encoding property on this compile task.

This Gradle build script allows me to compile, run tests, and assemble a JAR file for
my project by executing the single command gradle build. Because Gradle builds
are based on well-known conventions, build scripts contain only what is needed that
differentiates the build, helping to keep them small and maintainable. This simple
script shows how powerful and flexible Gradle can be, especially for Java projects that
have a more complicated build process. In that case, the up-front investment required
to understand the Gradle DSL for customization is well worth the time.

All three of these tools for building your Java project have their own strengths and
weaknesses. Choose a tool based on the needs of your project, the experience of
your team, and the flexibility required. Wrangling together a build script—however
you choose to do it—and with whatever tool you choose to do it, will increase

your efficiency by leaps and bounds. Building a Java project is a repetitive process consisting of numerous steps, ripe for human error, and marvelously suitable for automation. Reducing your project build to a single command saves ramp-up time for new developers, increases efficiency during development tasks in a local development environment, and paves the way for build automation, an integral component of an effective CI solution.

Continuously Build

The most telltale sign that code integration was unsuccessful is the failure of a build. Therefore, it stands to reason that a project should be built often in order to detect and resolve any issues as soon as possible. In fact, *every contribution to the mainline codebase should be expected to result in a build that compiles successfully and passes all unit tests.*

 When referring to building a project after code is merged into the mainline source code repository, I intentionally use the word *contribution* as opposed to *commit* or *check-in*. This is simply because your development team may have agreed to follow multiple development processes (all valid), and in some of these, a *contribution* to the mainline may be the merge of a branch or the merge of a pull request—both of which potentially consist of one or more commits.

The following is a typical developer workflow using test-driven development:

1. Check out the latest code from source control to a local workspace.
2. Build and run all tests for the project to ensure a clean start. (There should be a build script for this. Refer to "Declaratively Script Your Build" on page 114.)
3. Write the code and related unit tests for the new feature or bug fix.
4. Run the new unit tests to ensure that they pass.
5. Build and run *all* unit tests for the project to ensure that the new code doesn't result in negative side effects when integrated with the existing code. (Again, use a build script for this.)
6. Commit the new code along with the new tests to the codebase.

This process aims to prevent issues (including the introduction of bugs or loss of functionality) with integrating code before it leaves your local development workspace. However, problems can manifest during this workflow that will cause pain down the road. Some will be caused by the realities of human nature, and others arise because, regardless of how much effort is put into advanced planning, it is nearly impossible to prevent every potential incompatibility introduced by concurrent development. Do not misunderstand; I am *not* saying that this process is wrong and should be discarded altogether. Instead, this section explains how an automated CI implementation helps mitigate the problems that can arise during this workflow and bolster your efficiency and productivity as a developer.

It isn't enough for a developer to successfully build a project in their own local environment. Even if every developer diligently abides by the agreed-upon process and commits code changes only after all tests pass, you shouldn't rely on this alone. The simplest reason is that a developer might not have the latest changes from the mainline (an even more likely scenario when many developers are working in the same codebase). This could result in an incompatibility that isn't discovered until after the code is merged.

Sometimes issues with tests might surface only when someone else attempts to do a build or run tests in their own local development environment. For example, more than once I've embarrassingly forgotten to commit a new file or resource that I've created to the codebase. This means that the next developer who collects these changes gets to suffer through the annoyance of having either the build or tests fail immediately. Another issue I've seen is code written in such a way that it works in only a specific environment or a specific OS.

We all have bad days, and these problems slip by us from time to time even in the most ideal circumstances. But rather than let broken builds spread through the team like a virus, strategies can be put in place to help to mitigate integration issues like this. The most common is using automatic build servers, or CI servers. These servers are shared by development teams responsible for performing full builds, including running tests, and reporting the result of the build after code changes have been committed.

Popular CI servers you might recognize include Jenkins, CircleCI, TeamCity, Bamboo, and GitLab. More options are coming on the scene like JFrog Pipelines, and some have more features and capabilities than others, but the primary objective is to establish a referee for the code changes coming in to the shared repository by building frequently and reporting when a problem occurs. Utilizing a CI server for the purpose of running builds automatically is the best way to ensure that builds are happening regularly, revealing any integrations issues early.

Automate Tests

Outside of running individual tests during development, most often within an IDE, a developer should have a quick method of running the full suite of automated tests prior to checking in new code to the codebase.

The minimal build process outlined in "Declaratively Script Your Build" on page 114 includes a step for automatically running unit tests. Each build script example also includes this unit test step. This is no accident. In fact, this part of your build is absolutely essential for a healthy CI solution and is worthy of a decent amount of time and attention. One of the primary purposes of CI is having the ability to catch integration issues as early in the development process as possible.

Unit tests alone will not expose every single issue—that's an unrealistic expectation. But writing a strong set of unit tests is one of the best proactive approaches to detecting the most obvious problems early on. Because unit tests can be run even prior to the first stages of formal quality assurance, they are an extremely valuable part of the development cycle. They are the first set of safety measures that you can take to ensure that your software will behave correctly in production.

This section does not go into specifics on how to write unit tests in Java. I assume that you understand and accept their importance, that your project has unit tests, and that you utilize a framework that facilitates automatically running them like JUnit or TestNG. If you do not, immediately stop and write a simple unit test for your project that can be automatically run during your build for the sake of having this step available to expand on in your CI solution. Then, schedule a time to sit down with your development team and strategize how you will write and maintain unit tests moving forward.

Numerous test tools are available in the Java ecosystem, and this section is not meant to be an exhaustive comparison or an endorsement of one over another. Instead, I discuss how test automation should fit into your CI process, the qualities of your test suite to strive for, and how to avoid common pitfalls in the context of CI that will eat away at your efficiency.

Monitor and Maintain Tests

Checking out the latest code to your local development workspace is pretty straightforward. Compiling and running all of the unit tests is straightforward as well. But as you add more modules, and your project becomes more complicated, doing a complete build and running all of the tests will begin to take more time. The longer your development process takes, the more likely that other code changes have been introduced to the mainline ahead of yours.

To prevent a potential break, you would have to check out the newest changes and run all of the tests again—not a very efficient process. Frustration can lead to developers taking shortcuts and skipping running the tests in an effort to commit code to the mainline before it is changed out from under them. Obviously, this is a slippery slope that is guaranteed to result in broken code in the mainline more often, slowing the entire team.

It takes time to maintain tests, and this time should be regularly built in to the development schedule. Just like the rest of your codebase, tests require improvements and adjustments over time. When they become obsolete, they should be removed. When they break, they should be fixed. Often when browsing through various codebases, I'll come across test cases that are commented out. This happens for a few reasons; none of them good. Sometimes it's simply because a team was short on time and felt the need to force through a build to meet a deadline, with the promise of revisiting the tests at a later time. Sometimes, it's because a particular test case inconsistently fails, known as a *flaky* test. This could be due to a race condition or a dynamic value that the test erroneously expects to be static.

In either case, manipulating tests not to run is a dangerous business and indicates bigger problems afoot with the development team. A review of priorities is in order. Not addressing stale or brittle tests, or even worse, not writing them at all, removes the guardrails for your project and defeats the purpose of the CI process you have carefully put in place.

Sometimes tests are not run because it is determined they take too much time. Use your CI server to regularly record how long test runs take and determine your acceptable threshold. As your project grows and you see the amount of time for builds increase beyond your acceptable threshold, stop to review your tests. Look for obsolete tests, duplicates, and tests that could be run in parallel. Considering how often you expect your build server to run (potentially after every code change), every second counts.

Summary

This chapter presented continuous integration as an essential practice for a development team. Tools have developed over time that have helped increase our efficiency in building software projects. Automatically triggering builds as well as automatically running tests has helped developers better concentrate on coding and catch errant code earlier in the development process. It is easy to take for granted and enjoy the effort saved by automation, but it is important to understand the details underneath, especially when it comes to your test suite. Don't let poorly maintained tests take away the benefit of your continuous integration system.

## CHAPTER 6

Package Management

Ixchel Ruiz

Somewhere in the world, as you read this sentence, a line of code is being written. This line of code will ultimately become part of an artifact that will become a building block used internally by an organization in one or more enterprise products, or shared via a public repository, most notably Maven Central for Java and Kotlin libraries.

More libraries, binaries, and artifacts are available today than ever before, and this collection will continue to grow as developers around the world continue their next generation of products and services. Handling and managing these artifacts require more effort now than before—with an ever-increasing number of dependencies creating a complicated web of connectedness. Using an incorrect version of an artifact is an easy trap to fall into, causing confusion and broken builds, and ultimately thwarting carefully planned project release dates.

It's more important than ever for developers to understand not only the function and the idiosyncrasies of the source code directly in front of them, but also how their projects are packaged and how the building blocks are assembled into the final product. Having a deep understanding of the build process itself and how our automated build tools function under the hood is crucial to avert delays and hours of unnecessary troubleshooting—not to mention prevent a large category of bugs escaping into production.

Access to troves of third-party resources that provide solutions to common coding problems can help speed the development of our projects but introduces the risk of errant or unexpected behavior. Understanding how these components are brought into projects as well as where they come from will help in troubleshooting efforts. Ensuring that we are responsible managers of the artifacts we produce internally will allow us to improve our decision-making and prioritization when it comes to bug fixes and feature development as well as help pave the way to release to production. A developer can no longer be versed in only the semantics of the code in front of them, but also the complexities of package management.

Why Build-It-and-Ship-It Is Not Enough

Not so long ago, software developers viewed building an artifact as a culmination of hard, sometimes epic, efforts. Meeting deadlines sometimes meant using short-cuts and poorly documented steps. Since then, the requirements of the industry have changed to bring faster delivery cycles, diverse environments, tailored artifacts, exploding codebases and repositories, and multimodule packages. Today building an artifact is just one step of a bigger business cycle.

Successful leaders recognize that the best innovations emerge out of trial and error. That's why they've made testing, experimentation, and failure an integral part of their lives and their company's process.

One way to innovate, scale more quickly, launch more products, improve the quality or user experience of applications or products, and roll out new features is through A/B testing. What is A/B testing? According to Kaiser Fung, who founded the applied analytics program at Columbia University, *A/B testing* at its most basic is a century-old method used to compare two versions of something to figure out which performs better. Today several startups, well-established companies like Microsoft, and several other leading companies—including Amazon, Booking.com, Facebook, and Google—have been conducting (*https://oreil.ly/vRKPP*) more than 10,000 online controlled experiments annually.

Booking.com conducts comparative testing on every new feature on its website, comparing details from the selection of photos and content to button color and placement. By testing several versions against one another and tracking customer response, the company is able to constantly improve the user experience.

How do we deliver and deploy multiple versions of software composed of numerous artifacts? How do we find bottlenecks? How do we know we are moving in the right direction? How do we keep track of what is working well or what is working against us? How do we maintain a reproducible outcome but with enriched lineages? Answers to these questions can be found by capturing and analyzing relevant, contextual, clear, and specific information regarding the workflows and artifacts' inputs, outputs, and states. All of this is possible thanks to metadata.

It's All About Metadata

As W. Edwards Deming said, "In God we trust; all others bring data." *Metadata* is defined as a structured key/value storage of relevant information. In other words, it's a collection of properties or attributes applicable to a particular entity, which in our case applies to artifacts and processes.

Metadata enables the discovery of correlations and causations as well as insights into the organization's behavior and outcomes. As a result, metadata can show whether the organization is tuned in to its stakeholders' goals.

Additional data can be used in later stages to extract or derive more information. This data helps expand perspectives and create more stories, or narratives. It's important to choose which attributes, cardinality, and values to add—too many, and we harm performance; too few, and we miss information. With too many values, insights can be lost.

A good starting point is to answer the following questions concerning the main stages of each phase of the software development cycle: Who? What? How? Where? and When? Asking the right questions is only half of the effort, though. Having clear, relevant, specific, and clear answers that can be normalized or enumerated is always a good practice.

Key Attributes of Insightful Metadata

Insightful data should be all of the following:

Contextualized
> All data needs to be interpreted within a frame of reference. To extract and compare possible scenarios, it is important to have the right stage for analysis.

Relevant
> The variability in the values has an impact on the outcome or describes a specific stage or time in the outcome or process.

Specific
> The values describe a clear event (i.e., initial value, end value).

Clear
> The possible values are well-known or defined, computable, and comparable.

Unique
> Has a single, distinctive value.

Extensible
> Because the wealth of human knowledge is ever increasing, the data needs to define mechanisms so that standards can be evolved and extended to accommodate new properties.

Once you have defined what, when, why, and how to record the stages, inputs, outputs, and states of the software development cycle, you also need to keep in mind the consumers of subsets of the metadata. On one hand, you may have an intermediate private consumer who will consume and react in different ways to the set of values—from triggering sub pipelines, promoting builds, deploying in different environments, or publishing artifacts. On the other hand, you may have final external consumers who will be able to extract information and with skill and experience turn it into insights that will help fulfill the overall goals of the organization.

Metadata Considerations

The following are important considerations about metadata:

Privacy and security
> Think twice about exposing values.

Visibility
> Not all consumers are interested in all data.

Format and encoding
> One specific property may be exposed during different stages in different formats, but consistency is needed in the naming, meaning, and possibly the general value.

Let's turn our attention to generating and packaging metadata with build tools. The Java ecosystem has no shortage of options when it comes to build tools. Arguably, the most popular are Apache Maven and Gradle; hence it makes sense to discuss them in depth. However, should your build depend on a different build tool, the information presented in this section will likely still prove to be useful, as some of the techniques to gather and package metadata may be reused.

Now, before we jump into practical code snippets, we have to figure out three action items:

1. Determine the metadata that should be packaged with an artifact.
2. Find out how that metadata can be obtained during the build.
3. Process the metadata and record it in the appropriate format or formats.

The following subsections cover each of these aspects.

Determining the Metadata

The build environment has no shortage of information that can be converted into metadata and packaged alongside an artifact. A good example is the build timestamp that identifies the time and date when the build produced the artifact. Many timestamp formats can be followed, but I recommend using ISO 8601 (*https://oreil.ly/PsZkB*), whose formatted representation using `java.text.SimpleDateformat` is `yyyy-MM-dd'T'HH:mm:ssXXX`—useful when the captured timestamp relies on `java.util.Date`. Alternatively, the `java.time.format.DateTimeFormatter.ISO_OFF` `SET_DATE_TIME` may be used if the captured timestamp relies on `java.time.Local` `DateTime`. The build's OS details may also be of interest, as well as JDK information such as version, ID, and vendor. Luckily for us, these bits of information are captured by the JVM and exposed via `System` (*https://oreil.ly/CKMsE*) properties.

Consider including the artifact's ID and version as well (even though these values are usually encoded in the artifact's filename) as a precaution in case the artifact were to be renamed at some point. SCM information is also crucial. Useful information from source control includes the commit hash, tag, and branch name. Additionally, you may want to capture specific build information such as the user who runs the build; the build tool's name, ID, and version; and the hostname and IP address of the build machine. These key/value pairs are likely the most significant and commonly found metadata. However, you may select additional key/value pairs required by other tools and systems that will consume the produced artifacts.

 I can't stress enough how important it is to check your team's and organization's policies regarding access and visibility of sensitive data. Some of the key/value pairs mentioned before may be deemed a security risk if exposed to third parties or external consumers, though they may be of high importance to internal consumers.

Capturing Metadata

We must find a way to gather the metadata with our build tool of choice after we have determined which metadata we need to capture. Some of the key/value pairs can be obtained directly from the environment, system settings, and command flags exposed by the JVM as environment variables or `System` properties. Additional properties may be exposed by the build tool itself, whether they are defined as additional command-line arguments or as configuration elements in the tool's configuration settings.

Let's assume for the moment that we need to capture the following key/value pairs:

- JDK information such as version and vendor
- OS information such as name, arch, and version

- The build timestamp
- The current commit hash from SCM (assuming Git)

These values may be captured with Maven by using a combination of System properties for the first two items and a third-party plug-in for the last two. Both Maven and Gradle have no shortage of options when it comes to plug-ins that offer integration with Git; however, I recommend choosing git-commit-id-maven-plugin (*https:// oreil.ly/EwiLP*) for Maven and versioning (*https://oreil.ly/qjEOi*) for Gradle, as these plug-ins are the most versatile so far.

Now, Maven allows defining properties in a handful of ways, most commonly as key/value pairs inside the `<properties>` section found in the *pom.xml* build file. The value for each key is free text, although you can refer to System properties by using a shorthand notation or to environment variables by using a naming convention. Say you want to access the value for the `java.version` key found in System properties. This can be done by using the `${}` shorthand notation such as `${java.version}`. Conversely, for an environment variable, you may use the `${env.NAME}` notation. For example, the value of an environment variable named TOKEN can be accessed using the expression `${env.TOKEN}` in the *pom.xml* build file. Putting together the `git-commit-id` plug-in and build properties may result in a *pom.xml* similar to the following:

```
<project xmlns="http://maven.apache.org/POM/4.0.0"
  xmlns:xsi="http://www.w3.org/2001/XMLSchema-instance"
  xsi:schemaLocation="http://maven.apache.org/POM/4.0.0
  http://maven.apache.org/xsd/maven-4.0.0.xsd">
  <modelVersion>4.0.0</modelVersion>

  <groupId>com.acme</groupId>
  <artifactId>example</artifactId>
  <version>1.0.0-SNAPSHOT</version>

  <properties>
    <project.build.sourceEncoding>UTF-8</project.build.sourceEncoding>
    <build.jdk>${java.version} (${java.vendor} ${java.vm.version})</build.jdk>
    <build.os>${os.name} ${os.arch} ${os.version}</build.os>
    <build.revision>${git.commit.id}</build.revision>
    <build.timestamp>${git.build.time}</build.timestamp>
  </properties>

  <build>
    <plugins>
      <plugin>
        <groupId>pl.project13.maven</groupId>
        <artifactId>git-commit-id-plugin</artifactId>
        <version>4.0.3</version>
        <executions>
          <execution>
```

```
        <id>resolve-git-properties</id>
        <goals>
          <goal>revision</goal>
        </goals>
      </execution>
    </executions>
    <configuration>
      <verbose>false</verbose>
      <failOnNoGitDirectory>false</failOnNoGitDirectory>
      <generateGitPropertiesFile>true</generateGitPropertiesFile>
      <generateGitPropertiesFilename>
        ${project.build.directory}/git.properties
      </generateGitPropertiesFilename>
      <dateFormat>yyyy-MM-dd'T'HH:mm:ssXXX</dateFormat>
    </configuration>
  </plugin>
  </plugins>
  </build>
</project>
```

Note that the values for `build.jdk` and `build.os` already include formatting as they are composites of simpler values, whereas the `build.revision` and `build.timestamp` values come from the properties defined by the Git plug-in. We have yet to determine the final format and file or files that will contain the metadata, which is why we see it defined in the `<properties>` section. This setup allows these values to be reused and consumed by other plug-ins should they need it. Another reason to prefer this setup is that external tools (such as those found in a build pipeline) may read these values more easily as they are located at a specific section instead of at many places within the build file.

Also note the chosen value of version, `1.0.0-SNAPSHOT`. You may use any character combination for the version as you deem necessary. However, it's customary to at least use an alphanumeric sequence that defines two numbers in the *major.minor* format. A handful of versioning conventions are out there, with both advantages and drawbacks. This being said, the use of the `-SNAPSHOT` tag has a special meaning as it indicates the artifact is not yet ready for production. Some tools will behave differently when a snapshot version is detected; for example, they can prevent an artifact from ever being published to a production environment.

In contrast to Maven, Gradle has no shortage of options when it comes to defining and writing build files. To begin with, since Gradle 4, you have two choices for the build file format: Apache Groovy DSL or Kotlin DSL. Regardless of which one you pick, you will soon find that there are more options to capture and format metadata. Some of them may be idiomatic, some may require additional plug-ins, and some may even be considered outdated or obsolete. To keep this example short and basic, we'll go with Groovy and small idiomatic expressions. We'll capture the same metadata similarly as we did for Maven, with the first two values coming from System properties and the commit hash provided by the versioning Git plug-in, but the build timestamp will be calculated on the spot by using custom code. The following snippet shows how this can be done:

```
plugins {
  id 'java-library'
  id 'net.nemerosa.versioning' version '2.14.0'
}

version = '1.0.0-SNAPSHOT'

ext {
  buildJdk = [
    System.properties['java.version'],
    '(' + System.properties['java.vendor'],
    System.properties['java.vm.version'] + ')'
  ].join(' ')
  buildOs = [
    System.properties['os.name'],
    System.properties['os.arch'],
    System.properties['os.version']
  ].join(' ')
  buildRevision = project.extensions.versioning.info.commit
  buildTimestamp = new Date().format("yyyy-MM-dd'T'HH:mm:ssXXX")
}
```

These computed values will be available as dynamic project properties that may be consumed later in the build by additional configured elements such as extensions, tasks, closures (for Groovy), actions (for Groovy and Kotlin), and other elements exposed by the DSL. All that is left now is recording the metadata in a given format.

Writing the Metadata

You might need to record metadata in more than one format or file. The choice of format depends on the intended consumers. Some consumers require a unique format that no other consumer can read, whereas others may understand a variety of formats. Be sure to consult the documentation of a given consumer on its supported formats and options and also check whether integration with your build tool of choice is provided. You might discover that a plug-in for your build is available that eases the recording process of the metadata that you need. For demonstration purposes, we'll record the metadata by using two popular formats: a Java properties file and the JAR's manifest.

We can leverage Maven's resource filtering (*https://oreil.ly/X1x0q*), which is baked into the resources plug-in (*https://oreil.ly/YqOSO*), part of the core set of plug-ins that every build has access to. For this to work, we must add the following snippet to the previous *pom.xml* file, inside the <build> section:

```
<resources>
  <resource>
    <directory>src/main/resources</directory>
    <filtering>true</filtering>
  </resource>
</resources>
```

A companion properties file located at *src/main/resources* is also required. I've chosen *META-INF/metadata.properties* as the relative path and name of the properties file to be found inside the artifact JAR. Of course, you may choose a different naming convention as needed. This file relies on variable placeholder substitutions, variables that will be resolved from project properties such as those we set in the <properties> section. By convention, little configuration information is needed in the build file. The properties file looks like the following:

```
build.jdk       = ${build.jdk}
build.os        = ${build.os}
build.revision  = ${build.revision}
build.timestamp = ${build.timestamp}
```

Recording the metadata in the JAR's manifest requires tweaking the configuration of the jar-maven-plugin applicable to a build file. The following snippet must be included inside the <plugins> section found in the <build> section. In other words, it's a sibling of the git-commit-id plug-in we saw earlier in this section:

```
<plugin>
  <groupId>org.apache.maven.plugins</groupId>
  <artifactId>maven-jar-plugin</artifactId>
  <version>3.2.0</version>
  <configuration>
    <archive>
      <manifestEntries>
        <Build-Jdk>${build.jdk}</Build-Jdk>
        <Build-OS>${build.os}</Build-OS>
        <Build-Revision>${build.revision}</Build-Revision>
        <Build-Timestamp>${build.timestamp}</Build-Timestamp>
      </manifestEntries>
    </archive>
  </configuration>
</plugin>
```

Note that a specific plug-in version is defined even though this plug-in is part of the core plug-in set. The reason behind this is that it's imperative to declare all plug-in versions for the sake of reproducible builds. Otherwise, you will find builds may differ as different plug-in versions may be resolved depending on the specific version of Maven used to run the build. Each entry in the manifest is composed of a capitalized key and the captured value. Running the build with mvn package resolves the captured properties, copies the metadata properties file with resolved values into the *target/classes* directory where it will be added to the final JAR, and injects the metadata into the JAR's manifest. We can verify this by inspecting the contents of the generated artifact:

```
$ mvn verify
$ jar tvf target/example-1.0.0-SNAPSHOT.jar
      0 Sun Jan 10 20:41 CET 2021 META-INF/
    131 Sun Jan 10 20:41 CET 2021 META-INF/MANIFEST.MF
    205 Sun Jan 10 20:41 CET 2021 META-INF/metadata.properties
      0 Sun Jan 10 20:41 CET 2021 META-INF/maven/
      0 Sun Jan 10 20:41 CET 2021 META-INF/maven/com.acme/
      0 Sun Jan 10 20:41 CET 2021 META-INF/maven/com.acme/example/
   1693 Sun Jan 10 19:13 CET 2021 META-INF/maven/com.acme/example/pom.xml
    109 Sun Jan 10 20:41 CET 2021 META-INF/maven/com.acme/example/pom.properties
```

The two files are found inside the JAR file as expected. Extracting the JAR and looking at the contents of the properties file and the JAR manifest yield the following results:

```
build.jdk       = 11.0.9 (Azul Systems, Inc. 11.0.9+11-LTS)
build.os        = Mac OS X x86_64 10.15.7
build.revision  = 0ab9d51a3aaa17fca374d28be1e3f144801daa3b
build.timestamp = 2021-01-10T20:41:11+01:00

Manifest-Version: 1.0
Created-By: Maven Jar Plugin 3.2.0
Build-Jdk-Spec: 11
Build-Jdk: 11.0.9 (Azul Systems, Inc. 11.0.9+11-LTS)
Build-OS: Mac OS X x86_64 10.15.7
Build-Revision: 0ab9d51a3aaa17fca374d28be1e3f144801daa3b
Build-Timestamp: 2021-01-10T20:41:11+01:00
```

You've seen how to collect metadata with Maven. Let's see the same method of recording metadata by using a properties file and a JAR manifest with a different build tool: Gradle. For the first part, we'll configure the standard `processResources` task that's provided by the `java-library` plug-in we applied to the build. The additional configuration can be appended to the previously shown Gradle build file, and it looks like the following:

```
processResources {
  expand(
    'build_jdk'      : project.buildJdk,
    'build_os'       : project.buildOs,
    'build_revision' : project.buildRevision,
    'build_timestamp': project.buildTimestamp
  )
}
```

Note that the names of the keys use _ as a token separator, because of the default resource filtering mechanism appleid by Gradle. If we were to use . as we saw earlier with Maven, Gradle would expect to find a `build` object with matching `jdk`, `os`, `revision`, and `timestamp` properties during resource filtering. That object does not exist, which will cause the build to fail. Changing the token separator avoids that problem but also forces us to change the contents of the properties file to the following:

```
build.jdk       = ${build_jdk}
build.os        = ${build_os}
build.revision  = ${build_revision}
build.timestamp = ${build_timestamp}
```

Configuring the JAR manifest is a straightforward operation given that the `jar` task offers an entry point for this behavior, as shown by the following snippet that can also be appended to the existing Gradle build file:

```
jar {
  manifest {
    attributes(
      'Build-Jdk'       : project.buildJdk,
      'Build-OS'        : project.buildOs,
      'Build-Revision'  : project.buildRevision,
      'Build-Timestamp' : project.buildTimestamp
    )
  }
}
```

As seen before, each manifest entry uses a capitalized key and its corresponding captured value. Running the build with `gradle jar` should produce results similar to those provided by Maven: the properties file will be copied to a target location where it can be included in the final JAR, with its value placeholders substituted for the actual metadata values, and the JAR manifest will be enriched with metadata as well. Inspecting the JAR shows that it contains the expected files:

```
$ gradle jar
$ jar tvf build/libs/example-1.0.0-SNAPSHOT.jar
     0 Sun Jan 10 21:08:22 CET 2021 META-INF/
    25 Sun Jan 10 21:08:22 CET 2021 META-INF/MANIFEST.MF
   165 Sun Jan 10 21:08:22 CET 2021 META-INF/metadata.properties
```

Unpacking the JAR and looking inside each file yields the following results:

```
build.jdk       = 11.0.9 (Azul Systems, Inc. 11.0.9+11-LTS)
build.os        = Mac OS X x86_64 10.15.7
build.revision  = 0ab9d51a3aaa17fca374d28be1e3f144801daa3b
build.timestamp = 2021-01-10T21:08:22+01:00

Manifest-Version: 1.0
Build-Jdk: 11.0.9 (Azul Systems, Inc. 11.0.9+11-LTS)
Build-OS: Mac OS X x86_64 10.15.7
Build-Revision: 0ab9d51a3aaa17fca374d28be1e3f144801daa3b
Build-Timestamp: 2021-01-10T21:08:22+01:00
```

Perfect! That is all that there is to it. Let me encourage you to add or remove key/value pairs as needed as well as configure other plug-ins (for both Maven and Gradle) that may expose additional metadata or provide other means to process and record metadata into particular formats.

Dependency Management Basics for Maven and Gradle

Dependency management has been a staple of Java projects since Maven *1.x* came to light in 2002. The gist behind this feature is to declare artifacts that are required for compiling, testing, and consuming a particular project, relying on additional metadata attached to an artifact such as its group identifier, artifact identifier, version, and sometimes a classifier as well. This metadata is typically exposed using a well-known file format: the Apache Maven POM (*https://oreil.ly/1Kzp6*) expressed in a *pom.xml* file. Other build tools are capable of understanding this format, and can even produce and publish *pom.xml* files despite using a totally unrelated format for declaring build aspects, as is the case for Gradle with `build.gradle` (Groovy) or `build.gradle.kts` (Kotlin) build file.

Despite being a core feature provided by Maven since the early days, and also a core feature in Gradle, dependency management and dependency resolution remain a stumbling block for many. Even though the rules to declare dependencies are not complicated, you may find yourself at the mercy of published metadata with invalid, misleading, or missing constraints. The following subsections are a primer for dependency management using both Maven and Gradle, but it is by no means an exhaustive explanation—that would take a whole book on just this topic.

In other words, tread carefully, dear reader, there be dragons ahead. I'll do my best to point out the safest paths. We'll begin with Maven, as it is the build tool that defines the artifact metadata using the *pom.xml* file format.

Dependency Management with Apache Maven

You likely have encountered a POM file before—after all, it's ubiquitous. A POM file with model version 4.0.0 is responsible for defining the way artifacts are produced and consumed. In Maven version 4, these two capabilities are split, although the model version remains the same for compatibility reasons. It's expected that the model format will change when Maven version 5.0.0 is introduced. although there are no details on how this model will look at the time of writing. One thing is sure: the Maven developers are keen on keeping backward compatibility. Let's walk through the basics.

Dependencies are identified by three required elements: `groupId`, `artifactId`, and `version`. These elements are collectively known as *Maven coordinates*, or *GAV coordinates*, where GAV, as you may have guessed, stands for `groupId`, `artifactId`, `version`. From time to time, you may find dependencies that define a fourth element named `classifier`.

Let's break them down one by one. Both `artifactId` and `version` are straightforward; the former defines the "name" of the artifact, and the latter defines a version number. Many different versions may be associated with the same `artifactId`. The `groupId` is used to put together a set of artifacts that have some sort of relationship—that is, all of them belong to the same project or provide behavior that's germane to one another. The `classifier` adds another dimension to the artifact, albeit optional. Classifiers are often used to differentiate artifacts that are specific to a particular setting such as the operating system or the Java release. Examples of operating system classifiers are found in the JavaFX binaries, such as *javafx-controls-15-win.jar*, *javafx-controls-15-mac.jar*, and *javafx-controls-15-linux.jar*, which identify version 15 of the JavaFX control binaries that may be used with Windows, macOS, and Linux platforms.

Another set of common classifiers are `sources` and `javadoc`, which identify JAR files that contain sources and generated documentation (via the Javadoc tool). The combination of GAV coordinates must be unique; otherwise, the dependency resolution mechanism will have a hard time finding out correct dependencies to use.

POM files let you define dependencies inside the `<dependencies>` section, where you would list GAV coordinates for each dependency. In its simplest form, it looks something like this:

```xml
<?xml version="1.0" encoding="UTF-8"?>
<project
  xsi:schemaLocation="http://maven.apache.org/POM/4.0.0
  http://maven.apache.org/xsd/maven-4.0.0.xsd"
  xmlns="http://maven.apache.org/POM/4.0.0"
  xmlns:xsi="http://www.w3.org/2001/XMLSchema-instance">
  <modelVersion>4.0.0</modelVersion>
  <groupId>com.acme</groupId>
  <artifactId>example</artifactId>
  <version>1.0.0-SNAPSHOT</version>

  <dependencies>
    <dependency>
      <groupId>org.apache.commons</groupId>
      <artifactId>commons-collections4</artifactId>
      <version>4.4</version>
    </dependency>
  </dependencies>
</project>
```

Dependencies listed in this way are known as *direct dependencies*, as they are explicitly declared in the POM file. This classification holds true even for dependencies that may be declared in a POM that's marked as a parent of the current POM. What's a parent POM? It's just like another *pom.xml* file except that your POM marks it with a parent/child relationship by using the `<parent>` section. In this way, configuration defined by the parent POM can be inherited by the child POM. We can inspect the dependency graph by invoking the mvn dependency:tree command, which resolves the dependency graph and prints it out:

```
$ mvn dependency:tree
[INFO] Scanning for projects...
[INFO]
[INFO] -----------------------< com.acme:example >-----------------------
[INFO] Building example 1.0.0-SNAPSHOT
[INFO] -------------------------------[ jar ]--------------------------------
[INFO]
[INFO] --- maven-dependency-plugin:2.8:tree (default-cli) @ example ---
[INFO] com.acme:example:jar:1.0.0-SNAPSHOT
[INFO] \- org.apache.commons:commons-collections4:jar:4.4:compile
[INFO] -----------------------------------------------------------------------
[INFO] BUILD SUCCESS
[INFO] -----------------------------------------------------------------------
```

Here we can see that the current POM (identified by its GAV coordinates as com.acme:example:1.0.0-SNAPSHOT) has a single direct dependency. Two additional elements are found in the output of the commons-collections4 dependency: the first is jar, which identifies the type of the artifact, and the second is compile, which identifies the scope of the dependency. We'll come back to scopes in a moment, but suffice to say that if no explicit <scope> element is defined for a dependency, its default scope becomes compile. Now, when a POM that contains direct dependencies is consumed, it brings along those dependencies as transitive from the point of view of the consuming POM. The next example shows that particular setup:

```xml
<?xml version="1.0" encoding="UTF-8"?>
<project
  xsi:schemaLocation="http://maven.apache.org/POM/4.0.0
  http://maven.apache.org/xsd/maven-4.0.0.xsd"
  xmlns="http://maven.apache.org/POM/4.0.0"
  xmlns:xsi="http://www.w3.org/2001/XMLSchema-instance">
  <modelVersion>4.0.0</modelVersion>
  <groupId>com.acme</groupId>
  <artifactId>example</artifactId>
  <version>1.0.0-SNAPSHOT</version>

  <dependencies>
    <dependency>
      <groupId>commons-beanutils</groupId>
      <artifactId>commons-beanutils</artifactId>
      <version>1.9.4</version>
    </dependency>
  </dependencies>
</project>
```

Resolving and printing out the dependency graph using the same command as before yields this result:

```
$ mvn dependency:tree
[INFO] Scanning for projects...
[INFO]
[INFO] ------------------------< com.acme:example >------------------------
[INFO] Building example 1.0.0-SNAPSHOT
[INFO] --------------------------------[ jar ]--------------------------------
[INFO]
[INFO] --- maven-dependency-plugin:2.8:tree (default-cli) @ example ---
[INFO] com.acme:example:jar:1.0.0-SNAPSHOT
[INFO] \- commons-beanutils:commons-beanutils:jar:1.9.4:compile
[INFO]    +- commons-logging:commons-logging:jar:1.2:compile
[INFO]    \- commons-collections:commons-collections:jar:3.2.2:compile
[INFO] ----------------------------------------------------------------------
[INFO] BUILD SUCCESS
[INFO] ----------------------------------------------------------------------
```

This tells us that the commons-beanutils artifact has two dependencies set in the compile scope, which from the point of view of the com.acme:example:1.0.0-SNAPSHOT happen to be seen as transitive. These two transitive dependencies appear to have no direct dependencies of their own, as there's nothing listed for either of them. However, if you were to look at the commons-logging POM file, you'll find the following dependency declarations:

```
<dependencies>
  <dependency>
    <groupId>log4j</groupId>
    <artifactId>log4j</artifactId>
    <version>1.2.17</version>
    <optional>true</optional>
  </dependency>
  <dependency>
    <groupId>logkit</groupId>
    <artifactId>logkit</artifactId>
    <version>1.0.1</version>
    <optional>true</optional>
  </dependency>
  <dependency>
    <groupId>avalon-framework</groupId>
    <artifactId>avalon-framework</artifactId>
    <version>4.1.5</version>
    <optional>true</optional>
  </dependency>
  <dependency>
    <groupId>javax.servlet</groupId>
    <artifactId>servlet-api</artifactId>
    <version>2.3</version>
    <scope>provided</scope>
    <optional>true</optional>
  </dependency>
  <dependency>
    <groupId>junit</groupId>
    <artifactId>junit</artifactId>
```

```
        <version>3.8.1</version>
        <scope>test</scope>
      </dependency>
    </dependencies>
```

As you can see, there are actually five dependencies! However, four of them define an additional <optional> element, while two define a different value for <scope>. Dependencies marked as <optional> may be required for compiling and testing the producer (commons-logging in this case) but not necessarily for consumers; this is determined on a case-by-case basis.

It's time to discuss scopes now that we see them once again. *Scopes* determine whether a dependency is to be included in the classpath, as well as limit its transitivity. Maven defines six scopes as follows:

compile
> The default scope, used if none is specified, as we saw earlier. Dependencies in this scope will be used for all classpaths in the project (compile, runtime, test) and will be propagated to consuming projects.

provided
> Like compile, except that it does not affect the runtime classpath nor is it transitive. Dependencies set in this scope are expected to be provided by the hosting environment, as is the case for web applications packaged as WARs and launched from within an application server.

runtime
> This scope indicates the dependency is not required for compilation but for execution. Both the runtime and test classpaths include dependencies set in this scope, while the compile classpath is ignored.

test
> Defines dependencies required for compiling and running tests. This scope is not transitive.

system
> Similar to provided except that dependencies must be listed with an explicit path, relative or absolute. Therefore, this scope is seen as a bad practice and should be avoided at all costs. For a handful of use cases, it may come in handy, but you must bear the consequences. At best, it's an option left to the experts—in other words, imagine that this scope does not exist at all.

import
> Applies only to dependencies of type pom (the default is jar if not specified) and can be used only for dependencies declared inside the <dependencyManagement>

section. Dependencies in this scope are replaced by the list of dependencies found in their own <dependencyManagement> section.

The <dependencyManagement> section has three purposes: to provide version hints for transitive dependencies, to provide a list of dependencies that may be imported using the import scope, and to provide a set of defaults when used in a parent-child POM combination. Let's look at the first purpose. Say you have the following dependencies defined in your POM file:

```xml
<?xml version="1.0" encoding="UTF-8"?>
<project
  xsi:schemaLocation="http://maven.apache.org/POM/4.0.0
  http://maven.apache.org/xsd/maven-4.0.0.xsd"
  xmlns="http://maven.apache.org/POM/4.0.0"
  xmlns:xsi="http://www.w3.org/2001/XMLSchema-instance">
  <modelVersion>4.0.0</modelVersion>
  <groupId>com.acme</groupId>
  <artifactId>example</artifactId>
  <version>1.0.0-SNAPSHOT</version>

  <dependencies>
    <dependency>
      <groupId>com.google.inject</groupId>
      <artifactId>guice</artifactId>
      <version>4.2.2</version>
    </dependency>
    <dependency>
      <groupId>com.google.truth</groupId>
      <artifactId>truth</artifactId>
      <version>1.0</version>
    </dependency>
  </dependencies>
</project>
```

Both the guice and truth artifacts define guava as a direct dependency. This means guava is seen as a transitive dependency from the consumer's point of view. We get the following result if we resolve and print out the dependency graph:

```
$ mvn dependency:tree
[INFO] Scanning for projects...
[INFO]
[INFO] ----------------------< com.acme:example >----------------------
[INFO] Building example 1.0.0-SNAPSHOT
[INFO] --------------------------------[ jar ]---------------------------------
[INFO]
[INFO] --- maven-dependency-plugin:2.8:tree (default-cli) @ example ---
[INFO] com.acme:example:jar:1.0.0-SNAPSHOT
[INFO] +- com.google.inject:guice:jar:4.2.2:compile
[INFO] |  +- javax.inject:javax.inject:jar:1:compile
[INFO] |  +- aopalliance:aopalliance:jar:1.0:compile
[INFO] |  \- com.google.guava:guava:jar:25.1-android:compile
```

```
[INFO] |       +- com.google.code.findbugs:jsr305:jar:3.0.2:compile
[INFO] |       +- com.google.j2objc:j2objc-annotations:jar:1.1:compile
[INFO] |       \- org.codehaus.mojo:animal-sniffer-annotations:jar:1.14:compile
[INFO] \- com.google.truth:truth:jar:1.0:compile
[INFO]    +- org.checkerframework:checker-compat-qual:jar:2.5.5:compile
[INFO]    +- junit:junit:jar:4.12:compile
[INFO]    | \- org.hamcrest:hamcrest-core:jar:1.3:compile
[INFO]    +- com.googlecode.java-diff-utils:diffutils:jar:1.3.0:compile
[INFO]    +- com.google.auto.value:auto-value-annotations:jar:1.6.3:compile
[INFO]    \- com.google.errorprone:error_prone_annotations:jar:2.3.1:compile
[INFO] ------------------------------------------------------------------------
[INFO] BUILD SUCCESS
[INFO] ------------------------------------------------------------------------
```

The resolved version of guava turns out to be 25.1-android because that's the version found first in the graph. Look what happens if we invert the order of the dependencies and list truth before guice and resolve the graph once again:

```
$ mvn dependency:tree
[INFO] Scanning for projects...
[INFO]
[INFO] ------------------------< com.acme:example >------------------------
[INFO] Building example 1.0.0-SNAPSHOT
[INFO] --------------------------------[ jar ]---------------------------------
[INFO]
[INFO] --- maven-dependency-plugin:2.8:tree (default-cli) @ example ---
[INFO] com.acme:example:jar:1.0.0-SNAPSHOT
[INFO] +- com.google.truth:truth:jar:1.0:compile
[INFO] | +- com.google.guava:guava:jar:27.0.1-android:compile
[INFO] | | +- com.google.guava:failureaccess:jar:1.0.1:compile
[INFO] | | +- com.google.guava:listenablefuture:jar:
                       9999.0-empty-to-avoid-conflict
[INFO] | | +- com.google.code.findbugs:jsr305:jar:3.0.2:compile
[INFO] | | +- com.google.j2objc:j2objc-annotations:jar:1.1:compile
[INFO] | | \- org.codehaus.mojo:animal-sniffer-annotations:jar:1.17:compile
[INFO] | +- org.checkerframework:checker-compat-qual:jar:2.5.5:compile
[INFO] | +- junit:junit:jar:4.12:compile
[INFO] | | \- org.hamcrest:hamcrest-core:jar:1.3:compile
[INFO] | +- com.googlecode.java-diff-utils:diffutils:jar:1.3.0:compile
[INFO] | +- com.google.auto.value:auto-value-annotations:jar:1.6.3:compile
[INFO] | \- com.google.errorprone:error_prone_annotations:jar:2.3.1:compile
[INFO] \- com.google.inject:guice:jar:4.2.2:compile
[INFO]    +- javax.inject:javax.inject:jar:1:compile
[INFO]    \- aopalliance:aopalliance:jar:1.0:compile
[INFO] ------------------------------------------------------------------------
[INFO] BUILD SUCCESS
[INFO] ------------------------------------------------------------------------
```

Now the resolved version of guava happens to be 27.0.1-android because it's the one found first in the graph. This particular behavior is a constant source of head-scratching moments and frustration. As developers, we are used to versioning conventions, most notably semantic versioning (*https://semver.org*) when it applies to dependency versions.

Semantic versioning tells us that version tokens (separated by dots) have specific meaning based on their position. The first token identifies the major release, the second token identifies the minor release, and the third token identifies the build/patch/fix/revision release. It's also customary that version 27.0.1 is seen as more recent than 25.1.0 because the major number 27 is greater than 25. In our case, we have two versions for guava in the graph, 27.0.1-android and 25.1-android, and both are found at the same distance from the current POM—that is, just one level down in the transitive graph.

It's easy to assume that because we, as developers, are aware of semantic versioning and can clearly determine which version is more recent, so can Maven—and that is where assumption clashes with reality! Maven never looks at the version, but looks only at the location within the graph. This is why we get different results if we change the order of dependencies. We can use the <dependencyManagement> section to fix this issue.

Dependencies defined in the <dependencyManagement> section usually have the three main GAV coordinates. When Maven resolves dependencies, it will look at the definitions found in this section to see whether there's a match for groupId and artifactId, in which case the associated version will be used. It does not matter how deep in the graph a dependency may be, or how many times it may be found in the graph. If there's a match, that explicit version will be the chosen one. We can verify this claim by adding a <dependencyManagement> section to the consumer POM that looks like this:

```
<?xml version="1.0" encoding="UTF-8"?>
<project
  xsi:schemaLocation="http://maven.apache.org/POM/4.0.0
  http://maven.apache.org/xsd/maven-4.0.0.xsd"
  xmlns="http://maven.apache.org/POM/4.0.0"
  xmlns:xsi="http://www.w3.org/2001/XMLSchema-instance">
  <modelVersion>4.0.0</modelVersion>
  <groupId>com.acme</groupId>
  <artifactId>example</artifactId>
  <version>1.0.0-SNAPSHOT</version>

  <dependencyManagement>
    <dependencies>
      <dependency>
        <groupId>com.google.guava</groupId>
        <artifactId>guava</artifactId>
        <version>29.0-jre</version>
      </dependency>
    </dependencies>
  </dependencyManagement>
```

```
      <dependencies>
        <dependency>
          <groupId>com.google.truth</groupId>
          <artifactId>truth</artifactId>
          <version>1.0</version>
        </dependency>
        <dependency>
          <groupId>com.google.inject</groupId>
          <artifactId>guice</artifactId>
          <version>4.2.2</version>
        </dependency>
      </dependencies>
    </project>
```

We can see that the declaration for guava uses the com.google.guava:guava:29.0-jre coordinates, meaning that version 29.0-jre will be used if a transitive dependency happens to match the given groupId and artifactId. We know this will happen in our consumer POM, twice to be exact. We get the following result when resolving and printing out the dependency graph:

```
$ mvn dependency:tree
[INFO] Scanning for projects...
[INFO]
[INFO] ------------------------< com.acme:example >------------------------
[INFO] Building example 1.0.0-SNAPSHOT
[INFO] --------------------------------[ jar ]---------------------------------
[INFO]
[INFO] --- maven-dependency-plugin:2.8:tree (default-cli) @ example ---
[INFO] com.acme:example:jar:1.0.0-SNAPSHOT
[INFO] +- com.google.truth:truth:jar:1.0:compile
[INFO] |  +- com.google.guava:guava:jar:29.0-jre:compile
[INFO] |  |  +- com.google.guava:failureaccess:jar:1.0.1:compile
[INFO] |  |  +- com.google.guava:listenablefuture:jar:
[INFO]                         9999.0-empty-to-avoid-conflict
[INFO] |  |  +- com.google.code.findbugs:jsr305:jar:3.0.2:compile
[INFO] |  |  +- org.checkerframework:checker-qual:jar:2.11.1:compile
[INFO] |  |  \- com.google.j2objc:j2objc-annotations:jar:1.3:compile
[INFO] |  +- org.checkerframework:checker-compat-qual:jar:2.5.5:compile
[INFO] |  +- junit:junit:jar:4.12:compile
[INFO] |  |  \- org.hamcrest:hamcrest-core:jar:1.3:compile
[INFO] |  +- com.googlecode.java-diff-utils:diffutils:jar:1.3.0:compile
[INFO] |  +- com.google.auto.value:auto-value-annotations:jar:1.6.3:compile
[INFO] |  \- com.google.errorprone:error_prone_annotations:jar:2.3.1:compile
[INFO] \- com.google.inject:guice:jar:4.2.2:compile
[INFO]    +- javax.inject:javax.inject:jar:1:compile
[INFO]    \- aopalliance:aopalliance:jar:1.0:compile
[INFO] ------------------------------------------------------------------------
[INFO] BUILD SUCCESS
[INFO] ------------------------------------------------------------------------
```

Note that the chosen version for guava is indeed 29.0-jre and not the previous versions we saw earlier in this chapter, confirming that the <dependencyManagement> section is performing its job as expected.

The second purpose of <dependencyManagement>, listing dependencies that may be imported, is accomplished by using the import scope alongside dependencies of type pom. These types of dependencies usually define <dependencyManagement> sections of their own, although nothing stops these POMs from adding more sections. POM dependencies that define a <dependencyManagement> section and no <dependencies> section are known as bill of materials (BOM). Typically, BOM dependencies define a set of artifacts that belong together for a particular purpose. Although not explicitly defined in the Maven documentation, you can find two kinds of BOM dependencies:

Library
All declared dependencies belong to the same project even though they might have different group IDs, and possibly even different versions. An example can be seen at helidon-bom (*https://oreil.ly/bcMHI*), which groups all artifacts from the Helidon project.

Stack
Dependencies are grouped by behavior and the synergy they bring. Dependencies may belong to disparate projects. See an example at helidon-dependencies (*https://oreil.ly/wgmVx*), which groups the previous helidon-bom with other dependencies such as Netty, logging, and so on.

Let's take the helidon-dependencies as a source of dependencies. Inspecting this POM, we find dozens of dependencies declared inside its <dependencyManagement> section, only a few of which are seen in the following snippet:

```
<artifactId>helidon-dependencies</artifactId>
<packaging>pom</packaging>
<!-- additional elements elided -->
<dependencyManagement>
  <dependencies>
    <!-- more dependencies elided -->
    <dependency>
      <groupId>io.netty</groupId>
      <artifactId>netty-handler</artifactId>
      <version>4.1.51.Final</version>
    </dependency>
    <dependency>
      <groupId>io.netty</groupId>
      <artifactId>netty-handler-proxy</artifactId>
      <version>4.1.51.Final</version>
    </dependency>
    <dependency>
      <groupId>io.netty</groupId>
      <artifactId>netty-codec-http</artifactId>
```

```
        <version>4.1.51.Final</version>
      </dependency>
      <!-- more dependencies elided -->
    </dependencies>
  </dependencyManagement>
```

Consuming this BOM dependency in our own POM requires the use of the <depend
encyManagement> section once again. We'll also define an explicit dependency for
netty-handler as we have done before when defining dependencies, except that this
time we'll omit the <version> element. The POM ends up looking like this:

```
<?xml version="1.0" encoding="UTF-8"?>
<project
  xsi:schemaLocation="http://maven.apache.org/POM/4.0.0
  http://maven.apache.org/xsd/maven-4.0.0.xsd"
  xmlns="http://maven.apache.org/POM/4.0.0"
  xmlns:xsi="http://www.w3.org/2001/XMLSchema-instance">
  <modelVersion>4.0.0</modelVersion>
  <groupId>com.acme</groupId>
  <artifactId>example</artifactId>
  <version>1.0.0-SNAPSHOT</version>

  <dependencyManagement>
    <dependencies>
      <dependency>
        <groupId>io.helidon</groupId>
        <artifactId>helidon-dependencies</artifactId>
        <version>2.2.0</version>
        <type>pom</type>
        <scope>import</scope>
      </dependency>
    </dependencies>
  </dependencyManagement>

  <dependencies>
    <dependency>
      <groupId>io.netty</groupId>
      <artifactId>netty-handler</artifactId>
    </dependency>
  </dependencies>
</project>
```

Note how the helidon-dependencies dependency was imported. A key element must
be defined, <type>, which must be set as pom. Remember from earlier in this chapter
that dependencies will have type jar by default if no value is specified? Here we know
that helidon-dependencies is a BOM; thus it does not have a JAR file associated with
it. If we leave out the type element, Maven will complain with a warning and will fail
to resolve the version of netty-handler, so be sure not to miss setting this element
correctly. Resolving the dependency graph yields the following result:

```
$ mvn dependency:tree
[INFO] Scanning for projects...
[INFO]
[INFO] --------------------------< com.acme:example >--------------------------
[INFO] Building example 1.0.0-SNAPSHOT
[INFO] --------------------------------[ jar ]---------------------------------
[INFO]
[INFO] --- maven-dependency-plugin:2.8:tree (default-cli) @ example ---
[INFO] com.acme:example:jar:1.0.0-SNAPSHOT
[INFO] \- io.netty:netty-handler:jar:4.1.51.Final:compile
[INFO]    +- io.netty:netty-common:jar:4.1.51.Final:compile
[INFO]    +- io.netty:netty-resolver:jar:4.1.51.Final:compile
[INFO]    +- io.netty:netty-buffer:jar:4.1.51.Final:compile
[INFO]    +- io.netty:netty-transport:jar:4.1.51.Final:compile
[INFO]    \- io.netty:netty-codec:jar:4.1.51.Final:compile
[INFO] ------------------------------------------------------------------------
[INFO] BUILD SUCCESS
[INFO] ------------------------------------------------------------------------
```

We can see that the correct version was chosen and that every direct dependency of netty-handler is resolved as transitive as well.

The third and final purpose of the <dependencyManagement> section comes into play when a parent-child relationship exists between POMs. The POM format defines a <parent> section that any POM can use to establish a link with another POM seen as a parent. Parent POMs provide configuration that can be inherited by child POMs, the parent <dependencyManagement> section being one of them. Maven follows the parent link upward until it can no longer find a parent definition, then processes down the chain resolving configuration, with the POMs located at lower levels overriding configuration set by those POMs in higher levels.

This means a child POM always has the option to override configuration declared by a parent POM. Thus, a <dependencyManagement> section found in the parent POM will be visible to the child POM, as if it were defined on the child. We still get the same benefits from the two previous purposes of this section, which means we can fix versions for transitive dependencies and import BOM dependencies. The following is an example of a parent POM that declares helidon-dependencies and commons-lang3 in its own <dependencyManagement> section:

```
<?xml version="1.0" encoding="UTF-8"?>
<project
    xsi:schemaLocation="http://maven.apache.org/POM/4.0.0
    http://maven.apache.org/xsd/maven-4.0.0.xsd"
    xmlns="http://maven.apache.org/POM/4.0.0"
    xmlns:xsi="http://www.w3.org/2001/XMLSchema-instance">
  <modelVersion>4.0.0</modelVersion>
  <groupId>com.acme</groupId>
  <artifactId>parent</artifactId>
  <version>1.0.0-SNAPSHOT</version>
  <packaging>pom</packaging>
```

```
<dependencyManagement>
  <dependencies>
    <dependency>
      <groupId>io.helidon</groupId>
      <artifactId>helidon-dependencies</artifactId>
      <version>2.2.0</version>
      <type>pom</type>
      <scope>import</scope>
    </dependency>
    <dependency>
      <groupId>org.apache.commons</groupId>
      <artifactId>commons-lang3</artifactId>
      <version>3.11</version>
    </dependency>
  </dependencies>
</dependencyManagement>
</project>
```

Given that no JAR file is associated with this POM file, we also must explicitly define the value for the `<packaging>` element as pom. The child POM requires the use of the `<parent>` element to refer to this POM, shown in the following example:

```
<?xml version="1.0" encoding="UTF-8"?>
<project
  xsi:schemaLocation="http://maven.apache.org/POM/4.0.0
  http://maven.apache.org/xsd/maven-4.0.0.xsd"
  xmlns="http://maven.apache.org/POM/4.0.0"
  xmlns:xsi="http://www.w3.org/2001/XMLSchema-instance">
  <modelVersion>4.0.0</modelVersion>
  <parent>
    <groupId>com.acme</groupId>
    <artifactId>parent</artifactId>
    <version>1.0.0-SNAPSHOT</version>
  </parent>
  <artifactId>example</artifactId>

  <dependencies>
    <dependency>
      <groupId>io.netty</groupId>
      <artifactId>netty-handler</artifactId>
    </dependency>
    <dependency>
      <groupId>org.apache.commons</groupId>
      <artifactId>commons-lang3</artifactId>
    </dependency>
  </dependencies>
</project>
```

Perfect! With this setup ready, it's time to once again resolve the dependency graph and inspect its contents:

```
$ mvn dependency:tree
[INFO] Scanning for projects...
[INFO]
[INFO] ------------------------< com.acme:example >------------------------
[INFO] Building example 1.0.0-SNAPSHOT
[INFO] --------------------------------[ jar ]---------------------------------
[INFO]
[INFO] --- maven-dependency-plugin:2.8:tree (default-cli) @ example ---
[INFO] com.acme:example:jar:1.0.0-SNAPSHOT
[INFO] +- io.netty:netty-handler:jar:4.1.51.Final:compile
[INFO] |  +- io.netty:netty-common:jar:4.1.51.Final:compile
[INFO] |  +- io.netty:netty-resolver:jar:4.1.51.Final:compile
[INFO] |  +- io.netty:netty-buffer:jar:4.1.51.Final:compile
[INFO] |  +- io.netty:netty-transport:jar:4.1.51.Final:compile
[INFO] |  \- io.netty:netty-codec:jar:4.1.51.Final:compile
[INFO] \- org.apache.commons:commons-lang3:jar:3.11:compile
[INFO] ------------------------------------------------------------------------
[INFO] BUILD SUCCESS
[INFO] ------------------------------------------------------------------------
```

We have two direct dependencies as expected, with the correct GAV coordinates, as well as the transitive dependencies as seen earlier. A few additional items are related to dependency management and resolution, such as dependency exclusions (eject a transitive dependency by its GA coordinates) and failing the build on dependency conflicts (different versions of the same GA coordinates found in the graph). However, it's best to stop here and have a look at what Gradle offers in terms of dependency management.

Dependency Management with Gradle

As mentioned earlier, Gradle builds on top of the lessons learned from Maven and understands the POM format, allowing it to provide dependency resolution capabilities similar to Maven. Gradle also offers additional capabilities and finer-grained control. This section refers to topics already covered, so I recommend you read the preceding section first in the event you skipped it, or if you need a refresher on dependency management as provided by Maven. Let's have a look at what Gradle offers.

First, you must select the DSL for writing the build file. Your options are the Apache Groovy DSL or the Kotlin DSL. We'll continue with the former, as Groovy has more examples found in the wild. It's also easier to move from Groovy to Kotlin than vice versa, meaning that snippets written with Groovy can be used verbatim with Kotlin (with perhaps a few changes suggested by the IDE), whereas moving in the other direction requires knowledge of both DSLs. The next step is picking the format for recording dependencies, for which there are quite a few; the most common formats are a single literal with GAV coordinates, such as this:

```
'org.apache.commons:commons-collections4:4.4'
```

and the Map literal that splits each member of the GAV coordinates into its own element, such as this:

```
group: 'org.apache.commons', name: 'commons-collections4', version: '4.4'
```

Note that Gradle chose to go with `group` instead of `groupId`, and `name` instead of `artifactId`, though the semantics are the same.

The next order of business is declaring dependencies for a particular scope (in Maven's terms), though Gradle calls this *configuration*, and the behavior goes beyond what scopes are capable of. Assuming the `java-library` plug-in is applied to a Gradle build file, we gain access to the following configurations by default:

api

> Defines dependencies required for compiling production code and affects the compile classpath. It is equivalent to the `compile` scope and thus is mapped as such when a POM is generated.

implementation

> Defines dependencies required for compilation but deemed as implementation details; they are more flexible than dependencies found in the `api` configuration. This configuration affects the compile classpath but will be mapped to the `run time` scope when a POM is generated.

compileOnly

> Defines dependencies required for compilation but not for execution. This configuration affects the compile classpath, but these dependencies are not shared with other classpaths. Also, they are not mapped to the generated POM.

runtimeOnly

> Dependencies in this configuration are needed for execution only and affect only the runtime classpath. They are mapped to the `runtime` scope when a POM is generated.

testImplementation

> Defines dependencies required for compiling test code and affects the `testCompile` classpath. They are mapped to the `test` scope when a POM is generated.

testCompileOnly

> Defines dependencies required for compiling test code but not for execution. This configuration affects the `testCompile` classpath, but these dependencies are not shared with the testRuntime classpath. Also, they are not mapped to the generated POM.

testRuntimeOnly

> Dependencies with this configuration are needed for executing test code and affect only the `testRuntime` classpath. They are mapped to the `test` scope when a POM is generated.

You may see additional configurations depending on the Gradle version in use, including the following legacy ones (which were deprecated in Gradle 6 and removed in Gradle 7):

compile

> This configuration was split into `api` and `implementation`.

runtime

> Deprecated in favor of `runtimeOnly`.

testCompile

> Deprecated in favor of `testImplementation` to align with the `implementation` configuration name.

testRuntime

> Deprecated in favor of `testRuntimeOnly` to be consistent with `runtimeOnly`.

Similarly to Maven, the classpaths follow a hierarchy. The compile classpath can be consumed by the runtime classpath, thus every dependency set in either the `api` or `implementation` configurations is also available for execution. This classpath can also be consumed by the test compile classpath, enabling production code to be seen by test code. The runtime and test classpaths are consumed by the test runtime classpath, allowing test execution access to all dependencies defined in all the configurations so far mentioned.

As with Maven, dependencies can be resolved from repositories. Unlike Maven, in which both Maven local and Maven Central repositories are always available, in Gradle we must explicitly define the repositories from which dependencies may be consumed. Gradle lets you define repositories that follow the standard Maven layout, the Ivy layout, and even local directories with a flat layout. It also provides conventional options to configure the most commonly known repository, Maven Central. We'll use `mavenCentral` for now as our only repository. Putting together everything we have seen so far, we can produce a build file like the following:

```
plugins {
  id 'java-library'
}

repositories {
  mavenCentral()
}
```

```
dependencies {
    api 'org.apache.commons:commons-collections4:4.4'
}
```

We can print the resolved dependency graph by invoking the dependencies task. However, this will print the graph for every single configuration, so we'll print only the resolved dependency graph for the compile classpath for the sake of keeping the output short, as well as to showcase an extra setting that can be defined for this task:

```
$ gradle dependencies --configuration compileClasspath

> Task :dependencies

------------------------------------------------------------
Root project
------------------------------------------------------------

compileClasspath - Compile classpath for source set 'main'.
\--- org.apache.commons:commons-collections4:4.4
```

As you can see, only a single dependency is printed out, because commons-collections does not have any direct dependencies of its own that are visible to consumers.

Let's see what happens when we configure another dependency that brings in additional transitive dependencies, but this time using the implementation configuration that will show that both api and implementation contribute to the compile classpath. The updated build file looks like this:

```
plugins {
    id 'java-library'
}

repositories {
    mavenCentral()
}

dependencies {
    api 'org.apache.commons:commons-collections4:4.4'
    implementation 'commons-beanutils:commons-beanutils:1.9.4'
}
```

Running the dependencies task with the same configuration as before now yields the following result:

```
$ gradle dependencies --configuration compileClasspath

> Task :dependencies

------------------------------------------------------------
Root project
------------------------------------------------------------
```

```
compileClasspath - Compile classpath for source set 'main'.
+--- org.apache.commons:commons-collections4:4.4
\--- commons-beanutils:commons-beanutils:1.9.4
     +--- commons-logging:commons-logging:1.2
     \--- commons-collections:commons-collections:3.2.2
```

This tells us our consumer project has two direct dependencies contributing to the compile classpath, and that one of those dependencies brings two additional dependencies seen as transitive from our consumer's point of view. If for some reason you'd like to skip bringing those transitive dependencies into your dependency graph, you can add an extra block of configuration on the direct dependency that declares them, like this:

```
plugins {
  id 'java-library'
}

repositories {
  mavenCentral()
}

dependencies {
  api 'org.apache.commons:commons-collections4:4.4'
  implementation('commons-beanutils:commons-beanutils:1.9.4') {
    transitive = false
  }
}
```

Running the dependencies task once more now shows only the direct dependencies and no transitive dependencies:

```
$ gradle dependencies --configuration compileClasspath

> Task :dependencies

------------------------------------------------------------
Root project
------------------------------------------------------------

compileClasspath - Compile classpath for source set 'main'.
+--- org.apache.commons:commons-collections4:4.4
\--- commons-beanutils:commons-beanutils:1.9.4
```

The final aspect I'd like to cover before moving on is that unlike Maven, Gradle understands semantic versioning and will act accordingly during dependency resolution, choosing the highest version number as a result. We can verify this by configuring two versions of the same dependency, no matter whether they are direct or transitive, as shown in the following snippet:

```
plugins {
  id 'java-library'
```

```
}

repositories {
  mavenCentral()
}

dependencies {
  api 'org.apache.commons:commons-collections4:4.4'
  implementation 'commons-collections:commons-collections:3.2.1'
  implementation 'commons-beanutils:commons-beanutils:1.9.4'
}
```

In this case, we have declared a direct dependency for commons-collections version 3.2.1. We know from previous runs that commons-beanutils:1.9.4 brings in version 3.2.2 of commons-collections. Given that 3.2.2 is considered more recent than 3.2.1, we expect that 3.2.2 will be resolved. Invoking the dependencies task yields the following result:

```
$ gradle dependencies --configuration compileClasspath

> Task :dependencies

------------------------------------------------------------
Root project
------------------------------------------------------------

compileClasspath - Compile classpath for source set 'main'.
+--- org.apache.commons:commons-collections4:4.4
+--- commons-collections:commons-collections:3.2.1 -> 3.2.2
\--- commons-beanutils:commons-beanutils:1.9.4
     +--- commons-logging:commons-logging:1.2
     \--- commons-collections:commons-collections:3.2.2

(*) - dependencies omitted (listed previously)
```

As expected, version 3.2.2 was selected. The output even contains an indicator telling us when a dependency version was set to a different value other than the requested one. Versions may be also configured to be fixed regardless of their semantic versioning scheme, even to lower values. This is because Gradle offers more flexible options for dependency resolution strategies. However, that falls into the realm of advanced topics alongside dependency locking, strict versus suggested versions, dependency relocation, platforms and enforced platforms (Gradle's way to interact with BOM artifacts), and more.

Dependency Management Basics for Containers

Further along the line of the software development cycle, you may encounter a step where packaging your Maven and Gradle project into a container image is necessary. Just like other dependencies in your project, your container images must also be managed appropriately and in concert with other required artifacts. Containers are discussed in detail in Chapter 3, but this section focuses primarily on some of the subtleties of container image management. As with the dependency management in the automated build tools Maven and Gradle, even more dragons may lie ahead.

As you learned in Chapter 3, containers are launched using container images that are most commonly defined using a Dockerfile. The Dockerfile does the work of defining each layer of the image that will be used to build the running container. From this definition, you will get a base distribution layer, code libraries and frameworks, and any other needed files or artifacts required to run your software. Here you will also define any necessary configuration (for example, open ports, database credentials, and references to messaging servers) as well as any required users and permissions.

It's line 1 of the Dockerfile that we discuss in this section first, or in the case of multistage build Dockerfiles, the lines that begin with the directive FROM. Similarly to the Maven POM, an image can be built from a parent image, which may be built from another parent image—a hierarchy that goes all the way to a base image, the original ancestor. Here we must pay special attention to the way our images are composed.

As you may remember from Chapter 3, the versioning of Docker images is intended to provide flexibility during the development stage of your software, as well as a measure of confidence that you are using the latest maintenance update of an image when desired. Most often this is done by referencing the special image version latest (the default version if a version is not specified), a request for which will retrieve what is assumed to be the latest version of the image in active development. Although not a perfect comparison, this is most like using a snapshot version of a Java dependency.

This is all fine and good during development, but when it comes to troubleshooting a new bug in production, this type of versioning in a production image artifact can make troubleshooting more of a challenge. Once an image has been built with this default latest version in place for a parent or a base image, reproducing the build may be difficult or even impossible. Just as you would want to avoid using a snapshot dependency in a production release, I recommend locking down your image versions and avoiding using the default latest in order to limit the number of moving parts.

Simply locking down your image versions isn't sufficient from the context of security. Use only trusted base images when building your containers. This tip might seem like an obvious one, but third-party registries often don't have any governance policies for the images stored in them. It's important to know which images are available for use on the Docker host, understand their provenance, and review their content. You should also enable Docker Content Trust (DCT) for image verification and install only verified packages into images.

Use minimal base images that don't include unnecessary software packages that could lead to a larger attack surface. Having fewer components in your container reduces the number of available attack vectors, and a minimal image also yields better performance because there are fewer bytes on disk and less network traffic for images being copied. BusyBox and Alpine are two options for building minimal base images. Pay just as careful attention to any additional layers you build on top of your verified base image by explicitly specifying all versions of software packages or any other artifacts you pull into the image.

Artifact Publication

Up to now, I've discussed how artifacts and dependencies may be resolved, often from locations known as repositories, but what is a repository, and how do you publish artifacts to it? In the most basic sense, an *artifact repository* is file storage that keeps track of artifacts. A repository collects metadata on each published artifact and uses that metadata to offer additional capabilities such as search, archiving, access control lists (ACLs), and others. Tools can harness this metadata to offer other capabilities on top such as vulnerability scanning, metrics, categorization, and more.

We can use two types of repositories for Maven dependencies, those dependencies that can be resolved via GAV coordinates: local and remote. Maven uses a configurable directory found in the local file system to keep track of dependencies that have been resolved. These dependencies may have been downloaded from a remote repository or directly placed there by the Maven tool itself. This directory is typically referred to as *Maven Local*, and its default location is *.m2/repository*, found at the home directory of the current user. This location is configurable. On the other side of the spectrum are remote repositories, which are handled by repository software such as Sonatype Nexus Repository, JFrog Artifactory, and others. The most well-known remote repository is Maven Central, which is the canonical repository for resolving artifacts.

Let's discuss now how we can publish artifacts to local and remote repositories.

Publishing to Maven Local

Maven offers three ways to publish artifacts to the Maven Local repository. Two are explicit, and one is implicit. We've already covered the implicit one—it occurs whenever Maven resolves a dependency from a remote repository; as a result, a copy of the artifact and its metadata (the associated *pom.xml*) will be placed in the Maven Local repository. This behavior occurs by default since Maven uses Maven Local as a cache to avoid requesting artifacts over the network all over again.

The other two ways of publishing artifacts to Maven Local are by explicitly "installing" files into the repository. Maven has a set of lifecycle phases, of which *install* is one. This phase is well-known by Java developers, as it's used (and abused) to compile, test, package, and install artifacts to Maven Local. The Maven lifecycle phases follow a predetermined sequence:

```
Available lifecycle phases are: validate, initialize, generate-sources,
process-sources, generate-resources, process-resources, compile,
process-classes, generate-test-sources, process-test-sources,
generate-test-resources, process-test-resources, test-compile,
process-test-classes, test, prepare-package, package, pre-integration-test,
integration-test, post-integration-test, verify, install, deploy,
pre-clean, clean, post-clean, pre-site, site, post-site, site-deploy.
```

Phases are executed in sequence until the terminal phase is found. Thus invoking *install* typically results in an almost full build (except for *deploy* and *site*). I mentioned *install* is abused, as most times it's enough to invoke *verify*, the phase that's right before *install*, as the former will force compile, test, package, and integration-test but does not pollute Maven Local with artifacts if they are not needed. This is in no way a recommendation to drop *install* in favor of *verify* all the time, as sometimes a test will require resolving artifacts from Maven Local. The bottom line is to be aware of the inputs/outputs of each phase and their consequences.

Back to installing. The first way to install artifacts to Maven Local is simply invoking the *install* phase, like so:

```
$ mvn install
```

This will place copies of all of the *pom.xml* files renamed to follow the convention `artifactId-version.pom` as well as every attached artifact into Maven Local. Attached artifacts are typically the binary JARs produced by the build but can also include other JARs such as the `-sources` and `-javadoc` JARs. The second way to install artifacts is by manually invoking the `install:install-file` goal with a set of parameters. Let's say you have a JAR (*artifact.jar*) and a matching POM file (*artifact.pom*). Installing them can be done in the following way:

```
$ mvn install:install-file -Dfile=artifact.jar -DpomFile=artifact.pom
```

Maven will read the metadata found in the POM file and place the files in their corresponding location based on the resolved GAV coordinates. It's possible to override the GAV coordinates, generate the POM on the fly, and even omit the explicit POM if the JAR contains a copy inside. (That's typically the case for JARs built with Maven; Gradle, on the other hand, does not include the POM by default.)

Gradle has one way to publish artifacts to Maven Local, and that is by applying the `maven-publish` plug-in. This plug-in adds new capabilities to the project such as the `publishToMavenLocal` task; as the name indicates, it will copy the built artifacts and a generated POM to Maven Local. Unlike Maven, Gradle does not use Maven Local as a cache, as it has its own caching infrastructure. Thus, when Gradle resolves dependencies, the files are placed at a different location, usually *.gradle/ caches/modules-2/files-2.1*, located at the home directory of the current user.

That covers publishing to Maven Local. Now let's have a look at remote repositories.

Publishing to Maven Central

The *Maven Central* repository is the backbone that allows Java projects to be built on a daily basis. The software running Maven Central is *Sonatype Nexus Repository*, an artifact repository provided by Sonatype. Given its important role in the Java ecosystem, Maven Central has placed a set of rules that must be followed when publishing artifacts; Sonatype has published a guide (*https://oreil.ly/xfhNd*) explaining the prerequisites and rules. I highly recommend reading through the guide in case requirements have been updated since the publication of this book. In short, you must ensure the following:

- You must prove ownership of the reverse domain of the target groupId. If your groupId is com.acme.*, you must own acme.com.

- When publishing a binary JAR, you must also supply -sources and javadoc JARs, as well as a matching POM—that is, a minimum of four separate files.

- When publishing an artifact of type POM, only the POM file is needed.

- PGP signature files for all artifacts must be submitted as well. The PGP keys used for signing must be published in public-key servers to let Maven Central verify signatures.

- Perhaps the aspect that trips up most people at the beginning: POM files must comply with a minimum set of elements such as <license>, <developers>, <scm>, and others. These elements are described in the guide; omitting any of them will cause a failure during publication, and as result artifacts won't be published at all.

We can avoid the last problem or at least detect it much earlier during development by using the PomChecker (*https://oreil.ly/E7LP1*) project. PomChecker can be invoked in many ways: as a standalone CLI tool, as a Maven plug-in, or as a Gradle plug-in. This flexibility makes it ideal for verifying a POM at your local environment or at a CI/CD pipeline. Verifying a *pom.xml* file using the CLI can be done like so:

```
$ pomchecker check-maven-central --pom-file=pom.xml
```

If your project is built with Maven, you may invoke the PomChecker plug-in without having to configure it in the POM, like this:

```
$ mvn org.kordamp.maven:pomchecker-maven-plugin:check-maven-central
```

That command will resolve the latest version of `pomchecker-maven-plugin` and execute its `check-maven-central` goal right on the spot, using the current project as input. With Gradle, you'd have to explicitly configure the `org.kordamp.gradle` `.pomchecker` plug-in as Gradle does not offer an option for invoking an inlined plug-in as Maven does.

The last bit of configuration that must be applied to the build is the publication mechanism itself. Do that by adding the following to your *pom.xml* if you're building with Maven:

```
<distributionManagement>
  <repository>
    <id>ossrh</id>
    <url>https://s01.oss.sonatype.org/service/local/staging/deploy/maven2/</url>
  </repository>
  <snapshotRepository>
    <id>ossrh</id>
    <url>https://s01.oss.sonatype.org/content/repositories/snapshots</url>
  </snapshotRepository>
</distributionManagement>

<build>
  <plugins>
    <plugin>
      <groupId>org.apache.maven.plugins</groupId>
      <artifactId>maven-javadoc-plugin</artifactId>
      <version>3.2.0</version>
      cutions>
        cution>
        <id>attach-javadocs</id>
        <goals>
          <goal>jar</goal>
        </goals>
        <configuration>
          <attach>true</attach>
        </configuration>
        </execution>
      </executions>
    </plugin>
    <plugin>
      <groupId>org.apache.maven.plugins</groupId>
      <artifactId>maven-source-plugin</artifactId>
      <version>3.2.1</version>
      <executions>
        <execution>
          <id>attach-sources</id>
          <goals>
            <goal>jar</goal>
          </goals>
          <configuration>
            <attach>true</attach>
```

```
        </configuration>
      </execution>
    </executions>
  </plugin>
  <plugin>
    <groupId>org.apache.maven.plugins</groupId>
    <artifactId>maven-gpg-plugin</artifactId>
    <version>1.6</version>
    <executions>
      <execution>
        <goals>
          <goal>sign</goal>
        </goals>
        <phase>verify</phase>
        <configuration>
          <gpgArguments>
            <arg>--pinentry-mode</arg>
            <arg>loopback</arg>
          </gpgArguments>
        </configuration>
      </execution>
    </executions>
  </plugin>
  <plugin>
    <groupId>org.sonatype.plugins</groupId>
    <artifactId>nexus-staging-maven-plugin</artifactId>
    <version>1.6.8</version>
    <extensions>true</extensions>
    <configuration>
      <serverId>central</serverId>
      <nexusUrl>https://s01.oss.sonatype.org</nexusUrl>
      <autoReleaseAfterClose>true</autoReleaseAfterClose>
    </configuration>
  </plugin>
  </plugins>
</build>
```

Note that this configuration generates -`sources` and -`javadoc` JARs, signs all attached artifacts with PGP, and uploads all artifacts to the given URL, which happens to be one of the URLs supported by Maven Central. The `<serverId>` element identifies the credentials you must have in place in your *settings.xml* file (otherwise, the upload will fail), or you may define credentials as command-line arguments.

You may want to put the plug-in configuration inside a `<profile>` section, as the behavior provided by the configured plug-ins is needed only when a release is posted; there's no reason to generate additional JARs during the execution of the main lifecycle phase sequence. This way, your builds will execute only the minimum set of steps and thus be faster as a result.

On the other hand, if you're using Gradle for publication, you'd have to configure a plug-in that can publish to Sonatype Nexus Repository, the latest of such plug-ins being io.github.gradle-nexus.publish-plugin (*https://oreil.ly/MdCNh*). There's more than one way to configure Gradle to do the job. Idioms change more rapidly than what you must configure in Maven. I recommend you consult the official Gradle guides to find out what needs to be done in this case.

Publishing to Sonatype Nexus Repository

You may recall that Maven Central is run using Sonatype Nexus Repository, so it should be no surprise that the configuration shown in the previous section applies here as well, such that you have to change only the publication URLs to match the Nexus repository. There's one caveat though: the strict verification rules applied by Maven Central often do not apply to a custom Nexus installation. That is, Nexus has the option to configure the rules that govern artifact publication. These rules may be relaxed for a Nexus instance running within your organization, for example, or they may be stricter in other areas. It's a good idea to consult the documentation available at your organization regarding artifact publication to their own Nexus instance.

One thing is clear: if you are publishing artifacts to your organization's Nexus repository that eventually must be published to Maven Central, it's a good idea to follow the Maven Central rules from the start—as long as these rules do not clash with your organization's.

Publishing to JFrog Artifactory

JFrog Artifactory is another popular option for artifact management. It offers similar capabilities as Sonatype Nexus Repository while at the same time adding other features, including integration with other products that belong to the JFrog Platform, such as Xray and Pipelines. One particular feature I'm quite fond of is that artifacts do not need to be signed at the source before publication. Artifactory can perform the signing with your PGP keys or with a site-wide PGP key. This relieves you of the burden of setting up keys on your local and CI environments as well as transferring fewer bytes during publication. As before, the previous publication configuration we saw for Maven Central will work for Artifactory as well, by changing only the publication URLs to match the Artifactory instance.

As with Nexus, Artifactory allows you to sync artifacts to Maven Central, and you have to follow the rules for publishing to Maven Central once again. Thus publishing well-formed POMs, sources, and Javadoc JARs from the get-go is a good idea.

Summary

We've covered plenty of concepts in this chapter, but the main takeaway should be that artifacts on their own are not enough to get the best results when building software or to get ahead of the competition. Artifacts usually have metadata that can be associated with them such as their build time, dependency versions, and environment. This metadata may be used to trace the origins of a particular artifact, help turn it into a reproducible artifact, or enable the generation of a software bill of materials (SBOM), which happens to be yet another metadata format. Moreover, observability, monitoring, and other concerns regarding the health and stability of the build pipeline can be greatly enhanced by the existence of this metadata.

Specific to dependencies, we saw the basics of dependency resolution with popular Java build tools such as Apache Maven and Gradle. Of course, more depth than was discussed in this chapter is warranted; these topics could certainly fill a book on their own. Be sure to be on the lookout for improvements in this area as provided by later versions of these build tools.

Finally, we covered how to publish Java artifacts to the popular Maven Central repository, given that it requires adhering to a particular set of guidelines that must be followed for successful publication. Maven Central is the canonical repository, but it's not the only one. Sonatype offers Sonatype Nexus Repository, and JFrog offers JFrog Artifactory, also quite popular choices to manage artifacts at internal locations such as your own organization or company.

## CHAPTER 7

Securing Your Binaries

Sven Ruppert
Stephen Chin

Data is the pollution problem of the information age, and protecting privacy is the environmental challenge.
   —Bruce Schneier, *Data and Goliath*

Software security is a critical part of any comprehensive DevOps rollout. New breaches uncovered in the past year have called attention to the consequences of weak software security, and have prompted the creation of new government security regulations. The impact of meeting these new regulations spans across the entire software lifecycle, from development through production. As a result, DevSecOps is something that every software developer and DevOps professional needs to understand.

In this chapter, you will learn how to evaluate your product and organizational risk for security vulnerabilities. We will also cover static and dynamic techniques for security testing, and scoring techniques for risk assessment.

Regardless of your role, you will be better prepared to help secure your organization's software delivery lifecycle. But first let's look deeper into what happens if you don't have a focus on security and take steps to secure your software supply chain.

Supply Chain Security Compromised

It started in early December 2020, when FireEye noticed that it had become a victim of a cyberattack, which is remarkable because the company itself specializes in detecting and fending off cyberattacks. Internal analysis showed that the attackers managed to steal FireEye internal tools, which FireEye used to examine its customers' IT infrastructure for weak points. This highly specialized toolbox is optimized for breaking into networks and IT systems, which in the hands of hackers is a tremendous risk. It wasn't until later that this breach and a massive cyberattack known as the *SolarWinds hack* were discovered to be connected. (FireEye has since become Trellix, through a merger.)

SolarWinds, a company based in the United States, specializes in the management of complex IT network structures. For this, the company developed the Orion Platform. The company itself has over 300,000 active customers who use this software internally. The software for managing network components has to be equipped with generous administrative rights within the IT systems in order to be able to carry out its tasks, which is one of the critical points the hackers used in their strategy. It took some time to recognize the connection between the FireEye hack and the later, massive cyberattacks, because the chain of effects was not as direct as previous vulnerability breaches.

Because of the long gap between exploitation of the SolarWinds vulnerability and discovery of the breach, many companies and government organizations ended up being affected by this attack. Over a period of a few weeks 20,000 successful attacks were launched. Because the pattern of the attacks was similar, security researchers were able to identify that these attacks were related. One of the common characteristics was that all of the organizations that suffered an attack used SolarWinds software to manage their network infrastructure.

The attackers used FireEye tools to break into SolarWinds networks. They attacked the CI pipeline, which is responsible for creating the binaries for the Orion software platform. The software delivery production line was modified so that each time a new version was run through, the resulting binary was compromised and included a backdoor prepared by the hackers. The Orion Platform was used here as a Trojan horse to deliver the compromised binaries to thousands of networks. Any recipient who checked the fingerprint would see a valid binary because it was signed by SolarWinds, which is a vendor they trust. And this trust relationship is the flaw that this cyberattack takes advantage of to attack downstream networks.

The precise account of the way this attack was executed is as follows. The company, SolarWinds, created an update of its software and made these binaries available to all 300,000 customers via an automatic update process. Almost 20,000 customers then installed this update in a short period of time. The compromised software waited about two weeks after activation and then began to spread in the infected systems. As if that wasn't bad enough, over time, further malware was then dynamically loaded, making it impossible to repair the compromised system without a full rebuild.

Stepping back a bit, let's differentiate between the perspective of the SolarWinds company and the perspective of the affected customers. Whose responsibility is it to mitigate this attack, and what does the procedure look like if you are affected yourself? Which tools can you use to identify and address the vulnerability? Who can take action against such attacks, and at what point in the vulnerability timeline?

Security from the Vendor Perspective

First, let's start with the perspective of a software manufacturer (in this example, SolarWinds) that distributes software to its customers. When a supply-chain attack is carried out, you have to prepare yourself because you will be only the carrier of the viral software. Compared to a conventional attack, the damage is amplified because you are enabling hackers to open a security hole in thousands of your customers. Preventing this requires a stringent approach in your software development and distribution process.

Securing the tools used in your software delivery pipeline is one of the most important aspects, because they have access to your internal systems and can maliciously modify binaries in your software pipeline. However, this is challenging because the number of direct and indirect tools used in software delivery lifecycles is constantly increasing and expanding the attack surface.

Security from the Customer Perspective

As a customer of a vendor like SolarWinds, it is essential to consider all elements in the value chain, including all of the tools that a software developer uses daily. You also have to check the binaries generated from your CI/CD system for the possibility of modification or vulnerability injection. It is essential to keep an overview of all components used with a secure and traceable bill of materials. Ultimately, it helps only if you break your own products into their constituent parts and subject each element to a security review.

How can you protect yourself as a consumer? The approach that all elements in the value chain must be subjected to a critical review also applies here. As shown in the SolarWinds case, individual fingerprints and the exclusive use of confidential sources do not provide the best possible protection. The components used must be subjected to a deeper security inspection.

The Full Impact Graph

A *full impact graph* represents all areas of an application that are affected by the known vulnerability. Analyzing a full impact graph requires tools to check for known weak points. These tools can develop their full potential only if they can recognize and represent the interrelationships across technology boundaries. Without considering a full impact graph, it is easy to focus on just one technology, which can quickly lead to dangerous pseudosecurity.

As an example, let's say we are building a JAR with Maven; this JAR is used inside a WAR to be deployed inside a servlet container. Additionally, it is a best practice to pack this JAR inside a Docker image to deploy to production. The production configuration is also stored in Helm charts that are used to organize the Docker deployment. Suppose we can identify this compromised JAR inside the WAR that is part of the Docker image deployed by the Helm chart that is part of the active production environment. Tracing the vulnerability from a Helm chart through to the encapsulated JAR requires knowledge about the full impact graph.

The SolarWinds hack demonstrates the need to analyze a full impact graph in order to discover vulnerabilities in a supply chain. If you find a vulnerability in a binary file, the relevance of this vulnerability depends on how the file is used. You need to know where this file is used, and the potential risk caused by this weak point if used in an operational environment. If you don't use this binary anywhere, the vulnerability can't do any harm; however, if the use occurs in critical areas within a company, significant risk arises.

Assume that we are focusing on scanning Docker images only. We will get the information that the Docker image contains vulnerabilities and can mitigate the vulnerability in the Docker image. But we are missing information about all other places where this infected binary is used as well. We need to know the usage of this binary in all different layers and technologies. Just focusing on the usage inside Docker images could lead to open security holes in other parts of our environment where the binary is used directly.

In "The Common Vulnerability Scoring System" on page 181, we will show you how to use the environmental metric to precisely assess the context and use this information to make more-informed risk assessments.

Securing Your DevOps Infrastructure

Now that you understand the impact of security vulnerabilities, it is time to look at countermeasures we can utilize to improve the security of our full software development lifecycle. First, let's shed some light on the procedures and roles used in a DevOps environment.

The Rise of DevSecOps

Let's briefly go over how development and operations merged to become DevOps, because it plays a central role in introducing security. DevOps started with the basic recognition that the two areas of developers and operations have to work closer together in order to improve productivity. The fundamental stages of DevOps map directly to the process of building and delivering software to production.

Before DevOps, a big split existed in responsibilities, with a release build used as the handover point between groups. DevOps changes the roles to be more inclusive; developers need to understand the intricacies of doing production deployments, and vice versa. This change requires more-advanced automated tooling and repositories, as well as shared knowledge and processes.

But what about security? Security is not and should never be an explicit step in software development. Safety is a crosscutting issue that goes through all phases of production through operation. This, in turn, brings the realization that no dedicated safety officer can do this work alone. The team as a whole is entrusted with the issue of safety, just as they are, for example, with the issue of quality.

The outcome of this realization was the creation of the term *DevSecOps*. However, some subtleties here cannot be ignored. Not everyone in the production chain can do all things equally well. Everyone has their own idiosyncrasies and is more efficient in some areas. Accordingly, even in a DevSecOps organization, some team members care more about the dev area, and others have their strengths in the ops area.

The Role of SREs in Security

An exception to the dev and ops specialization is the *site reliability engineer* (SRE) role. The term originally comes from Google and describes the people on a team who deal with the reliability of services. The metric against which an SRE works is called the *failure budget*. It is assumed that the software has failures and that this is exactly what leads to downtimes. A service has a specific failure budget, or downtime budget. The SRE aims to keep service uptime within the defined budget by reducing downtime due to bugs, damage, or cyberattacks. To meet these goals, the SRE may choose to invest downtime on upgrades that can be used to deploy quality and security improvements to the system.

Therefore, an SRE is a team member whose role is to ensure the balance between the robustness of the systems and the introduction of new features. For this purpose, the SRE is given up to a maximum of 50% of their working time to focus on the operations tasks and responsibilities. This time should be used to automate the systems and improve quality and security. The rest of the SRE's time is spent working as a developer and involved in implementing new features. And now we come to the exciting question: is an SRE also responsible for security?

This role of an SRE can be in the middle of a DevSecOps structure since the working hours and skills are almost evenly split between the dev and ops areas, so both concepts can coexist inside the same organization.

SREs are usually developers with many years of experience who now specialize in the ops area, or an administrator with many years of professional experience who is now deliberately entering into software development. With this in mind, the position of an SRE is a perfect place to merge the dev and ops strategies for crosscutting issues.

Considering the example of SolarWinds again, the question arises of who has the most influence within the value chain to take action against vulnerabilities. For this purpose, we will look at the two areas dev and ops and the options available there.

Static and Dynamic Security Analysis

Two main types of security analysis exist: static application security testing and dynamic application security testing. Let's examine what these mean and how the two approaches differ.

Static Application Security Testing

Static application security testing (SAST) analyzes an application at a specific point in time. It's static. The focus is on recognizing and localizing the known vulnerabilities.

SAST is a so-called clear-testing process in which you look at the system internals to do the analysis. For this procedure, you need to have access to the source code of the application to be tested. However, an operational runtime environment does not have to be available. The application does not have to be executed for this procedure, which is why the term *static* is also used. Three types of security threats can be identified using SAST:

- Does the source code have gaps in the functional area that allow, for example, "tainted code" to be smuggled in? These are lines that can later infiltrate malware.

- Do any source code lines allow you to connect to files or certain object classes? The focus is also on detecting and preventing the introduction of malware.

- Do gaps exist on the application level that allow you to interact with other programs unnoticed?

However, it should be noted that the analysis of the source code is itself a complex matter. The area of static security analysis also includes the tools that enable you to determine and evaluate all contained direct and indirect dependencies.

As a rule, various SAST tools should check the source code at regular intervals. The SAST source code scanners must also be adapted to your organizational needs with an initial implementation to adjust the scanner to your respective domain. The Open Web Application Security Project (OWASP) Foundation offers assistance; it not only lists typical security vulnerabilities, but also recommends suitable SAST tools.

Advantages of the SAST approach

In comparison with security tests done at later stages in the software delivery process, a static security analysis approach offers the following advantages:

- Because vulnerability detection testing takes place in the development phase, removing the weak points can be carried out much more cost-effectively compared to detection that takes place only at runtime. By accessing the source code, you can also understand how this vulnerability came about and prevent it from recurring in the future. These findings cannot be obtained using an opaque-testing process.

- Partial analysis can be done, which means that even non-executable source text can be analyzed. The static security analysis can be carried out by the developers themselves, which significantly reduces the need for security experts.

A 100% analysis of the system at the source code level is also possible, which cannot be guaranteed with a dynamic approach. Opaque-testing systems can perform only penetration tests, which are an indirect analysis.

Disadvantages of the SAST approach

Since you are starting with the source code, SAST seems like it has the potential to be the most comprehensive security scanning approach. However, in practice it has fundamental problems:

- The programming work often suffers, which in turn manifests itself in domain-specific bugs. The developers focus too much on the security tests and related bug fixes.

- The tools can be problematic. This happens especially if the scanners have not been adapted to your entire tech stack. Most systems are polyglot these days. To get a complete list of known vulnerabilities, you need a tool that supports all direct or indirect technologies.

- SAST often replaces the subsequent security tests completely. However, all problems that are directly related to an application in operation remain undetected.

- Focusing on your source code is not enough. The static scan must analyze the binaries and additionally the source code if possible.

In "How Much Is Enough?" on page 186, we will show why you should focus on scanning binaries first.

Dynamic Application Security Testing

Dynamic application security testing (DAST) is security analysis of a running application (usually a running web application). A wide variety of attack scenarios are performed in order to identify as many of the weak points as possible in the application. The term *dynamic* indicates that a running application must be available to carry out the tests. It is critical that the test system behaves the same as the production environment. Even minor variations can represent serious differences, including different configurations or upstream load balancers and firewalls.

DAST is an opaque-testing process in which the application is viewed only from the outside. The technologies used do not play a role in the type of security check, as the application is accessed only generically and externally. This means that all information that could be obtained from the source code is invisible for this type of test. It is, therefore, possible for the person testing to test for the typical problems with a generic set of tools. The benchmark OWASP project offers reasonable assistance for selecting a scanner for your own project. This evaluates the performance of the individual tools in relation to the specific application background.

Advantages of DAST

The DAST process has the following advantages:

- Security analysis works in a technology-neutral manner.
- The scanners find errors in the runtime environment in which the test is carried out.
- The rate of false positives is low.
- The tools find faulty configurations in basically functional applications. For example, you can identify performance problems that other scanners cannot.
- The DAST programs can be used in all phases of development and in a later operation.

DAST scanners are based on the same concepts that real attackers use for their malware. They, therefore, provide reliable feedback on weaknesses. Tests have consistently shown that the majority of DAST tools can identify the top 10 most common threats (*https://oreil.ly/3MmBn*) listed by the OWASP Foundation.

Disadvantages of DAST

Using DAST tools has several disadvantages:

- The scanners are programmed to carry out specific attacks on functional web apps and can usually be adapted only by security experts with the necessary product knowledge. They, therefore, offer little space for individual scaling.
- DAST tools are slow; they can take several days to complete their analysis.

- DAST tools find some security gaps very late in the development cycle that could have been discovered earlier via SAST. The costs of fixing the related problems are therefore higher than they should be.

- DAST scans are based on known bugs. Scanning for new types of attacks takes a relatively long time. Therefore, modifying the existing tool is often not possible. If it is doable, it requires in-depth knowledge about the attack vector itself and how to implement it inside the DAST tool.

Comparing SAST and DAST

Table 7-1 summarizes the differences between the SAST and DAST testing approaches.

Table 7-1. SAST versus DAST

SAST	DAST
Clear security testing • The tester has access to the underlying framework, design, and implementation. • The application is tested from the inside out. • This type of testing represents the developer approach.	Opaque security testing • The tester has no knowledge of the technologies or framework that the application is built on. • The application is tested from the outside in. • This type of testing represents the hacker approach.
Requires source code • SAST doesn't require a deployed application. • It analyzes the source code or binary without executing the application.	Requires a running application • DAST doesn't require source code or binaries. • It analyzes by executing the application.
Find vulnerabilities earlier in the SDLC • The scan can be executed as soon as code is deemed feature complete.	Finds vulnerabilities toward the end of the SDLC • Vulnerabilities can be discovered after the development cycle is complete.
Less expensive to fix vulnerabilities • Since vulnerabilities are found earlier in the SDLC, remediating them is easier and faster. • Finding can often be fixed before the code enters the QA cycle.	More expensive to fix vulnerabilities • Since vulnerabilities are found toward the end of the SDLC, remediation often gets pushed into the next development cycle. • Critical vulnerabilities may be fixed as an emergency release.
Can't discover runtime and environmental issues • Since the tool scans static code, it cannot discover runtime vulnerabilities.	Can discover runtime and environmental issues • Since the tool uses dynamic analysis on a running application, it is able to find runtime vulnerabilities.
Typically supports all kinds of software • Examples include web applications, web services, and thick clients.	Typically scans only web apps and web services • DAST is not useful for other types of software.

If you look at the advantages and disadvantages of these two types of security testing, you can see that they are not mutually exclusive. On the contrary, these approaches complement each other perfectly. SAST can be used to identify known vulnerabilities. DAST can be used to identify vulnerabilities that are not yet known. This is primarily the case if the new attack is based on the pattern of common vulnerabilities. You also gain knowledge about the overall system if you carry out these tests on the production system. However, as soon as you run DAST on test systems, you lose these last-mentioned capabilities again.

Interactive Application Security Testing

Interactive application security testing (IAST) uses software tools to evaluate application performance and identify vulnerabilities. IAST takes an "agent-like" approach; agents and sensors run to continuously analyze application functions during automated tests, manual tests, or a mixture of both.

The process and feedback occur in real-time in the IDE, CI or QA environment, or during production. The sensors have access to the following:

- All source code
- Data and control flow
- System configuration data
- Web components
- Backend connection data

The main difference between IAST, SAST, and DAST is that IAST runs inside the application. Access to all static components as well as the runtime information enables a comprehensive picture. It is a combination of static and dynamic analysis. However, the part of the dynamic analysis is not a pure opaque test, as it is implemented at DAST.

IAST helps identify potential problems earlier, so IAST minimizes the cost of eliminating potential costs and delays. This is due to a *shift left* approach, meaning it is carried out in the early stages of the project lifecycle. Similar to SAST, the IAST analysis provides complete lines of data-rich code so that security teams can immediately look out for a specific bug. With the wealth of information that the tool has access to, the source of vulnerabilities can be precisely identified. Unlike other dynamic software tests, IAST can be easily integrated into CI/CD pipelines. The evaluations take place in real time in the production environment.

On the other hand, IAST tools can slow the operation of the application. This is because the agents change the bytecode themselves. This leads to a lower performance of the overall system. The change itself can also lead to problems in the production environment. The use of agents represents a potential source of danger since these agents can also be compromised as happened in the SolarWinds hack.

Runtime Application Self-Protection

Runtime application self-protection (RASP) is the approach to secure the application from within. The check takes place at runtime and generally consists of looking for suspicious commands when they are executed.

With the RASP approach, you can examine the entire application context on the production machine in real time. Here all commands that are processed are examined for possible attack patterns. Therefore, this procedure aims to identify existing security gaps and attack patterns and those that are not yet known. Here it goes clearly into the use of AI and machine learning (ML) techniques.

RASP tools can usually be used in two operating modes. The first operating mode (monitoring) is limited to observing and reporting possible attacks. The second operating mode (protection) then includes implementing defensive measures in real time and directly on the production environment. RASP aims to fill the gap left by application security testing and network perimeter controls. SAST and DAST do not have sufficient visibility into real-time data and event flows to prevent vulnerabilities from sliding through the verification process or to block new threats that were overlooked during development.

RASP is similar to IAST. The main difference is that IAST focuses on identifying vulnerabilities in the applications, and RASP focuses on protecting against cybersecurity attacks that can exploit these vulnerabilities or other attack vectors.

The RASP technology has the following advantages:

- RASP complements SAST and DAST with an additional layer of protection after the application is started (usually in production).
- RASP can be easily applied with faster development cycles.
- Unexpected entries are checked and identified in RASP.
- RASP enables you to react quickly to an attack by providing comprehensive analysis and information about the possible vulnerabilities.

However, since RASP tools sit on the application server, they can adversely affect application performance. In addition, the RASP technology may not be compliant with regulations or internal guidelines, because it allows the installation of other software or the automatic blocking of services. The use of this technology can also give a false sense of security and is not a substitute for application security testing, because it cannot provide comprehensive protection. Finally, the application must also be switched offline until the vulnerability is eliminated.

While RASP and IAST have similar methods and uses, RASP does not perform extensive scans but instead runs as part of the application to examine traffic and activity. Both report attacks as soon as they occur; with IAST, this happens at the time of the test, whereas with RASP, it takes place at runtime in production.

SAST, DAST, IAST, and RASP Summary

All approaches result in a wide range of options for arming yourself against known and unknown security gaps. Reconciling your own needs and those of the company is essential when choosing your approach.

With RASP, the application can protect itself against attacks at runtime. The permanent monitoring of your activities and the data transferred to the application enable an analysis based on the runtime environment. Here you can choose between pure monitoring or alerting, and active self-protection. However, software components are added to the runtime environment with RASP approaches to manipulate the system independently. This has an impact on performance. With this approach, RASP concentrates on the detection and defense of current cyberattacks. So it analyzes the data and user behavior in order to identify suspicious activities.

The IAST approach combines the SAST and DAST approaches and is already used within the SDLC—that is, within the development itself. This means that the IAST tools are already further "to the left" compared to the RASP tools. Another difference to the RASP tools is that IAST consists of static, dynamic, and manual tests. Here it also becomes clear that IAST is more in the development phase. The combination of dynamic, static, and manual tests promises a comprehensive security solution. However, we should not underestimate the complexity of the manual and dynamic security tests at this point.

The DAST approach focuses on how a hacker would approach the system. The overall system is viewed as opaque, and the attacks occur without knowing the technologies used. The point here is to harden the production system against the most common vulnerabilities. However, we must not forget at this point that this technology can be used only at the end of the production cycle.

If you have access to all system components, the SAST approach can be used effectively against known security gaps and license problems. This procedure is the only guarantee that the entire tech stack can be subjected to direct control. The focus of the SAST approach is on static semantics and, in turn, is completely blind to security holes in the dynamic context. A huge advantage is that this approach can be used with the first line of source code.

In my experience, if you start with DevSecOps or security in IT in general, the SAST approach makes the most sense. This is where the greatest potential threat can be eliminated with minimal effort. It is also a process that can be used in all steps of the production line. Only when all components in the system are secured against known security gaps do the following methods show their highest potential. After introducing SAST, I would use the IAST approach and, finally, the RASP approach. This also ensures that the respective teams can grow with the task and that no obstacles or delays occur in production.

The Common Vulnerability Scoring System

The basic idea behind the *Common Vulnerability Scoring System* (CVSS) is to provide a general classification of the severity of a security vulnerability. The weak points found are evaluated from various points of view. These elements are weighed against each other to obtain a standardized number from 0 to 10.

A rating system, like CVSS, allows us to evaluate various weak points abstractly and derive follow-up actions from them. The focus is on standardizing the handling of these weak points. As a result, you can define actions based on the value ranges.

In principle, CVSS can be described so that the probability and the maximum possible damage are related using predefined factors. The basic formula for this is risk = probability of occurrence × damage.

These CVSS metrics are divided into three orthogonal areas that are weighted differently from one another, called Basic Metrics, Temporal Metrics, and Environmental Metrics. Different aspects are queried in each area, which must be assigned a single value. The weighting and the subsequent composition of the three group values gives the final result. The next section explores these metrics in detail.

CVSS Basic Metrics

The *basic metrics* form the foundation of the CVSS rating system. The aim of querying aspects in this area is to record technical details of the vulnerability that will not change over time, so the assessment is independent of other changing elements. Different parties can carry out the calculation of the base value. It can be done by the discoverer, the manufacturer of the project or product concerned, or by a computer emergency response team (CERT) charged with eliminating this weak point. We can imagine that, based on this initial decision, the value itself will turn out different since the individual groups pursue different goals.

The base value evaluates the prerequisites necessary for a successful attack via this security gap. This is the distinction between whether a user account must be available on the target system or whether the system can be compromised without the knowledge about a system user. These prerequisites play a significant role in whether a system is vulnerable over the internet or whether physical access to the affected component is required.

The base value should also reflect how complex the attack is to carry out. In this case, the complexity relates to the necessary technical steps and includes assessing whether the interaction with a regular user is essential. Is it sufficient to encourage any user to interact, or does this user have to belong to a specific system group (e.g., administrator)? The correct classification is not a trivial process; the assessment of a new vulnerability requires exact knowledge of this vulnerability and the systems concerned.

The basic metrics also take into account the damage that this attack could cause to the affected component. The three areas of concern are as follows:

Confidentiality
    Possibility of extracting the data from the system

Integrity
    Possibility of manipulating the system

Availability
    Completely preventing the system's use

However, you have to be careful concerning the weighting of these areas of concern. In one case, having stolen data can be worse than changed data. In another case, the unusability of a component can be the worst damage to be assumed.

The *scope metric* has also been available since CVSS version 3.0. This metric looks at the effects of an affected component on other system components. For example, a compromised element in a virtualized environment enables access to the carrier system. A successful change of this scope represents a greater risk for the overall system and is therefore also evaluated using this factor. This demonstrates that the interpretation of the values also requires adjusting to one's situation, which brings us to the temporal and environment metrics.

CVSS Temporal Metrics

The time-dependent components of the vulnerability assessment are brought together in the *temporal metrics* group.

The elements that change over time influence these temporal metrics. For example, the availability of tools that support the exploitation of the vulnerability may change. These can be exploits code or step-by-step instructions. A distinction must be made on whether a vulnerability is theoretical or whether a manufacturer has officially confirmed it. All of these events change the base value.

Temporal metrics are unique in that the base value can be only reduced and not increased. The initial rating is intended to represent the worst-case scenario. This has both advantages and disadvantages if you bear in mind that it is during the initial assessment of a vulnerability that interests are competing.

The influence on the initial evaluation comes about through external framework conditions. These take place over an undefined time frame and are not relevant for the actual basic assessment. Even if an exploit is already in circulation during the base values survey, this knowledge will not be included in the primary assessment. However, the base value can only be reduced by the temporal metrics.

And this is where a conflict arises. The person or group who has found a security gap tries to set the base value as high as possible. A high-severity loophole will sell for a higher price and receive more media attention. The reputation of the person/group who found this gap increases as a result. The affected company or the affected project is interested in exactly the opposite assessment. Therefore, it depends on who finds the security gap, how the review process should take place, and by which body the first evaluation is carried out. This value is further adjusted by the environmental metrics.

CVSS Environmental Metrics

For *environmental metrics*, your own system landscape is used to evaluate the risk of the security gap. The evaluation is adjusted based on the real situation. In contrast to temporal metrics, environmental metrics can correct the base value in both directions. The environment can therefore lead to a higher classification and must also be constantly adapted to your own environment changes.

Let's take an example of a security hole that has an available patch from the manufacturer. The mere presence of this modification leads to a reduction of the total value in the temporal metrics. However, as long as the patch has not been activated in your own systems, the overall value must be drastically corrected upward again via the environmental metrics. This is because as soon as a patch is available, it can be used to better understand the security gap and its effects. The attacker has more detailed information that can be exploited, which reduces the resistance of the not-yet-hardened systems.

At the end of an evaluation, the final score is obtained, calculated from the three previously mentioned values. The resulting value is then assigned to a value group. But one more point is often overlooked. In many cases, the final score is simply carried over without individual adjustments utilizing the environmental score. This behavior leads to a dangerous evaluation that is incorrect for the overall system concerned.

CVSS in Practice

With CVSS, we have a system for evaluating and rating security gaps in software. Since there are no alternatives, CVSS has become a de facto standard; the system has been in use worldwide for over 10 years and is constantly being developed. The evaluation consists of three components.

First, the basic score depicts a purely technical worst-case scenario. The second component is the evaluation of the time-dependent corrections based on external influences—including further findings, tools, or patches for this security gap—which can be used to reduce the value. The third component of the assessment is your own system environment with regard to this vulnerability. With this consideration, the security gap is adjusted in relation to the real situation on site. Last but not least, an overall evaluation is made from these three values, which results in a number from 0.0 to 10.0.

This final value can be used to control your own organizational response to defend against the security gap. At first glance, everything feels quite abstract, so it takes some practice to get a feel for the application of CVSS, which can be developed through experience with your own systems.

Scoping Security Analysis

As soon as we deal with security, the following questions always come up: how much effort is enough, where should you start, and how quickly can you get the first results? In this section, we deal with how to take these first steps. For this, we look at two concepts and consider the associated effects.

Time to Market

You have probably heard of the term *time to market*, but how does this relate to security? In general terms, this expression means that the desired functionality is transferred as quickly as possible from conception through development into the production environment. This allows the customer to start benefiting from the new functionality, which increases business value.

At first glance, time to market seems focused on business use cases only, but it is equally relevant when applied to security remediation. Activating the required modifications to the overall system as quickly as possible is also optimal. In short, the term *time to market* is a common and worthwhile goal for security implementation.

The process for business use cases should be the same as remediating security vulnerabilities. They both require as much automation as possible, and all human interaction must be as short as possible. All interactions that waste time increase the potential that the vulnerability will be used against the production system.

Make or Buy

Across all layers of a cloud native stack, the majority of the software and technology is bought or acquired rather than made. We will go through the layers in Figure 7-1 and talk about the software composition at each.

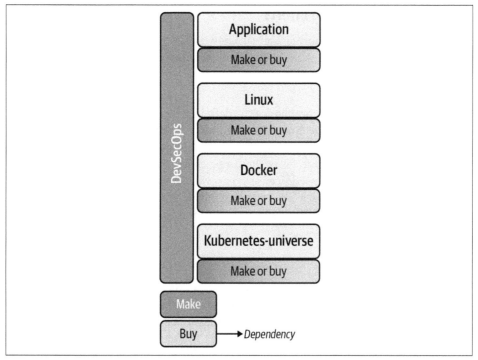

Figure 7-1. DevSecOps components that you can decide to build or purchase

The first layer is the development of the application itself. Assuming that we are working with Java and using Maven as a dependency manager, we are most likely adding more lines of code indirectly as dependencies compared to the number of lines we are writing ourselves. The dependencies are the more prominent part, and third parties develop them. We have to be careful, and it is good advice to check these external binaries for known vulnerabilities. We should have the same behavior regarding compliance and license usage.

The next layer is the operating system, which is typically Linux. And again, we are adding configuration files, and the rest are existing binaries. The result is an application running inside the operating system that is a composition of external binaries based on our configuration.

The two following layers, Docker and Kubernetes, lead us to the same result. Until now, we are not looking at the tool stack for the production line itself. All programs and utilities that are directly or indirectly used under the hood for DevSecOps create dependencies. All layers' dependencies are the most significant part by far. Checking these binaries against known vulnerabilities is the first logical step.

One-Time and Recurring Efforts

Comparing the effort of scanning against known vulnerabilities and for compliance issues, we see a few differences. Let's start with the compliance issues.

Compliance issues

The first step in scoping compliance is defining which licenses are allowed at which part of the production line. This definition of allowed licenses includes the dependencies during development and the usage of tools and runtime environments. Defining the noncritical license types should be checked by a specialized compliance process. With this list of allowed license types, we can start using the build automation to scan the full tool stack on a regular basis. After the machine has found a violation, we have to remove this element, and it must be replaced by another that is licensed.

Vulnerabilities

The ongoing effort to scan for vulnerabilities is low compared to the amount of work required to fix vulnerabilities. A slightly different workflow is needed for the handling of discovered vulnerabilities. With more significant preparations, the build automation can do the work on a regular basis as well. The identification of a vulnerability will trigger a workflow that includes human interaction. The vulnerability must be classified internally, which leads to a decision about the next action to take.

How Much Is Enough?

So let's come back to the initial question in this section. How much scanning is enough? No change is too small, because all changes that have to do with adding or changing dependencies will cause you to reevaluate the security and run a new scan. Checking for known vulnerabilities or checking the license being used can be carried out efficiently by automation.

Another point that should not be underestimated is that the quality with which such an examination is carried out is constant, as nobody is involved at this point. If the value chain's speed is not slowed by constantly checking all dependencies, this is a worthwhile investment.

Compliance Versus Vulnerabilities

One other difference exists between compliance issues and vulnerabilities. If a compliance issue exists, it is a singular point inside the overall environment. Just this single part is a defect and is not influencing other elements of the environment, as shown in Figure 7-2.

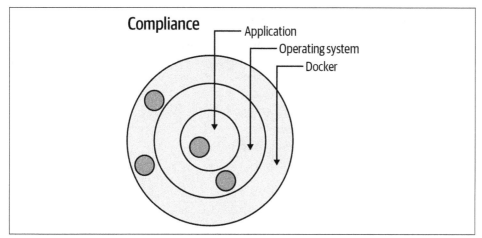

Figure 7-2. Layers of an application where compliance issues can be found

Vulnerabilities Can Be Combined into Different Attack Vectors

Vulnerabilities are a bit different. They do not exist only at the point where they are located. Additionally, they can be combined with other existing vulnerabilities in any additional layer of the environment, as shown in Figure 7-3. Vulnerabilities can be combined into different attack vectors. Every possible attack vector itself must be seen and evaluated. A set of minor vulnerabilities in different layers of the application can be combined into a highly critical risk.

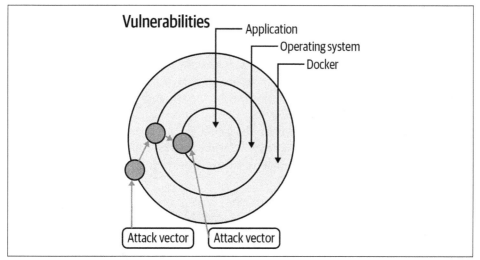

Figure 7-3. Vulnerabilities in multiple layers of an application

Vulnerabilities: Timeline from Inception Through Production Fix

Again and again, we read something in the IT news about security gaps that have been exploited. The more severe the classification of this loophole, the more attention this information will get in the general press. Most of the time, we hear and read nothing about all the security holes found that are not as well-known as the Solar-Winds hack. The typical timeline of a vulnerability is shown in Figure 7-4.

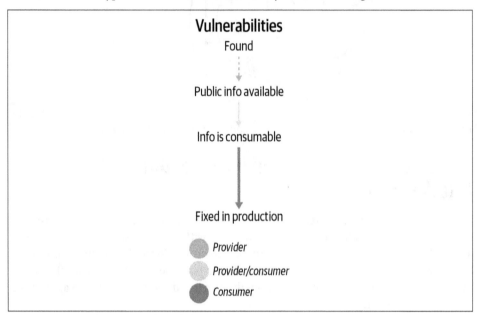

Figure 7-4. Timeline of a vulnerability

Creation of a vulnerability

Let's start with the birth of a vulnerability. This can be done in two ways. On the one hand, it can happen to any developer who has an unfortunate combination of source code pieces that creates a security hole. On the other hand, it can also be based on targeted manipulation. However, this has essentially no effect on the further course of the lifeline of a security vulnerability. In the following, we assume that a security hole has been created and that it is now active in some software. These can be executable programs or libraries integrated into other software projects as a dependency.

Discovery of the vulnerability

In most cases, it is not possible to understand precisely when a security hole was created, but let's assume that a security hole exists and that at some point it will be discovered. A few different scenarios could occur, depending on who finds the security hole first.

If a malicious actor finds the security hole, they will probably try to keep it a secret so they can profit from it. The two ways to profit are either to exploit the security hole themselves or to sell information about the security hole to an interested party. In either case, the quicker they are able to profit from the security hole, the less likely it is discovered and patched.

Conversely, if the security hole is found by ethical attackers, they will first verify that the security hole can be exploited without doing any damage, and then disclose it to the affected parties. Often a financial motivation exists for this as well. These can be driven by bug bounties and rewards by companies aware of their potential for security holes and willing to pay to have them disclosed to the company rather than to attackers. Also, companies that maintain vulnerability databases are incentivized to find security holes and disclose them to their customer base in advance of making them publicly known.

And yet another possibility is that the company discovers the security vulnerability by itself. In this case, the company may be inclined to either hide the vulnerability or present it as harmless. However, the best approach is to fix the vulnerability as soon as possible, because a malicious actor could soon discover the vulnerability or perhaps already knows about it and is waiting to exploit it.

Regardless of the route via which the knowledge comes to the vulnerability databases, only when the information has reached one of these points can we assume that this knowledge will be available to the general public over time.

Public availability of the vulnerability

Each provider of security vulnerabilities has a subset of all publicly disclosed vulnerabilities. To get a more holistic set of vulnerabilities, you need to aggregate multiple sources. Furthermore, since the vulnerability databases are constantly being updated, this needs to be an automated process.

It is also crucial that the vulnerabilities are processed in such a way that further processing by machines is possible. Critical meta-information such as the CVE or the CVSS value needs to be included. For example, the CVSS value can be used in CI environments to interrupt further processing when a specific threshold value is reached.

As an end user, there is really only one way to go here. Instead of contacting the providers directly, you should rely on services that integrate a wide variety of sources and offer a processed and merged database. Since the information generally represents a considerable financial value, commercial providers of such data sets invest a lot of resources to make sure it is accurate and up-to-date.

Fixing the vulnerability in production

Once the information is publicly disclosed and made available to you through one of many security providers, you can start to take action. The key factor is the amount of time it takes for your organization to identify and mitigate the security vulnerability.

The first step is the consumption of the vulnerability from your chosen security provider. This is hopefully fully automated with an API that you can use to consume vulnerabilities, security scanners that are continuously scanning your production deployments, and reporting that notifies you quickly about any new vulnerabilities.

The next step is to develop, test, and deploy a fix that solves the security vulnerability. Only those who have implemented a high degree of automation can enable short response times in the delivery processes. It is also an advantage if the team concerned can easily make the necessary decisions. Lengthy approval processes are counterproductive at this point and can also cause extensive damage to the company.

Another point that can improve the response time is to catch security vulnerabilities in earlier stages of development. By providing security information in all production stages, vulnerabilities can be caught earlier, lowering the cost of mitigation. We'll come back to this in more detail in "Shift Security Left" on page 195.

Test Coverage Is Your Safety Belt

The best knowledge of security gaps is of no use if this knowledge cannot be put to use. But what tools do you have in software development to take efficient action against known security gaps? I want to highlight one metric in particular: the test coverage of your own source code parts. If you have strong test coverage, you can make changes to the system and rely on the test suite. If a smooth test of all affected system components has taken place, nothing stands in the way of making the software available from a technical point of view.

But let's take a closer look at the situation. In most cases, known security vulnerabilities are removed by changing the version used for the same dependency. Therefore, efficient version management gives you the agility you need to be able to react quickly. In very few cases, the affected components have to be replaced by semantic equivalents from other manufacturers. And to classify the new composition of versions of the same components as valid, strong test coverage is required. Manual tests would go far beyond the time frame and cannot be carried out with the same quality in every run. Mutation testing gives you much more concrete test coverage than is usually the case with the conventional line or branch coverage.

To get a picture of the full impact graph based on all known vulnerabilities, it is crucial to understand all package managers included by the dependencies. Focusing on just one layer in the tech stack is by far not enough. Package managers like Artifactory provide information, including vendor-specific metadata. This can be augmented with security scanning tools like JFrog Xray that consume this knowledge and can scan all binaries hosted inside the repositories managed by your package manager.

Quality Gate Methodology

With respect to a security response, the success of IT projects is dependent on participation and involvement of end users as early as possible, the support of higher management, and the formulation of clear business goals. By managing these factors, a software project can quickly address security vulnerabilities and mitigate risk to the corporation.

The demand for comprehensive support from higher management provides, among other things, systematic control of the quality and progress of IT projects in good time by using criteria in order to be able to intervene. By specifying criteria, management has two ways of controlling the software development process:

- The criteria are project management specifications that the developer must adhere to.
- Project management can intervene in the event of a deviation from the defined target.

The group responsible for setting and enforcing these criteria can be different depending on the management system. The distribution of roles is also controversially discussed again and again. However, it turns out that a more substantial involvement of all team members leads to dynamic and successful structures.

In the context of project control, measures can be taken to counteract undesirable developments within a project. The ideal case for project participants is that security risks do not impact the continuation of the project. In extreme cases, however, it is also possible to cancel the project. Timeliness means being able to take action before significant financial damage can occur.

At the same time, however, this presupposes that relevant and measurable results are available to make effective project control sensible and possible. The end of activity within a project is a suitable time for this, as results are available that can be checked. However, because of the large number of activities within a project, too frequent checks by the project management team would slow the project's progress. In addition, there would be a more significant burden on project management with many parallel projects (which would all have to be monitored).

A middle ground is to establish control and steering at specific significant points as binding for each project. For this purpose, quality gates offer an opportunity to check the degree of fulfillment of the individual quality goals. A *quality gate* is a special point in time in a project at which a decision about the continuation or termination of a project is made based on a formal examination of quality-related criteria.

Metaphorically speaking, quality gates are barriers between the various process steps of a project: once the quality gate has been reached, a project can be continued only if all criteria, or at least a sufficiently large number of criteria, are met. This ensures that all results of the project at the time of the quality gate are good enough to be able to continue working with them. Using the criteria of a quality gate, the results on the one hand and the qualitative requirements for the results on the other can be determined. They can then be used to define the interfaces between individual project phases. To establish quality gates, certain structures, activities, roles, documents, and resources are necessary, which are summarized in a quality gate reference process.

The precise design of the quality gate reference process is based on the company's needs. Quality gates have their origins in automobile development and in the production of technical goods, but they have increasingly found their way into system development projects and recently also into pure software development projects.

Quality gates in series production rely on statistically determined values that can be used as a target for control activities in future projects. Such a starting position does not exist in software development, since software development projects are highly individual. As a result, a quality gate reference process practiced in assembly-line production can be transferred to software development to only a limited extent. Instead, a suitable quality gate reference process must be designed differently in order to do justice to the particular problems of software development. However, it makes sense to use the quality gate reference processes from other domains as they have been developed and optimized over the years.

Quality Gate Strategies

When using quality gates, two basic strategies have been identified. Depending on the objective, a company can choose one of these two strategies, described next, when designing a quality gate reference process.

Quality gates as uniform quality guideline

In the first approach, every project has to go through the same quality gates and is measured against the same criteria. The adaptation of a quality gate reference process that follows this strategy is permissible to a minimal extent (if at all). The aim is to achieve at least the same level of quality in every project; a qualitative guideline is thus established for every project.

Quality gates can therefore be used as a uniform measure of progress. We can compare progress between projects by checking which tasks have already passed a particular quality gate and which have not. Management can easily recognize when a project is behind another project (qualitatively) and act accordingly. Quality gates can thus easily be used as an instrument for multiproject management.

Quality gates as a flexible quality strategy

In the second approach, the number, arrangement, and selection of quality gates or criteria can be adapted to the needs of a project. Quality gates and standards can thus be tailored more precisely to a project's qualitative requirements, improving the quality of results. However, this makes comparing multiple projects more difficult. Fortunately, similar projects will have comparable quality gates and can be measured against similar criteria.

Researching the topic of quality gates on the internet and in the literature (dissertations, standard works, and conference volumes) reveals a wide range of terms. Because synonymous terms are used in many places, quality gates are often mistakenly equated with various other concepts. A *review* or *milestone*, for example, should not be equated with a quality gate.

Fit with Project Management Procedures

The question arises whether this methodology can be applied to other project management processes. The answer here is a resounding yes. The quality gate methodology can be integrated into cyclical as well as acyclical project methods. The time sequence is irrelevant at this point and can therefore also be used in classic waterfall projects at the milestone level.

The significant advantage is that this method can still be used in the case of a paradigm shift in project management. The knowledge built up in a team can continue to be used and does not lose its value. This means that the measures described here can be introduced and used regardless of the current project implementation.

Implementing Security with the Quality Gate Method

We will introduce, define, and use a greatly simplified approach to integrate the crosscutting issue of security. In the following, we assume that the quality gate methodology is suitable for implementing any cross-sectional topic. The temporal component is also irrelevant and can therefore be used in any cyclical project management methodology. This approach is therefore ideally suited for integration into the DevSecOps project organization methodology.

The DevOps process is divided into stages. The individual phases are seamlessly connected to one another. It makes no sense to install something at these points that interferes with the entire process. However, there are also much better places where cross-cutting issues are located. We are talking about the automated process derivation that can be found in a CI route. Assuming that the necessary process steps to go through a quality gate can be fully automated, a CI route is ideal for doing this regularly occurring work.

Assuming that the CI line carries out an automated process step, two results can occur.

Green: Quality gate has passed

One possible result of this processing step is that all checks have passed successfully. Processing can continue uninterrupted at this point. Only a few log entries are made to ensure complete documentation.

Red: Failed the quality gate

Another possible result is that the check has found something indicating a failure. This interrupts the process, and the cause of the failure must be identified, as well as a way to remediate it. The automatic process usually ends at this point and is replaced by a manual process.

Risk Management in Quality Gates

Since the quality gate is blocked by identifying a defect, someone needs to be responsible for the following steps:

- Risk assessment (identification, analysis, assessment, and prioritization of risks)
- Design and initiation of countermeasures
- Tracking of risks in the course of the project

The risk determination was already completed with the creation of the criteria and their operationalization by weighing the requirements on a risk basis. This takes place during the gate review itself.

The conception and initiation of countermeasures is an essential activity of a gate review, at least in the event that a project is not postponed or canceled before going to production. The countermeasures to be taken primarily counteract the risks that arise from criteria that are not met.

The countermeasures of risk management can be divided into preventive measures and emergency measures. The *preventive measures* include meeting the criteria as quickly as possible. If this is not possible, appropriate countermeasures must be designed. The design of the countermeasures is a creative act; it depends on the risk, its assessment, and the possible alternatives.

The effectiveness of the countermeasures must be tracked to ensure that they are successful. This spans all phases of the project and is critical to ensuring that security vulnerabilities are caught and addressed early in the process.

Practical Applications of Quality Management

Let's go through a practical example of quality management in the context of a software release. For this purpose, all required components are generated and collected in the repository, and every binary has an identity and version. All elements necessary for a release are put together in a deployment bundle after they have been created successfully. In this case, a release is a composition of different binaries in their respective versions. The technology plays a subordinate role here, as the most diverse artifacts can come together in a release.

You can also imagine that all crucial documents are part of this compilation at this point. This can include documents such as the release notes and build information that provides information about the manufacturing process itself—for example, which JDK was used on which platform and much more. All information that can be automatically collated at this point increases the traceability and reproduction quality if a postmortem analysis has to be carried out.

We now have everything together and would like to start making the artifacts available. We are talking about promoting the binaries here. This can be done in your own repositories or generally available global repositories. Now the last time has come when you can still make changes.

We are talking about a security check as a promotional gateway. The tools used here should finally check two things. First, known vulnerabilities in the binaries need to be removed. Second, all the licenses used in all the artifacts contained must be adequate for the purpose. What becomes immediately clear here is the need for the check to be carried out independently of the technology used. This brings us back to the full impact graph. At this point, we have to get the full impact graph in order to be able to achieve a high-quality result. The repository manager, who is responsible for providing all dependent artifacts, must be seamlessly integrated with the binary scanner. One example is the combination of Artifactory and Xray.

But is a security check a gateway for the promotion of binaries at the earliest possible time? Where can you start earlier? We now come to the concept of shift left.

Shift Security Left

Agile development, DevOps, and the implementation of security have long been considered mutually exclusive. Classic development work was always confronted with the problem that the security of a software product could not be adequately defined as a final, static, end state. This is the *security paradox* in software development.

It may seem that Agile development is too dynamic to be able to carry out a detailed security analysis of the software product to be developed in every development cycle. The opposite is the case because Agile and secure development techniques complement each other very well. One of the key points of Agile development is the ability to implement changes on short notice as well as changes to requirements within a short period of time.

In the past, security has tended to be viewed as a static process. Accordingly, application of Agile concepts to the security domain is required. The general handling of security requirements must adapt to this development in order to be able to be implemented efficiently. However, we must note that Agile development is feature-oriented. Security requirements are mostly from the category of nonfunctional features, though, and are therefore available in only an implicitly formulated form in most cases. The consequence of this, in combination with faulty security requirements engineering results, is miscalculated development cycles with increased time pressure; the sprint is canceled because of incorrect budget calculations, increased technical debts, persistent weak points, or specific security gaps within the codebase.

Let's now focus on how the necessary conditions can be created in an Agile development team that improves the codebase's security level as early as possible. Regardless of the specific project management method used, the following approaches are not restricted in their validity.

It is essential to set the security level so that the respective development team should achieve a security increment when performing a product increment. A team with an implicit and pronounced security focus can immediately gain a different level of security than a team without this focus. Regardless of the experience of each team, a general minimum standard must be defined and adhered to.

The OWASP Top 10 (*https://owasp.org/Top10*) is a list of general security vulnerabilities that developers can avoid with simple measures. Accordingly, they serve as an introduction to the topic and should be part of every developer's security repertoire. However, code reviews often reveal that teams are not adequately considering the top 10, so this is a good area to focus teams on improvement.

It should also be recognized that developers can do an excellent job in their field but are not security experts. In addition to different levels of experience, developers and security experts have different approaches and ways of thinking that are decisive for their respective tasks. Therefore, the development team must be aware of their limitations with regard to the assessment of attack methods and security aspects. When developing critical components or in the event of problems, the organizational option of calling in a security expert must therefore be determined in advance. Nevertheless, developers should generally be able to evaluate typical security factors and take simple steps to improve the security of the code.

Ideally, each team has a member who has both development and detailed security knowledge. In the context of supported projects, the relevant employees are referred to as security managers (SecMs). They monitor the security aspects of the developed code sections, define the attack surface and attack vectors in each development cycle, support you in assessing the user stories' effort, and implement mitigation strategies.

To get a global overview of the codebase and its security level, aiming for a regular exchange between the SecMs of the teams involved makes sense. Since a company-wide synchronization of the development cycle phases is unrealistic, SecMs should meet at regular, fixed times. In small companies or with synchronized sprints, the teams particularly benefit from an exchange during development cycle planning. In this way, cross-component security aspects and the effects of the development cycle on the security of the product increment can be assessed. The latter can currently be achieved only through downstream tests. Based on the development cycle review, a SecM meeting should also occur after implementing new components. In preparation for the next sprint, the participants evaluate the security level according to the increment.

OWASP Security Champions are implemented differently. These are often developers, possibly junior developers, who acquire additional security knowledge that can be very domain-specific depending on experience. Conceptual overlap occurs with the SecMs; however, a key difference is that a SecM is a full-fledged security expert with development experience who acts on the same level as the senior developer. When implementing secure software, however, it is crucial to take into account the security-relevant effects of implementation decisions and cross-thematic specialist knowledge.

Regardless of whether a team can create a dedicated role, basic measures should be taken to support the process of developing secure software. These are the following best practice recommendations and empirical values.

Not All Clean Code Is Secure Code

Clean Code by Robert Martin (Pearson), also known as Uncle Bob, coined the term *clean code*. However, a common misconception among decision makers is that clean code also covers the security of the code.

Safe and clean code overlap but are not the same. *Clean code* promotes understandability, maintainability, and reusability of code. *Secure code*, on the other hand, also requires predefined specifications and compliance with them. However, clean code is often a requirement for safe code. The code can be written cleanly without any security features. However, only a clean implementation opens up the full potential for security measures.

Well-written code is also easier to secure because the relationships between components and functions are clearly defined and delimited. Any development team looking for reasons to promote adherence to and implementation of the clean code principles will find good arguments in the security of the code, which can also be explained economically to decision makers in cost and time savings for security hardening.

Effects on Scheduling

In general, and particularly in Agile development, teams do not allow enough time to improve the codebase when planning the next version. In sprint planning, the focus on effort assessment is primarily on time to develop a new function. Hardening is considered explicitly only when a special requirement exists.

The amount of time teams need to implement a function safely depends on the functionality, the status of the product increment, the existing technical debt, and the prior knowledge of the developer. However, as intended in Agile development, it should be up to the team to estimate the actual time required. Since miscalculations are to be expected, especially at the beginning, it can make sense to reduce the number of user stories adopted compared to the previous sprints.

The Right Contact Person

Every team must have access to security professionals, but it can be hard to find the right contact person in large organizations. IT security is divided into numerous, sometimes highly specific and complex, subareas for which full-time security experts are responsible. Good programmers are full-time developers and even after IT security training, cannot replace dedicated security experts.

It is the responsibility of project management to ensure that organizational, structural, and financial requirements are met so that teams can quickly draw on technical expertise when needed and during an assessment. This is not the case by default in most organizations.

Dealing with Technical Debt

Technical debt is an integral part of development, and project owners should treat it as such—both in terms of time and budget. Technical debt has a negative impact on the maintainability, development, and security of the codebase. This means a significant increase in individual (new) implementation costs and a sustained slowdown in overall production by blocking developers for a more extended period of time with individual projects. Therefore, it is in the interest of everyone involved—especially management—to keep the technical debt of a codebase low and to continuously reduce it.

Alternatively, the substrategy is to set a fixed portion of the estimated project time for servicing technical debt. The approach is minor, as there is a risk that teams will use the time spent processing technical debt to implement a function instead and misjudge the extent of technical debt under the development cycle pressure.

Advanced Training on Secure Coding

A misconception exists that security can be learned in passing and that everyone has access to the necessary materials. Typically, a list of secure coding guidelines is in a public folder somewhere. In addition, the OWASP Top 10 is often published to the general public. As a rule, however, employees do not read such documents or, at best, skim them. Often, after a while, teams no longer know where such documents are, let alone what use they should get from them. Admonitions to encourage reading the guidelines are not very helpful if companies cannot create extra time to focus on secure coding.

Milestones for Quality

Quality gates in development help check compliance with quality requirements. Analogous to the *definition of done* (DoD), the team-wide definition of when a task can be viewed as completed, quality gates should not be available only in stationary paper form. Ideally, automated checks are integrated into the CI/CD pipeline through static code analyses (SAST) or the evaluation of all dependencies.

For developers, however, it can be helpful to receive feedback on the code and its dependencies in addition to feedback from the CI/CD pipeline during programming. Language- and platform-dependent IDE plug-ins and separate code analysis tools are available, such as FindBugs/SpotBugs, Checkstyle, and PMD. When using JFrog Xray, the IDE plug-in can be used to make it easier to compare against known vulnerabilities and compliance issues.

An additional upstream process for checking the code in the IDE pursues the goal of familiarizing developers with security aspects during development. As a result, the code security is improved at the points identified by the plug-in and in the entire code since developers are given a security orientation. Another side effect is the reduction in the number of false positives on the build server. The latter is exceptionally high for security quality gates, as security gaps in the code are often context-dependent and require manual verification, which leads to a considerable increase in the development effort.

The Attacker's Point of View

Evil user stories (also called *bad user stories*) present the desired functionality from an attacker's perspective. Analogous to user stories, they are designed so that their focus is not on the technical implementation. Accordingly, people with a limited technical background in IT security can write bad user stories. However, this increases the effort required to generate tasks from the possibly unspecific (bad) user stories.

Ideally, bad user stories try to depict the attack surface. They enable the development team to process identified attack methods in a familiar workflow. This creates awareness of possible attack vectors, but these are limited. Evil user stories are limited not only by the knowledge and experience of their respective authors and their imagination, but also by the developer's ability to fend off the attack vector in the context of the sprint. It's not just about whether the developers develop the right damage-control strategy, but also about correctly and comprehensively identifying the use case in the code.

Like conventional user stories, the evil variants are not always easy to write. Teams with little experience in developing secure software, in particular, can encounter difficulties creating meaningful nasty user stories. If a SecM is on the team, that person should take on the task or offer support. Teams without a SecM should either look for external technical expertise or plan a structured process for creating the evil user stories.

Methods of Evaluation

To establish security as a process within Agile development, regular code reviews must be carried out, with the focus on the security level of the code, both component by component and across segments. Ideally, errors that are easy to avoid and can cause security breaches can be identified and corrected as part of the CI/CD pipeline through quality gates and automated tests. In this case, the component-by-component test is primarily concerned with the investigation of the attack surface of the respective component and the weakening of attack vectors. A cheat sheet for analyzing the attack surface can be found on the OWASP Cheat Sheet Series on GitHub (*https://oreil.ly/kHLm1*).

The teams must regularly redefine the attack surface, as it can change with each development cycle. The cross-component check is used to monitor the attack surface of the overall product, as it can also change with every development cycle. Ultimately, only a cross-component view enables the search for attack vectors that result from interactions between components or even dependencies.

If SecMs are not available, a security assessment can be carried out through a structured approach and joint training in the team. The OWASP Cornucopia card game (*https://oreil.ly/dhQK3*) can, among other things, promote such an approach. The players try to apply the attack scenarios depicted on the cards to a domain selected in advance by the team or, if necessary, only to individual methods, such as the codebase. The team must then decide whether the attack scenario of the card played is conceivable. Therefore, the focus is on identifying attack vectors; because of time constraints, mitigation strategies should be discussed elsewhere. The winner of the card game is the one who can successfully play the most difficult cards. The team must document the resulting security analysis at the end.

One benefit of Cornucopia is that it increases awareness of code vulnerabilities across the team. The game also improves the developer's expertise in IT security. The focus is on the ability of the developer and thus reflects Agile guidelines. Cornucopia sessions are an excellent tool to generate evil user stories afterward.

The problem with Cornucopia sessions is that they present especially inexperienced teams with a steep learning curve at the beginning. There is also a risk that the team will incorrectly discard a potential attack vector. If the preparation is poor (e.g., components are too large, or the team doesn't have enough technical knowledge about possible attack vectors), Cornucopia can be inefficient in terms of time. Therefore, it is advisable, especially in the first few sessions, to examine small independent components and, if necessary, to consult security experts.

Be Aware of Responsibility

Overall, developers should not allow the code security scepter to be taken out of their hands. Ideally, the team should jointly insist on sufficient time and financial resources to implement basic security aspects.

Current developers will largely define and shape the world for the years to come. Because of expected digitization and networking, security must not fall victim to budget and time constraints. According to the Agile Manifesto, the codebase remains the product of the team responsible for the outcome.

Summary

With the proliferation of supply chain attacks in the industry, addressing security is more critical than ever for the success of your project and organization. The best way to mitigate vulnerabilities quickly is to shift left and start addressing security as a primary concern from day one of every software development project. This chapter introduced you to the basics of security, including various analysis approaches, such as SAST, DAST, IAST, and RASP. You also learned about basic scoring systems like the CVSS. With this knowledge, you will be able to put the right quality gates and criteria in place to improve the security of every project that you work on going forward.

## CHAPTER 8

Deploying for Developers

Ana-Maria Mihalceanu

However beautiful the strategy, you should occasionally look at the results.
—Sir Winston Churchill

When computers were extremely large and expensive, manufacturers often bundled together the software with the hardware. With the development of mass-market software, this type of operation was time-consuming, and new forms of software distribution emerged. Today's development processes focus on decoupling build and deployment activities to facilitate fast software distribution and parallel activities in teams.

The deployment of an application represents the transformation of that software from a packaged artifact to an operational working state. Modern development days require this transformation to happen as fast as possible in order to get rapid feedback about the running state of our system.

As a developer, your focus is mainly on writing performant application code. Yet DevOps is collaboration centric, and your work should flawlessly blend within the infrastructure. While looking at your deployment process, you should continuously ask yourself, "What instructions would a machine need to execute this deployment as I envisioned it?" and share those with the colleagues or experts in charge of the infrastructure and automation. When planning a deployment process, you can make a wish list that you can later scale to more components of the distributed system:

- To gradually extend the functionalities of your system, conduct small deployments often. Using this approach, you can easily roll back to a previously working state in case of failures.

- Isolate deployment of each microservice, as you should be able to scale or replace it individually.

- You should be able to reuse in another environment an already deployed microservice.

- Automate infrastructure deployment and evolve it with your application features.

Regardless of the container orchestration platform where you will deploy any of your microservices, you likely will start by packaging the application and continue with the following:

1. Building and pushing a container image

2. Choosing and implementing a deployment strategy

As the application deployment progresses throughout various stages or environments, is likely for you to get involved in the following:

Workload management
Refine health checks and the amount of CPU and memory used to avoid slow or nonresponsive functionalities.

Observability aspects
Use metrics, logs, and traces to provide visibility into internals of your distributed systems and measure its outputs.

This chapter walks you through these activities and explores their impact at scale.

Building and Pushing Container Images

Deploying applications to containers requires creating the Java application artifacts and building container images. By leveraging the recommended artifact formats and practices shared in Chapter 6, we can focus on producing container images.

Starting with Docker's appearance in 2013, building container images using Dockerfiles became popular. A *Dockerfile* is a standardized image format consisting of the base operating system, application artifacts to be added, and required runtime configurations. Essentially, this file is the blueprint for how your future container will behave. As explained in Chapter 3, besides Docker, you can build container images with tools like Podman (*https://podman.io*), Buildah (*https://buildah.io*), and kaniko (*https://oreil.ly/X1A8A*).

As DevOps methodology relies on good communication among application developers and infrastructure engineers, some teams find it best to keep the Dockerfiles at the repository root. Moreover, scripts or pipelines can further use that location when instrumenting a container image build. In addition to writing your Dockerfile, Java-specific options can help you make container images part of your standard build processes, such as Eclipse JKube or Jib.

Using Java-specific tools to generate and push container images might tempt you to control the entire runtime from application code. To avoid tight coupling between infrastructure and application code, you should configure those tools with parameters that can be overwritten at build or runtime. Modern Java frameworks provide customization of configuration files under *src/main/resources*. The examples from this chapter use parameters in project configuration files to showcase this approach.

Managing Container Images by Using Jib

Google's Jib (*https://oreil.ly/nWoWY*) is one of the tools that you can use to containerize Java applications without writing a Dockerfile. It provides a Java library, and Maven and Gradle plug-ins for creating OCI-compatible container images. Additionally, the tool does not require running the Docker daemon locally in order to produce a container image.

Jib takes advantage of image layering and registry caching to achieve fast, incremental builds. The tool can create reproducible build images as long as the inputs remain the same.

To begin using Jib within your Maven project, set up the authentication method for the target container registry by using any of the following:

- System properties `jib.to.auth.username` and `jib.to.auth.password`
- `<to>` section in the plug-in configuration with `username` and `password` elements
- A `<server>` configuration in *~/.m2/settings.xml*
- Previous login into a registry with Docker login (credentials in a credential helper or in *~/.docker/config.json*)

If you are using a specific base image registry, you can set up its credentials by using the `<from>` section in the plug-in configuration or `jib.from.auth.username` and `jib.from.auth.password` system properties.

Next, let's configure the Maven plug-in in your *pom.xml*:

```
<project>
    ...
    <build>
        <plugins>
            ...
            <plugin>
                <groupId>com.google.cloud.tools</groupId>
```

```
                <artifactId>jib-maven-plugin</artifactId>
                <version>3.1.4</version>
                <configuration>
                    <to>
                        <image>${pathTo.image}</image>
                    </to>
                </configuration>
            </plugin>
            ...
        </plugins>
    </build>
    ...
</project>
```

The image tag configuration is mandatory and is the target path in the container registry. Now you can build the image to a container registry with a single command:

```
mvn compile jib:build -DpathTo.image=registry.hub.docker.com/myuser/repo
```

If you would like to build and push the container image by using Gradle, you can configure the authentication in one of these ways:

- Use the to and from section in the plug-in configuration in *build.gradle*.

- Connect into a registry with a Docker login command (store credentials in a credential helper or in *~/.docker/config.json*).

Next, add the plug-in to your *build.gradle*:

```
plugins {
    id 'com.google.cloud.tools.jib' version '3.1.4'
}
```

And invoke the following command in a terminal window:

```
gradle jib --image=registry.hub.docker.com/myuser/repo
```

To simplify container image customization when using Jib, some frameworks have integrated the plug-in as a dependency library. For example, Quarkus provides the *quarkus-container-image-jib* extension for personalizing the container image build process. Using this extension, we can revisit the Quarkus example from Chapter 4 and add it using the following Maven command:

```
mvn quarkus:add-extension -Dextensions="io.quarkus:quarkus-container-image-jib"
```

Furthermore, you can customize the image details in *src/main/resources/application.properties*:

```
quarkus.container-image.builder=jib ❶

quarkus.container-image.registry=quay.io ❷
quarkus.container-image.group=repo ❸
```

```
quarkus.container-image.name=demo ❹
quarkus.container-image.tag=1.0.0-SNAPSHOT ❺
```

❶ The extension used for building (and pushing) container images.

❷ The container registry to use.

❸ The container image will be part of this group.

❹ The name of the container image is optional; if not set, it defaults to the application name.

❺ The tag of the container image is also optional; if not set, it defaults to the application version.

Finally, you can build and push the container image:

```
mvn package -Dquarkus.container-image.push=true
```

In Chapter 3, you read about keeping the container images small. The size of a container image influences the time spent by the orchestrating platform to pull that image from the registry. Often, the size of the base image used by the FROM instruction influences the size of your container image, and Jib allows you to control it by changing the baseImage configuration. Moreover, when using Jib, you can also control the ports you expose or the entry point of your container image.

 Changing the JVM base image is also helpful when performing JDK upgrades. In addition, the Quarkus extension supports customization of the JVM base image (quarkus.jib.base-jvm-image) and the native base image (quarkus.jib.base-native-image) used for the native binary build.

The code sample referenced in this section is available on GitHub (*https://oreil.ly/AshKo*).

Building Container Images with Eclipse JKube

An alternative tool that a Java developer can use to containerize Java applications without writing Dockerfiles is Eclipse JKube (*https://oreil.ly/Fp5xx*). This community project, supported by the Eclipse Foundation and Red Hat, can help you build container images and cooperate with Kubernetes. The project contains a Maven plug-in that is the refactored and rebranded version of the Fabric8 Maven plug-in (*https://oreil.ly/dHtw8*). At the time of writing this chapter, Gradle plug-ins are available for technical preview, and support is planned for the future.

To start using the Eclipse JKube Maven plug-in within your project, please add the Kubernetes Maven plug-in to your *pom.xml*:

```
<plugin>
    <groupId>org.eclipse.jkube</groupId>
    <artifactId>kubernetes-maven-plugin</artifactId>
    <version>${jkube.version}</version>
</plugin>
```

Let's add the snippet to the sample Spring Boot application from Chapter 4.

Example 8-1. pom.xml configuration file for sample Spring Boot project

```
<?xml version="1.0" encoding="UTF-8"?>
<project xmlns:xsi="http://www.w3.org/2001/XMLSchema-instance"
        xmlns="http://maven.apache.org/POM/4.0.0"
        xsi:schemaLocation="http://maven.apache.org/POM/4.0.0
    https://maven.apache.org/xsd/maven-4.0.0.xsd">
    <modelVersion>4.0.0</modelVersion>
    <parent>
        <groupId>org.springframework.boot</groupId>
        <artifactId>spring-boot-starter-parent</artifactId>
        <version>2.5.0</version>
    </parent>
    <groupId>com.example</groupId>
    <artifactId>demo</artifactId>
    <version>0.0.1-SNAPSHOT</version>
    <name>demo</name>
    <description>Demo project for Spring Boot</description>
    <properties>
        <java.version>11</java.version>
        <spring-native.version>0.10.5</spring-native.version>
        <jkube.version>1.5.1</jkube.version>
        <jkube.docker.registry>registry.hub.docker.com</jkube.docker.registry> ❶
        <repository>myuser</repository> ❷
        <tag>${project.version}</tag> ❸
        <jkube.generator.name>
            ${jkube.docker.registry}/${repository}/${project.name}:${tag}
        </jkube.generator.name>
    </properties>
    <dependencies>
        ...
    </dependencies>
    <build>
        <plugins>
            <plugin>
                <groupId>org.eclipse.jkube</groupId>
                <artifactId>kubernetes-maven-plugin</artifactId>
                <version>${jkube.version}</version>
            </plugin>
            ...
        </plugins>
```

```
    </build>
    ...
</project>
```

❶ You can provide a default value for the container registry property and override it at build time.

❷ You can provide a default value for the repository property and override it at build time.

❸ You can provide a default value for the tag property and override it at build time. The default image name will be the project name.

To produce a container image for that application, run the following at the command line:

```
mvn k8s:build
```

JKube selects opinionated defaults like base images and handcrafted startup scripts, depending on the type of technology stack you are using. For this case, JKube uses the current local Docker build context for pulling and pushing the container images.

In addition, the image name results from concatenating the values of the Maven properties `${jkube.docker.registry}`, `${repository}`, `${project.name}`, and `${tag}`: `registry.hub.docker.com/myuser/demo:0.0.1-SNAPSHOT`.

Yet, in order to separate the development part from the operational side, we will customize these details and override them at build time. By customizing the property, `jkube.generator.name`, you can include a remote registry, repository, image name, and tag of choice:

```
<jkube.generator.name>
    ${jkube.docker.registry}/${repository}/${project.name}:${tag}
</jkube.generator.name>
```

Now, we can build an image for a remote container registry by using the following command:

```
mvn k8s:build -Djkube.docker.registry=quay.io -Drepository=repo -Dtag=0.0.1
```

If you would like to build and push the image to the remote container registry, you can use this:

```
mvn k8s:build k8s:push -Djkube.docker.registry=quay.io \
    -Drepository=repo -Dtag=0.0.1
```

This command builds the image *quay.io/repo/demo:0.0.1* and pushes it to the respective remote registry.

When using remote registries, you need to provide credentials. Eclipse JKube will search for these locations to obtain credentials:

- The system properties `jkube.docker.username` and `jkube.docker.password`
- The `<authConfig>` section in the plug-in configuration with the `<username>` and `<password>` elements
- A `<server>` configuration in *~/.m2/settings.xml*
- Previous login into a registry with Docker login (credentials in a credential helper or in *~/.docker/config.json*)
- OpenShift configuration in *~/.config/kube*

You can use the same steps to build and push container images using the Eclipse JKube Kubernetes Gradle plug-in (*https://oreil.ly/CeYVl*). In that case, you should configure the plug-in in *build.gradle*:

```
plugins {
    id 'org.eclipse.jkube.kubernetes' version '1.5.1'
}
```

At the command line, you can build the container image by using `gradle k8sBuild` and push the result with `gradle k8sPush`.

You can add `k8s:watch` goal to the plug-in configuration in order to automatically re-create images or copy new artifacts into running containers when your code changes.

Deploying to Kubernetes

With a good understanding of building and pushing container images, you can focus on running containers. When working with distributed systems, containers help you achieve deployment independency and can isolate application code from failures.

Because a distributed system will likely have more than one microservice, you will need to figure out how to manage those using containers. Orchestration tools can help you manage a large number of containers as they typically provide the following:

- A declarative system configuration
- Container provisioning and discovery

- System monitoring and crash recovery
- Instruments for defining rules and constraints on container placement and performance.

Kubernetes is an open source platform automating deployment, scaling, and management of containerized workloads. With Kubernetes, you can organize your deployments in such a way that the platform can spin up or remove instances to match the load demand. Furthermore, Kubernetes can replace and reschedule containers when nodes die.

Features like portability and extensibility increased the popularity of Kubernetes, stimulating community contributions and vendors' support. The proven success of Kubernetes to support increasingly complex categories of applications continues to enable enterprise transition to both hybrid cloud and microservices.

With Kubernetes, you can deploy your application(s) in such a way to have Kubernetes run more instances of your service if load increases, stop instances if load decreases, or spin up new instances should existing ones fail. As a developer, when you want to deploy to Kubernetes, you need access to a Kubernetes cluster. A *Kubernetes cluster* consists of a set of nodes that run containerized applications, as shown in Figure 8-1.

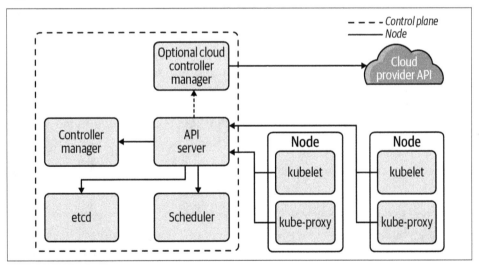

Figure 8-1. Kubernetes components (image adapted from Kubernetes documentation (https://oreil.ly/nyzh7))

Every cluster has at least one worker node, and each worker hosts Pods. Within a cluster, namespaces are used to isolate groups of resources (Pods included). Pods are the components in direct contact with your running containers, instantiated from container images previously built and pushed to a container registry.

When you work with Kubernetes, you are using a set of objects that are validated and accepted by the system. To work with Kubernetes objects, you need to use the Kubernetes API. Nowadays it's possible to instrument Kubernetes deployments by using visual helpers, command-line interfaces, or Java add-ons like Dekorate and JKube to generate and deploy Kubernetes manifests.

Local Setup for Deployment

As a developer, you are used to configuring a local setup to implement application features. Typically, this local setup involves having access to a version control system, and installing and configuring the following:

- A JDK

- Maven or Gradle

- An IDE like IntelliJ IDEA, Eclipse, or Visual Studio Code

- Optionally, a database or middleware that integrates with your code

- One or more tools for building, running, and pushing container images: Docker, Podman, Buildah, Jib, JKube, etc.

- A Kubernetes development cluster: minikube (*https://oreil.ly/SfNR3*), kind (*https://oreil.ly/BcYHp*), or Red Hat CodeReady Containers (*https://oreil.ly/iIkzu*). For development purposes, Docker Desktop (*https://oreil.ly/gmh6B*) also offers a single-node Kubernetes cluster that runs locally within your Docker instance. Rancher Desktop (*https://oreil.ly/09wOS*) is another great tool that can help you locally with container management and running Kubernetes. If running a local development cluster consumes too many resources, you may prefer to have development namespaces in remote Kubernetes cluster(s) or use an already provisioned one like Developer Sandbox for Red Hat OpenShift (*https://oreil.ly/14VUx*).

Before creating any Kubernetes resources, let's summarize some Kubernetes concepts:

Cluster
A set of nodes where you can instruct Kubernetes on deploying containers.

Namespace
A Kubernetes object responsible for isolating groups' resources based on different permissions.

User
Interaction with the Kubernetes API requires a form of authentication managed through users.

Context

A specific combination that contains a Kubernetes cluster, a user, and a name-space.

Kubelet

The main agent that runs on each cluster node and ensures that containers are running and healthy, according to pod specifications.

Deployment

A resource that instructs Kubernetes on creating or modifying instances of pods with a containerized application.

ReplicaSet

Every time Kubernetes creates a deployment, this resource instantiates a Replica-Set and delegates to it counting pods.

Service

A way to expose an application having multiple instances in different pods as a network service.

Keeping in mind these concepts, let's investigate how you can generate Kubernetes objects and deploy them.

Generate Kubernetes Manifests by Using Dekorate

Dekorate (*http://dekorate.io*) can generate Kubernetes manifests at compile time, using Java annotations and standard Java framework configuration mechanisms. Table 8-1 shows Dekorate Maven dependencies available for Quarkus, Spring Boot, or a generic Java project.

Table 8-1. Dekorate Maven dependencies

Framework	Dependency
Quarkus	```<dependency>` ` <groupId>io.quarkus</groupId>` ` <artifactId>quarkus-kubernetes</artifactId>` `</dependency>```
Spring Boot	```<dependency>` ` <groupId>io.dekorate</groupId>` ` <artifactId>kubernetes-spring-starter</artifactId>` ` <version>2.7.0</version>` `</dependency>```
Generic Java Application	```<dependency>` ` <groupId>io.dekorate</groupId>` ` <artifactId>kubernetes-annotations</artifactId>` ` <version>2.7.0</version>` `</dependency>```

Let's create some Kubernetes resources by adding Dekorate to Example 8-1:

```xml
<?xml version="1.0" encoding="UTF-8"?>
<project xmlns:xsi="http://www.w3.org/2001/XMLSchema-instance"
         xmlns="http://maven.apache.org/POM/4.0.0"
         xsi:schemaLocation="http://maven.apache.org/POM/4.0.0
    https://maven.apache.org/xsd/maven-4.0.0.xsd">
    <modelVersion>4.0.0</modelVersion>
    <parent>
        <groupId>org.springframework.boot</groupId>
        <artifactId>spring-boot-starter-parent</artifactId>
        <version>2.5.0</version>
    </parent>
    <groupId>com.example</groupId>
    <artifactId>demo</artifactId>
    <version>0.0.1-SNAPSHOT</version>
    <name>demo</name>
    <description>Demo project for Spring Boot</description>
    <properties>
        <java.version>11</java.version>
        <spring-native.version>0.10.5</spring-native.version>
        <kubernetes-spring-starter.version>
            2.7.0
        </kubernetes-spring-starter.version>
    </properties>
    <dependencies>
        <dependency>
            <groupId>io.dekorate</groupId>
            <artifactId>kubernetes-spring-starter</artifactId>
            <version>${kubernetes-spring-starter.version}</version>
        </dependency>
        ...
    </dependencies>
    ...
</project>
```

If no configuration is provided, Dekorate will produce a Deployment and Service resource in the manifest created under *target/classes/META-INF/dekorate*. This generated Service type is `ClusterIP` and makes the application available only within the Kubernetes cluster. If you want to expose the service externally, using the load balancer of a cloud provider, you can do that by using a Service resource of type `Load Balancer`, as explained in the Kubernetes documentation (*https://oreil.ly/uPUm6*).

When working with Dekorate, you can customize the generation of Kubernetes resources by using the following approaches:

- Specifying configurations in `application.properies`

- Adding the `@KubernetesApplication` annotation to the `DemoApplication` class

To avoid tight coupling between infrastructure and application code, we customize the Service resource *src/main/resources/application.properties* by using the following:

```
dekorate.kubernetes.serviceType=LoadBalancer
```

To generate the Kubernetes objects, you can package the application like this:

```
mvn clean package
```

After packaging the application, you will notice among the other files that are created, two files named *kubernetes.json* and *kubernetes.yml* in the *target/classes/META-INF/dekorate* directory. Either of these manifests can be used to deploy to Kubernetes:

```
---
apiVersion: apps/v1
kind: Deployment ❶
metadata:
  annotations:
    app.dekorate.io/vcs-url: <<unknown>>
  labels:
    app.kubernetes.io/version: 0.0.1-SNAPSHOT ❷
    app.kubernetes.io/name: demo ❷
  name: demo ❸
spec:
  replicas: 1
  selector:
    matchLabels:
      app.kubernetes.io/version: 0.0.1-SNAPSHOT ❷
      app.kubernetes.io/name: demo ❷
  template:
    metadata:
      annotations:
        app.dekorate.io/vcs-url: <<unknown>>
      labels:
        app.kubernetes.io/version: 0.0.1-SNAPSHOT ❷
        app.kubernetes.io/name: demo ❷
    spec:
      containers:
        - env:
            - name: KUBERNETES_NAMESPACE
              valueFrom:
                fieldRef:
                  fieldPath: metadata.namespace
          image: repo/demo:0.0.1-SNAPSHOT ❹
          imagePullPolicy: IfNotPresent
          name: demo
          ports:
            - containerPort: 8080 ❺
              name: http
              protocol: TCP
---
apiVersion: v1
kind: Service ❻
```

```
    metadata:
      annotations:
        app.dekorate.io/vcs-url: <<unknown>>
      labels:
        app.kubernetes.io/name: demo ❷
        app.kubernetes.io/version: 0.0.1-SNAPSHOT ❷
      name: demo
    spec:
      ports:
        - name: http
          port: 80 ❼
          targetPort: 8080 ❺
      selector:
        app.kubernetes.io/name: demo
        app.kubernetes.io/version: 0.0.1-SNAPSHOT
      type: LoadBalancer ❽
```

❶ A Deployment provides declarative updates for Pods and ReplicaSets.

❷ Labels are used by selectors to connect the Service to the Pods, but also to align the specifications of Deployment to ReplicaSets and Pods.

❸ Name of the Deployment object.

❹ Container image used by the Deployment.

❺ Port exposed by the container and targeted by the Service.

❻ A Service exposes the application running on a set of Pods as a network service.

❼ Port used to serve incoming traffic.

❽ Expose the service externally using the load balancer of a cloud provider.

Assuming you have previously logged in a Kubernetes cluster, you can deploy to it using the command-line interface:

```
kubectl apply -f target/classes/META-INF/dekorate/kubernetes.yml
```

As a result, you can access the application by using the external IP (LoadBalancer Ingress) and port by Kubernetes after applying the manifests.

Generate and Deploy Kubernetes Manifests with Eclipse JKube

Eclipse JKube can also generate and deploy Kubernetes/OpenShift manifests at com-pile time. In addition to creating Kubernetes descriptors (YAML files), you can adjust the output by using the following:

- Inline configuration within the XML plug-in configuration
- External configuration templates of deployment descriptors

"Building Container Images with Eclipse JKube" on page 207 explored building container images with JKube and with Docker daemon integration. We will reuse the Quarkus sample code from "Managing Container Images by Using Jib" on page 205 to generate and deploy Kubernetes resources with Eclipse JKube and Jib.

Example 8-2. pom.xml configuration file for sampled Quarkus project

```xml
<?xml version="1.0"?>
<project xsi:schemaLocation="http://maven.apache.org/POM/4.0.0
https://maven.apache.org/xsd/maven-4.0.0.xsd"
         xmlns="http://maven.apache.org/POM/4.0.0"
         xmlns:xsi="http://www.w3.org/2001/XMLSchema-instance">
    <modelVersion>4.0.0</modelVersion>
    <groupId>com.example.demo</groupId>
    <artifactId>demo</artifactId>
    <name>demo</name>
    <version>1.0-SNAPSHOT</version>
    <properties>
        <compiler-plugin.version>3.8.1</compiler-plugin.version>
        <maven.compiler.parameters>true</maven.compiler.parameters>
        <maven.compiler.target>11</maven.compiler.target>
        <maven.compiler.source>11</maven.compiler.source>
        <project.build.sourceEncoding>UTF-8</project.build.sourceEncoding>
        <quarkus-plugin.version>2.5.0.Final</quarkus-plugin.version>
        <quarkus.platform.artifact-id>quarkus-bom</quarkus.platform.artifact-id>
        <quarkus.platform.group-id>io.quarkus</quarkus.platform.group-id>
        <quarkus.platform.version>2.5.0.Final</quarkus.platform.version>
        <surefire-plugin.version>3.0.0-M5</surefire-plugin.version>
        <jkube.version>1.5.1</jkube.version>
        <jkube.generator.name>
            ${quarkus.container-image.registry}/${quarkus.container-image.group}
            /${quarkus.container-image.name}:${quarkus.container-image.tag} ❶
        </jkube.generator.name>
        <jkube.enricher.jkube-service.type>
            NodePort
        </jkube.enricher.jkube-service.type> ❷
    </properties>
    <dependencyManagement>
        <dependencies>
            <dependency>
                <groupId>${quarkus.platform.group-id}</groupId>
                <artifactId>${quarkus.platform.artifact-id}</artifactId>
                <version>${quarkus.platform.version}</version>
                <type>pom</type>
                <scope>import</scope>
            </dependency>
```

```
            </dependencies>
        </dependencyManagement>
        <dependencies>
            <dependency>
                <groupId>io.quarkus</groupId>
                <artifactId>quarkus-container-image-jib</artifactId>
            </dependency>
            ...
        </dependencies>
        <build>
            <plugins>
                <plugin>
                    <groupId>org.eclipse.jkube</groupId>
                    <artifactId>kubernetes-maven-plugin</artifactId>
                    <version>${jkube.version}</version>
                    <configuration>
                        <buildStrategy>jib</buildStrategy> ❸
                    </configuration>
                </plugin>
                ...
            </plugins>
        </build>
        ...
</project>
```

❶ For consistency, you can reuse the Quarkus extension properties within the
    JKube image name.

❷ Expose the service on each node's IP at a static port (the NodePort).

❸ Specify that the build strategy is Jib.

We can now invoke the container image build (k8s:build) and create a Kubernetes
resource (k8s:resource) in a single command:

```
mvn package k8s:build k8s:resource \
    -Dquarkus.container-image.registry=quay.io \
    -Dquarkus.container-image.group=repo \
    -Dquarkus.container-image.name=demo \
    -Dquarkus.container-image.tag=1.0.0-SNAPSHOT
```

The following structure will appear under *target/classes/META-INF/jkube*:

```
|-- kubernetes
|   |-- demo-deployment.yml
|   `-- demo-service.yml
`-- kubernetes.yml
```

kubernetes.yml contains both the Deployment and the Service resource definition,
while in the *kubernetes* folder you have them separated in two distinct files.

As we did for the Dekorate manifest, we can deploy *kubernetes.yml* by using the command-line interface:

```
kubectl apply -f target/classes/META-INF/jkube/kubernetes.yml
```

Or you can use the k8s:apply Maven goal of the JKube plug-in to achieve the same result:

```
mvn k8s:apply
```

This goal will search for the previously generated files and apply them to the connected Kubernetes cluster. The application will be reachable using the cluster IP and the assigned node port.

Furthermore, you can model the interaction between the generated resources and the Kubernetes cluster with more plug-in goals. Table 8-2 lists other goals available with the Kubernetes Maven plug-in.

Table 8-2. Eclipse JKube additional goals

Goal	Description
k8s:log	Gets the logs from your running container in Kubernetes
k8s:debug	Opens the debug port so that you can debug the application deployed in Kubernetes from your IDE
k8s:watch	Does an automatic deployment of your application by watching your application context
k8s:deploy	Forks the Install goal and applies your generated manifests onto a Kubernetes cluster
k8s:undeploy	Deletes all of the resources applied with k8s:apply

Now that you have seen how to deploy to Kubernetes, let's see how we can refine this by choosing and implementing a deployment strategy.

Choose and Implement a Deployment Strategy

Deploying a single application to Kubernetes can be an easy task when using the right tools. As developers, we should also think ahead and decide how we might replace an old version of a microservice with a newer one without downtime.

When you choose a deployment strategy to Kubernetes, you need to look into establishing these quotas:

- Number of desired instances for your application
- Minimum healthy running instances
- Maximum instances

The ideal situation is to have the number of desired running instances in the shortest time possible while using minimal resources (CPU, memory). But let's try the already established methodologies and compare their performance.

All-in-one deployment using the `Recreate` strategy is the simplest available when using Kubernetes Deployment objects:

```
apiVersion: apps/v1
kind: Deployment
metadata:
  labels:
    app: demo
  name: demo
spec:
  strategy:
    type: Recreate ❶
  revisionHistoryLimit: 15 ❷
  replicas: 4
  selector:
    matchLabels:
      app: demo
  template:
    metadata:
      labels:
        app: demo
    spec:
      containers:
      - image: quay.io/repo/demo:1.0.0-SNAPSHOT
        imagePullPolicy: IfNotPresent
        name: quarkus
        ports:
        - containerPort: 8080
          name: http
          protocol: TCP
```

❶   The deployment strategy is `Recreate`.

❷   You can set `revisionHistoryLimit` to specify the number of old ReplicaSets for this deployment that you want to retain. By default, Kubernetes stores the last 10 ReplicaSets.

Whenever the preceding specification is applied in a cluster, Kubernetes will take down all the current running pod instances, and once they are terminated, will bring up new ones. We do not need to set up a minimum and maximum number of instances, only the number of desired instances (4).

In this example, Kubernetes does not delete the previous ReplicaSet immediately after performing an update. Instead, it keeps the ReplicaSet around with a replicas count of 0. If the deployment introduced a change that breaks the stability of the system, we can roll back to a previous working version by choosing from the old ReplicaSets.

You can find out the previous revisions by running the following command:

```
kubectl rollout history deployment/demo
```

And roll back to a previous version by using the following:

```
kubectl rollout undo deployment/demo --to-revision=[revision-number]
```

Although this strategy is efficient in terms of memory and amount of CPU consumption, it introduces a gap in time when the microservice is unavailable.

Another Kubernetes built-in strategy is RollingUpdate, where the current running instances are slowly replaced by the new ones:

```
apiVersion: apps/v1
kind: Deployment
metadata:
  labels:
    app: demo
  name: demo
spec:
  strategy:
    type: RollingUpdate
    rollingUpdate:
      maxUnavailable: 1 ❶
      maxSurge: 3 ❷
  replicas: 4 ❸
  selector:
    matchLabels:
      app: demo
  template:
    metadata:
      labels:
        app: demo
    spec:
      containers:
      - image: quay.io/repo/demo:1.0.0-SNAPSHOT
        imagePullPolicy: IfNotPresent
        name: quarkus
        ports:
        - containerPort: 8080
          name: http
          protocol: TCP
```

❶ Maximum number of Pods that can be unavailable when performing the deployment

❷ Maximum number of Pods that can be created over the desired number of Pods

❸ Desired number of Pods

By focusing on the maximum number of the unavailable Pods, this strategy safely upgrades your deployment, without experiencing any downtime. But, depending on your microservice startup time, the entire transition to the newer version of the deployment can take longer to complete. If the deployment introduces a change that breaks the stability of the system, Kubernetes will update the Deployment template but will keep the previous running Pods.

The rolling deployment is the standard default deployment to Kubernetes if you do not fill in a strategy in the object spec.

If your application is using a database, you should consider the impact of having two application versions running simultaneously. Another disadvantage with this strategy is that during the upgrade, there will be a mix of old and new versions of the application. If you want to keep the zero downtime and avoid mixing application versions in production, take a look at the blue/green deployment technique.

Blue/green deployment is a strategy that reduces downtime and risk of failure by running two identical (production) environments named Blue and Green; see Figure 8-2. When using this deployment strategy, no new instances will serve user requests until all become available; at that moment, all old instances become instantly unavailable. You can achieve this by orchestrating services and routing requests.

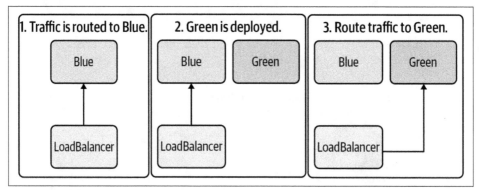

Figure 8-2. Blue/green strategy

Let's observe how we can implement blue/green deployments by using standard Kubernetes objects:

1. Apply the blue version of the microservice having the label version: blue. We will associate the convention of *blue deployment* by using the value of the label version:

```
kubectl apply -f blue_deployment_sample.yml

apiVersion: apps/v1
kind: Deployment
metadata:
  creationTimestamp: null
  labels:
    app: demo
    version: blue
  name: demo-blue
spec:
  replicas: 1
  selector:
    matchLabels:
      app: demo
      version: blue
  template:
    metadata:
      creationTimestamp: null
      labels:
        app: demo
        version: blue
    spec:
      containers:
        - image: nginx:1.14.2
          name: nginx-demo
          imagePullPolicy: IfNotPresent
          ports:
            - containerPort: 80
          resources: {}
```

2. Expose this deployment by using a Kubernetes Service. After this, traffic is served from the blue version:

```
kubectl expose deployment demo-blue --selector="version=blue"
        --type=LoadBalancer
```

3. Apply the *green deployment* of a microservice having the label version: green:

```
kubectl apply -f green_deployment_sample.yml

apiVersion: apps/v1
kind: Deployment
metadata:
  creationTimestamp: null
  labels:
    app: demo
    version: green
  name: demo-green
spec:
  replicas: 1
  selector:
```

```
      matchLabels:
        app: demo
        version: green
    template:
      metadata:
        creationTimestamp: null
        labels:
          app: demo
          version: green
      spec:
        containers:
          - image: nginx:1.14.2
            name: nginx-demo
            imagePullPolicy: IfNotPresent
            ports:
              - containerPort: 80
            resources: {}
```

4. Switch the traffic from blue deployment to green by patching the Service object:

```
kubectl patch svc/demo -p '{"spec":{"selector":{"version":"green"}}}'
```

5. If the blue deployment is no longer needed, you can remove it by using `kubectl delete`.

Although this deployment strategy is more complex and requires more resources, you can shorten the time between software development and user feedback. This approach is less disruptive for experimenting with features; if any issues appear after a deployment, you can quickly route to a previous stable version.

 You can explore a blue/green deployment strategy with more cloud native tools that are compatible with Kubernetes, such as Istio (*https://istio.io*) and Knative (*https://knative.dev*).

The last strategy that we will look at is a *canary deployment*. This is a way to reduce risk and validate new system features by releasing software to a small percentage of users. Performing a canary deployment allows you to try out the new version of a microservice with a small user audience without replacing any of the existing instances of the application. To evaluate the behavior of the deployments (canary and existing), you should implement a load balancer configuration on top of the service instances and add weighted routing to choose how much traffic is routed to each resource.

Currently, the canary strategy can be achieved by adding an extra layer of tools (Figure 8-3). API gateways with weighted routing support let you manage your API endpoints and decide the amount of traffic routed toward them. Service mesh control planes like Istio are a solution compatible with Kubernetes that can help you to control service-to-service communication over a network and the percentage of user traffic to each service version.

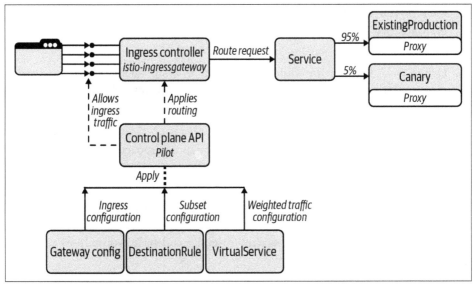

Figure 8-3. Canary strategy using weighted traffic routing in Istio

If you still struggle to choose a deployment mechanism, check out Table 8-3, which summarizes characteristics of the previously discussed strategies.

Table 8-3. Characteristics of the deployment strategies

	Re-create	Rolling update	Blue/green	Canary
Out of the box in Kubernetes	Yes	Yes	No	No
Downtime occurrence	Yes	No	No	No
Rollback process	Manually roll out a previous version	Stop rollout and keep the previous version	Switch traffic to previous version	Delete canary instance
Traffic control	No	No	Yes	Yes
Traffic sent simultaneously to old and new version	No	Yes	No	Yes

Managing Workloads in Kubernetes

An application running on Kubernetes is a *workload*. In the cluster, your workload will run on one or several Pods having a defined lifecycle. To simplify Pod lifecycle management, Kubernetes provides several built-in workload resources:

Deployment and ReplicaSet
> Help manage a stateless application workload.

StatefulSet
> Enables you to run a stateful application either as a single instance or as a replicated set.

Job and CronJob
> Define tasks that run to completion and then stop. These types of resources are useful when implementing batch-processing activities. Jobs are one-off tasks, while CronJobs run according to a schedule.

DaemonSet
> Can help you to define Pods with functionalities impacting the entire node. Scheduling the workload using this type of resource is rare.

Earlier, we generated and deployed Kubernetes manifests containing a Deployment specification, as typically microservices are stateless applications. But how can we prevent failure for those microservices that depend on an external service or persist their data in a database? Moreover, as a microservice codebase evolves, how can it use a fair share of memory and CPU?

Setting Up Health Checks

Another benefit of working with distributed systems and in the cloud is that microservices independence often stimulates automated deployments. As automated deployments can occur several times per day, on multiple instances, you need a way to validate that your application is available and running as expected. Each increase in the number of components in the system brings with it an increase in the probability of failure: a deadlock, a host becoming unavailable, a hardware failure, etc. To detect issues before they propagate as outages, we can validate the status of a microservice by using health checks.

Health checks should span across the entire system, from application code to infrastructure. Infrastructure can use application health checks to determine when to serve traffic using readiness probes or to restart the container via liveness probes. You should know that a liveness probe does not always execute after the readiness probe succeeds. When your application needs additional time to initialize, you can define the amount of time in seconds to wait before executing the probe or use a startup probe to check if the container has started.

At the Kubernetes level, the *kubelet* is the component that uses liveness, readiness, and startup probes to assess the state of your containers. The kubelet uses readiness probes to check when a container is ready to start accepting traffic, and liveness probes to know when to restart it. You can use any of these three mechanisms to implement liveness, readiness, or startup probes:

- Opening a TCP socket against a container

- Making an HTTP request against a containerized application that exposes API endpoints

- Running a command inside a container in case your application uses a protocol different from HTTP or TCP

 With Kubernetes v1.23, a gRPC health probe mechanism is available as an alpha feature. Please keep an eye on the evolution of the Kubernetes health probe documentation (*https://oreil.ly/IDsqC*).

The simplest way of implementing a health check is to periodically evaluate the running application by sending requests to some of its API endpoints. You can determine the health of the system based on the response payload. Typically, these health endpoints are HTTP GET or HEAD requests that do not change the state of the system and perform a lightweight task. You can define a */health* endpoint in a RESTful API to check the internal status of your microservice or you can use framework-compatible dependencies:

The Actuator (*https://oreil.ly/rNxMx*) module provides useful insight into a Spring environment running applications. Actuator has functions for health checking and gathers metrics by exposing multiple endpoints over HTTP and Java Management Extensions (JMX).

You can add the Actuator module to your Spring Boot project as a Maven or Gradle dependency (see Table 8-4) and can access the default health endpoints at */actuator/ health*.

Table 8-4. Actuator as Maven or Gradle dependency

Build tool	Definition

Maven	```<dependency>```
	``` <groupId>org.springframework.boot</groupId>```
	``` <artifactId>spring-boot-starter-actuator</artifactId>```
	```</dependency>```

Gradle	```dependencies {```
	``` compile("org.springframework.boot:spring-boot-starter-actuator")```
	```}```

With Actuator, you can check the health of individual components with health indicators or have a composite health check with composite health contributors. You can work with several predefined health indicators, including `DataSourceHealth`

Indicator, MongoHealthIndicator, RedisHealthIndicator, and CassandraHealth
Indicator. These implement the HealthIndicator interface, which enables you to
check the health of that component. For example, if your application is using a
database to persist data, the database health indicator will be automatically added
by Spring Boot if it detects a datasource. The health check consists of creating a
connection to a database to perform a simple query.

Although using the built-in health indicators saves you development time, sometimes
you should investigate the health of dependent systems aggregated together. Spring
Boot will aggregate all health indicators it finds in the application context under
the /actuator/health endpoint. Yet, if a health check on one of the dependent
systems is unsuccessful, the composite probe will fail. For such cases, you should
consider implementing the CompositeHealthContributor interface in a Spring bean
or treating the potential failure by offering a fallback response.

The MicroProfile Health module allows services to report their health, and it pub-
lishes the overall health status to a defined endpoint. Quarkus applications can use
the SmallRye Health extension (*https://oreil.ly/r9QuE*), which is an implementation
of the Eclipse MicroProfile Health Check specification. You can add the extension to
your Maven or Gradle configuration by using snippets from Table 8-5.

Table 8-5. SmallRye Health as Maven or Gradle dependency

Build tool	Definition
Maven	```<dependency>` ` <groupId>io.quarkus</groupId>` ` <artifactId>quarkus-smallrye-health</artifactId>` `</dependency>```
Gradle	```dependencies {` ` implementation 'io.quarkus:quarkus-smallrye-health'` `}```

All health-check procedures in the application are accumulated in the /q/health
REST endpoint. Some Quarkus extensions provide default health checks. This means
that the extension can automatically register its health checks.

For example, when using a Quarkus datasource, the quarkus-agroal extension automatically registers a readiness health check that will validate that datasource. You
can disable automatic registration of the extension health check via the property
quarkus.health.extensions.enabled.

When you investigate the health of dependent systems, you can define your own
health checks by implementing org.eclipse.microprofile.health.HealthCheck
and use @Liveness, @Readiness, and @Startup to distinguish the role of each check.
A composite health check inspects the condition of the dependent systems aggregated

together. Yet this approach is counterproductive if one of the dependent systems fails. A more proactive strategy involves offering a fallback response and monitoring a set of metrics showing the application's health. These are more useful as they offer early notifications about a system's deteriorating health, giving us time to take mitigating measures.

Besides the automatic readiness probes when adding specific extensions, Quarkus comes with some health-check implementations for you to check the status of various components:

- `SocketHealthCheck` checks if the host is reachable using a socket.

- `UrlHealthCheck` checks if the host is reachable using an HTTP URL connection.

- `InetAddressHealthCheck` checks if the host is reachable using the `InetAddress.isReachable` method.

When you implement health checks using REST endpoints at the application level, you will likely invoke those using an HTTP request from a probe. Kubernetes probes consult these endpoints to determine the health of your container. A probe has configuration parameters to control its behavior, including the following:

- How often to execute the probe (`periodSeconds`)

- How long to wait after starting the container to initiate the probe (`initialDelay Seconds`)

- Number of seconds after which the probe is considered failed (`timeoutSeconds`)

- Number of times the probe can fail before giving up (`failureThreshold`)

- Minimum consecutive successes for the probe to be considered successful after having failed (`successThreshold`)

The tools we have previously used to generate Kubernetes manifests (Dekorate and Eclipse JKube) can help you start working with health probes. For example, let's add the Actuator dependency to the Spring Boot project and package the application by using the following:

```
mvn clean package
```

The Kubernetes manifest file from *target/classes/dekorate/* will contain specifications for health probes:

```
---
apiVersion: v1
kind: Service
#[...]
```

```
---
apiVersion: apps/v1
kind: Deployment
metadata:
  annotations:
    app.dekorate.io/vcs-url: <<unknown>>
  labels:
    app.kubernetes.io/version: 0.0.1-SNAPSHOT
    app.kubernetes.io/name: demo
  name: demo
spec:
  replicas: 1
  selector:
    matchLabels:
      app.kubernetes.io/version: 0.0.1-SNAPSHOT
      app.kubernetes.io/name: demo
  template:
    metadata:
      annotations:
        app.dekorate.io/vcs-url: <<unknown>>
      labels:
        app.kubernetes.io/version: 0.0.1-SNAPSHOT
        app.kubernetes.io/name: demo
    spec:
      containers:
        - env:
            - name: KUBERNETES_NAMESPACE
              valueFrom:
                fieldRef:
                  fieldPath: metadata.namespace
          image: repo/demo:0.0.1-SNAPSHOT
          imagePullPolicy: IfNotPresent
          livenessProbe: ❶
            failureThreshold: 3 ❷
            httpGet: ❸
              path: /actuator/info
              port: 8080
              scheme: HTTP
            initialDelaySeconds: 0 ❹
            periodSeconds: 30 ❺
            successThreshold: 1 ❻
            timeoutSeconds: 10 ❼
          name: demo
          ports:
            - containerPort: 8080
              name: http
              protocol: TCP
          readinessProbe: ❶
            failureThreshold: 3 ❷
            httpGet: ❸
              path: /actuator/health
              port: 8080
```

```
      scheme: HTTP
      initialDelaySeconds: 0  ❹
      periodSeconds: 30  ❺
      successThreshold: 1  ❻
      timeoutSeconds: 10  ❼
```

❶ Declaration of readiness and liveness probe is within the container specification.

❷ The probe can fail three times before giving up.

❸ The probe should make an HTTP GET request against the container.

❹ Wait 0 seconds after starting the container to initiate the probe.

❺ Execute the probe every 30 seconds.

❻ Minimum one consecutive success for the probe to be considered successful after having failed.

❼ After 10 seconds, the probe is considered failed.

> Depending on the tech stack that you use, Eclipse JKube (*https://oreil.ly/guUR9*) has a list of enrichers that can help you adjust health checks.

Now that you have used application health checks to ensure that the system is performing as expected, we can look into fine-tuning resource quotas for containerized applications.

Adjusting Resource Quotas

A common practice is to have several users or teams share a cluster with a fixed number of nodes. To facilitate a fair share of resources for each deployed application, cluster administrators establish a `ResourceQuota` object. This object provides constraints that limit resource consumption for a namespace.

When you define specifications for a Pod, you can specify the amount of resources each container will need. Requests define the minimum amount of resources that containers need, while limits define the maximum amount of resources that the container can consume. The kubelet enforces those limits for the running container.

For a container, the common resources to specify are CPU and memory. For each container of a Pod, you can define them as follows:

- `spec.containers[].resources.limits.cpu`

- `spec.containers[].resources.limits.memory`

- `spec.containers[].resources.requests.cpu`

- `spec.containers[].resources.requests.memory`

In Kubernetes, the CPU is assigned with values in millicores or millicpu, and memory is measured in bytes. The kubelet collects metrics such as CPU and memory from your Pods and can check them using Metrics Server (*https://oreil.ly/31lKM*).

As your containers start to compete for resources, you should carefully divide the CPU and memory based on limits and requests. To achieve that, you need the following:

- A tool or practice to programmatically generate traffic for your application. For local development purposes, you can start with tools like hey (*https://oreil.ly/rJK0q*) or Apache JMeter (*https://oreil.ly/pvNfd*).

- A tool or practice to collect metrics and decide how to set requests and limits for CPU and memory. For example, on local minikube installations, you can enable the `metrics-server` add-on (*https://oreil.ly/9Ix3p*).

Next, you can add the resource limits and requests to your existing container specification. You can also have them generated if you are using Dekorate and have them defined at the application configuration level. For example, in the case of Quarkus, you can add the Kubernetes extension that includes Dekorate:

```
mvn quarkus:add-extension -Dextensions="io.quarkus:quarkus-kubernetes"
```

and configure them in *src/main/resources/application.properties*:

```
quarkus.kubernetes.resources.limits.cpu=200m
quarkus.kubernetes.resources.limits.memory=230Mi
quarkus.kubernetes.resources.requests.cpu=100m
quarkus.kubernetes.resources.requests.memory=115Mi
```

These configurations can be customized when packaging the application. After running `mvn clean package`, note that the newly generated Deployment object includes resource specifications:

```
apiVersion: apps/v1
kind: Deployment
metadata:
  annotations:
    app.quarkus.io/build-timestamp: 2021-12-11 - 16:51:44 +0000
  labels:
    app.kubernetes.io/version: 1.0.0-SNAPSHOT
    app.kubernetes.io/name: demo
  name: demo
```

```
spec:
  replicas: 1
  selector:
    matchLabels:
      app.kubernetes.io/version: 1.0.0-SNAPSHOT
      app.kubernetes.io/name: demo
  template:
    metadata:
      annotations:
        app.quarkus.io/build-timestamp: 2021-12-11 - 16:51:44 +0000
      labels:
        app.kubernetes.io/version: 1.0.0-SNAPSHOT
        app.kubernetes.io/name: demo
    spec:
      containers:
        - env:
            - name: KUBERNETES_NAMESPACE
              valueFrom:
                fieldRef:
                  fieldPath: metadata.namespace
          image: quay.io/repo/demo:1.0.0-SNAPSHOT
          imagePullPolicy: Always
          name: demo
          resources:
            limits:
              cpu: 200m
              memory: 230Mi
            requests:
              cpu: 100m
              memory: 115Mi
```

 The container is limited to use maximum 200 millicores (m) and 230 mebibytes (MiB).

 The container can request a minimum 100 m and 115 MiB.

 If a container specifies a memory limit but does not specify a memory request, Kubernetes automatically assigns a memory request that matches the limit. If a container specifies a CPU limit but does not specify a CPU request, Kubernetes automatically assigns a CPU request that matches the limit.

Working with Persistent Data Collections

A basic principle of microservices is that each service manages its own data. If services share the same underlying data schemas, unintentional coupling between services can occur, thus endangering independent deployments.

If you are working with NoSQL databases, like CouchDB or MongoDB, don't worry about database changes, as altering the data structure can be performed from application code.

On the other hand, if you are using a standard SQL database, you can use tools like Flyway (*https://flywaydb.org*) or Liquibase (*https://liquibase.org*) to handle schema changes. These tools can help you generate migration scripts and keep track of which of those were run in the database and which were not yet applied. When any of these migration tools is invoked, it will scan the available migration scripts, identify ones that have not been run on a particular database, and then execute those.

When investigating the options from "Choose and Implement a Deployment Strategy" on page 219, you should consider the following:

- Both database schema versions must work well with the application versions used during the deployment phase.

- Ensure that you have a schema compatibility with the previous working version of your containerized application.

- Changing a column's data type requires converting all values stored according to the old column definition.

- Renaming a column, a table, or a view are backward-incompatible operations unless you use triggers or a programmatic migration script.

By separating application deployments from applying migration scripts, you can independently manage your microservices. Most of the time, cloud providers offer several datasources as part of their cloud service. These types of offerings might be the right option for your workloads if you are looking for database solutions without having to manage and maintain the underlying layers. Nevertheless, also consider how to protect, manage, and secure sensitive data when using a managed database service.

Should databases run in Kubernetes? The answer to this question depends on how the Kubernetes way to manage workload and traffic aligns with operational steps to maintain the database. Because maintaining databases requires more complex sequences of actions, the Kubernetes community resolved these challenges by implementing operators that incorporate logical domain and operational runbooks needed to run databases in Kubernetes. OperatorHub.io (*https://operatorhub.io*) has an extensive list of operators.

Best Practices for Monitoring, Logging, and Tracing

So far, we've been focusing on making containerized applications operational. On your local machine, you are the only end user of your work, but your application will face the rest of the world in production. To have your application aligned to the expectations of all your end users, you should observe its evolution in time under different conditions and environment instances.

In recent years, the term *observability* has become popular in the IT industry, but chances are that you have already been working on *observable* Java applications. Observability is the ability to measure a system's current state based on the telemetry data it generates, such as logs, metrics, and traces. If you have implemented auditing, exception handling, or event logging, you have already started to observe your application behavior. Furthermore, to build observability for your distributed system, you will likely use different tools to implement monitoring, logging, and tracing practices.

> You should observe applications, networks, and infrastructures that you and your team(s) are responsible for, regardless of the tools used to implement them.

Applications and the underlying infrastructure can produce useful metrics, logs, and traces to correctly observe a system. As shown in Figure 8-4, collecting this telemetry data contributes to visualizing the state of the system and to triggering notifications when a part of your system is underperforming.

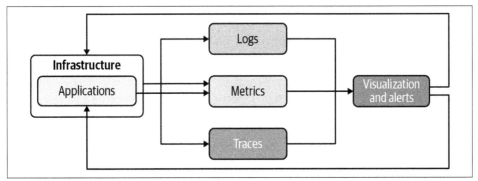

Figure 8-4. Gathering metrics, logs, and traces from applications and infrastructure

Alerts help you acknowledge an unforeseen scenario and implement a recovery mechanism if the unexpected conditions reoccur. You can use distribution of notifications to identify a pattern in the normal workflow of the system. This pattern can further help you automate the recovery mechanism and use it whenever the alert is received.

As observability measures the state of a distributed system, you can have it as input to repair the faulty states of your microservices; see Figure 8-5. Kubernetes has a built-in self-healing mechanism that includes restarting failed containers, disposing of unhealthy containers, or not routing traffic to Pods that are not ready to serve traffic. At the node level, the control plane watches over the state of the worker nodes. Some practices for automating the recovery mechanism involve extending the Kubernetes self-healing mechanism by utilizing Job and DaemonSet resources. For example, you can use a DaemonSet to run a node-monitoring daemon on every worker, while a Job creates one or more Pods and retries execution of those until a specified number successfully terminate.

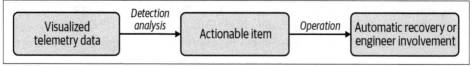

Figure 8-5. Improving from observation to automating recovery

Observability also helps you measure the state of the system when traffic spikes occur. Applications that respond with delay induce frustrations in end users. In such cases, you should investigate how you can scale your containerized applications. Moreover, autoscaling eliminates the need to respond manually to traffic spikes that need new resources and instances by automatically changing their active number.

In Kubernetes, a HorizontalPodAutoscaler (HPA) resource automatically updates a workload resource like Deployment, aiming to scale the workload to match demand automatically. A HorizontalPodAutoscaler resource responds to increased load by deploying more Pods. If the load diminishes and the number of Pods is above the minimum configured, the HorizontalPodAutoscaler requires the Deployment resource to scale down.

As explained in the Kubernetes documentation (*https://oreil.ly/UWebg*), the algorithm HorizontalPodAutoscaler uses the ratio of the desired metric value to the current metric value:

```
wantedReplicas = ceil[currentReplicas * (currentMetricValue / wantedMetricValue)]
```

To demonstrate how the preceding algorithm works when you set up a HorizontalPodAutoscaler resource, let's reuse the example from "Adjusting Resource Quotas" on page 231, where we adjusted resource quotas:

```
quarkus.kubernetes.resources.limits.cpu=200m
quarkus.kubernetes.resources.limits.memory=230Mi
quarkus.kubernetes.resources.requests.cpu=100m
quarkus.kubernetes.resources.requests.memory=115Mi
```

Each Pod using the previous configuration can request a minimum 100 m for CPU. You can set up the HorizontalPodAutoscaler to maintain an average CPU utilization across all Pods of 80% for this deployment by using the following command:

```
kubectl autoscale deployment demo --cpu-percent=80 --min=1 --max=10
```

Assuming that the current metric value for CPU is 320 m and the desired value is 160 m, the number of replicas needed is 320 / 160 = 2.0. Based on the Horizontal-PodAutoscaler configuration, the Deployment updates the ReplicaSet and then the ReplicaSet adds Pods to match the workload need. If the current metric value for CPU decreases at 120 m, the number of replicas needed will be 120 / 160 = 0.75, and the scale-down to one replica will occur gradually.

Another option to scale with Kubernetes is to use *vertical scaling*, which means to match the workload by assigning more resources to the Pods that are already running. VerticalPodAutoscaler (*https://oreil.ly/vTegk*) (VPA) needs to be installed and enabled in order to further use its policies. To avoid undefined behavior over your Pods, do not use VerticalPodAutoscaler and HorizontalPodAutoscaler simultaneously to adjust CPU or memory of resources.

Let's look into some monitoring, logging, and tracing recommendations to understand observability better when deploying, scaling, and maintaining containerized applications.

Monitoring

You can use monitoring to observe a system in near real-time. Typically, this practice involves setting up a technical solution that can gather logs and predefined sets of metrics, as shown in Figure 8-6.

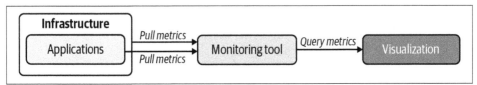

Figure 8-6. Pulling and querying metrics

Metrics are numeric values of system properties over time, like maximum Java heap memory available or the total number of garbage collections that occurred. Table 8-6 shows which metrics can help you when monitoring a system.

Table 8-6. General types of metrics

Name	Description
Counter	A cumulative value based on incrementing an integer
Timer	Measures both the count of timed events and the total time of all timed events
Gauge	A single numerical value that can go up and down arbitrarily
Histogram	Measures distribution of values in a stream of data
Meter	Indicates the rate at which a set of events occur

A few popular Java libraries for working with metrics include MicroProfile Metrics, Spring Boot Actuator, and Micrometer. For a better overview of your system behavior, you can collect and query these metrics with tools such as Prometheus (*https://prometheus.io*).

To provide you with an example, we will reuse Example 8-1, expose its metrics under */actuator/prometheus*, and send those to Prometheus by generating the container image and Kubernetes resources using Eclipse JKube.

Let's start by adding the Micrometer registry dependency, which specifically enables Prometheus support:

```
<dependency>
    <groupId>io.micrometer</groupId>
    <artifactId>micrometer-registry-prometheus</artifactId>
    <scope>runtime</scope>
</dependency>
```

Next, you need to instruct Spring Boot's Actuator which endpoints it should expose by adding this line to *src/main/resources/application.properties*:

```
management.endpoints.web.exposure.include=health,info,prometheus
```

The Spring Boot application exposes the metrics under */actuator/prometheus*. Metrics related to JVM are also available at */actuator/prometheus*, such as `jvm.gc.pause` that measures garbage collection pause times. To further expose these metrics at the container and Kubernetes resource level, we can customize the Eclipse JKube setup with the following:

```
<?xml version="1.0" encoding="UTF-8"?>
<project xmlns:xsi="http://www.w3.org/2001/XMLSchema-instance"
        xmlns="http://maven.apache.org/POM/4.0.0"
        xsi:schemaLocation="http://maven.apache.org/POM/4.0.0
    https://maven.apache.org/xsd/maven-4.0.0.xsd">
    <modelVersion>4.0.0</modelVersion>
    <groupId>com.example</groupId>
    <artifactId>demo</artifactId>
    <version>0.0.1-SNAPSHOT</version>
    <name>demo</name>
    <!--[...]-->
    <build>
        <plugins>
            <plugin>
                <groupId>org.eclipse.jkube</groupId>
                <artifactId>kubernetes-maven-plugin</artifactId>
                <version>${jkube.version}</version>
                <executions>
                    <execution>
                        <id>resources</id>
                        <phase>process-resources</phase>
                        <goals>
```

```
                             <goal>resource</goal> ❶
                          </goals>
                       </execution>
                    </executions>
                    <configuration>
                       <generator> ❷
                          <config>
                             <spring-boot>
                                <prometheusPort> ❸
                                   9779
                                </prometheusPort>
                             </spring-boot>
                          </config>
                       </generator>
                       <enricher> ❹
                          <config>
                             <jkube-prometheus>
                                <prometheusPort> ❸
                                   9779
                                </prometheusPort>
                             </jkube-prometheus>
                          </config>
                       </enricher>
                    </configuration>
                 </plugin>
              </plugins>
           </build>
        </project>
```

❶ Execute this configuration with the `k8s:resource` goal.

❷ Adjust the generated Docker image to expose the Prometheus port.

❸ Expose the 9779 port at the container-image level and have it in Kubernetes resources annotations.

❹ Generate Kubernetes resources helpful for Spring Boot applications.

To build the container image and generate the Kubernetes resources, run the following command:

```
mvn clean package k8s:build k8s:resource \
    -Djkube.docker.registry=quay.io \
    -Drepository=repo \
    -Dtag=0.0.1
```

The Kubernetes resources generated at *target/classes/META-INF/jkube/kubernetes.yml* will contain the Prometheus annotations controlling the metrics collection process:

```
apiVersion: v1
kind: List
```

```
items:
- apiVersion: v1
  kind: Service
  metadata:
    annotations:
      prometheus.io/path: /metrics
      prometheus.io/port: "9779"
      prometheus.io/scrape: "true"
```

Once you deploy the generated resources, you can use a custom Prometheus query (PromQL) to query different metrics. For example, you can pick the `jvm.gc.pause` metric and run the following PromQL query to check the average time spent in garbage collection by cause:

```
avg(rate(jvm_gc_pause_seconds_sum[1m])) by (cause)
```

When generating and capturing metrics, several best practices should be followed:

- As metrics can be defined at both the application and infrastructure level, have team members collaborate on defining those.

- Always expose internal JVM metrics, such as number of threads, CPU usage, how often the garbage collector ran, heap, and nonheap memory usage.

- Make an effort to create metrics for application-specific implementations that impact nonfunctional requirements. For example, cache statistics like size, hits, and entry time-to-live can offer you insights when assessing the performance of a functionality.

- Tailor metrics that can support key performance indicators (KPIs) used by business people. For example, the number of end users who used a new functionality is a KPI that can be proven with software metrics.

- Measure and expose details about errors and exceptions that occur within your system. You can use these details later to establish error patterns and thus perform an enhancement.

Logging

At the Java application level, developers use logging to record exceptional cases. Logs are useful to obtain insights with additional context information and can complement existing metrics. When it comes to logging, three formats are available: plain text, JSON or XML, and binary.

Besides the Java language built-in log, several logging frameworks can help you achieve this task: Simple Logging Facade for Java (SLF4J) (*http://www.slf4j.org*) and Apache Log4j 2 (*https://oreil.ly/foEtO*). Some logging best practices include the following:

- Be conservative; log only details that are relevant to a particular functionality of your system.

- Write meaningful information in the log message in order to help you and your colleagues troubleshoot future issues.

- Use the correct log level: TRACE for capturing fine-grained insights, DEBUG for statements helpful when troubleshooting, INFO for general information, WARN and ERROR to signal events that might require action.

- Make sure you use guard clauses or lambda expressions to log messages if the corresponding log level is enabled.

- Have the log level customizable via variables that can be set at container runtime.

- Set appropriate permissions to locations where your log files will live.

- Customize layout of your logs to have region-specific formats.

- Protect sensitive data when logging. For example, logging personally identifiable information (PII) can lead not only to compliance violations, but also to security vulnerabilities.

- Periodically rotate logs to prevent log files from growing too large or have them automatically discarded. Container and Pod logs are transient by default. This means that the container logs are gone when Pods are deleted, crashed, or scheduled on a different node. But you can stream your logs asynchronously to a centralized storage or service and keep locally a fixed number of rotated log files.

Tracing

Within a distributed system, a request traverses multiple components. Tracing helps you capture metadata and timing details concerning the flow of a request to identify slow transactions or where failures occur.

Finding the right instrumentation to capture traces can be challenging for a developer. Proprietary agents can help you with that, but you should look into solutions aligned to vendor-neutral, open standards like OpenCensus (*https://opencensus.io*) or OpenTracing (*https://opentracing.io*). Many developers found it difficult to choose the best option for an application and have it work across vendors and projects, so OpenTracing and OpenCensus projects merged and formed another CNCF (*https://www.cncf.io*) incubating project called OpenTelemetry (*https://oreil.ly/QyOhu*). This collection of tools, APIs, and SDKs standardizes the way you collect and transmit metrics, logs, and traces. The OpenTelemetry tracing specification defines the following terms:

Trace
A single transaction request that uses other services and resources as it moves through a distributed system.

Span
A named, timed operation representing a workflow piece. A trace contains multiple spans.

Attributes
Key/value pairs that you can use to query, filter, and comprehend trace data.

Baggage items
Key/value pairs that cross process boundaries.

Context propagation
A common subsystem shared by traces, metrics, and baggage. A developer can pass additional context information to a span by using attributes, logs, and baggage items.

Figure 8-7 illustrates the trace for a transaction that begins with microservice Blue and traverses microservices Violet and Green. The trace has three spans, and attributes are set on the Violet and Green spans.

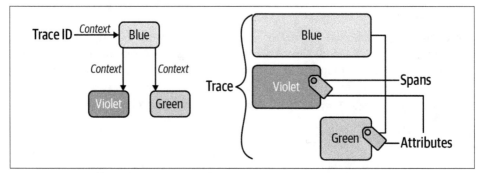

Figure 8-7. Distributed tracing example

To give an example that incorporates both metrics and traces, we will enhance Example 8-2 by tracing the request to the */greeting* endpoint and detecting the time spent to return a response with a Timer metric.

Next, let's export the metrics to Prometheus and for further processing include OpenTelemetry support by adding the following Quarkus extensions:

```
mvn quarkus:add-extension \
    -Dextensions="quarkus-micrometer-registry-prometheus,
                  quarkus-opentelemetry-exporter-otlp"
```

Next, let's customize the endpoint for sending spans by adding the following:

```
custom.host = ${exporter.host:localhost}  ❶
quarkus.kubernetes.env.vars.otlp-exporter=${custom.host:localhost}  ❷
quarkus.opentelemetry.tracer.exporter.otlp.endpoint=http://${custom.host}:4317  ❸
```

Define the host as a configuration that you can parametrize. The default value for the host of the endpoint is localhost, but you can override it with -Dexporter.host: mvn package -Dexporter.host=myhost.

❷ At compile time, the quarkus-kubernetes extension that is already in the project will take into account this environment variable and autogenerate the configuration of the Kubernetes resources. The configuration reuses the value of custom.host.

❸ The gRPC endpoint for sending spans that reuses the previous host definition. The configuration reuses the value of custom.host.

To measure the duration of a request sent to the */greeting* endpoint, we will annotate it with @Timed and instrument its traces by customizing a Span with two attributes:

```
package com.example.demo;


import io.micrometer.core.annotation.Timed;
import io.opentelemetry.api.trace.*;
import io.opentelemetry.context.Context;

import javax.ws.rs.*;
import java.util.logging.Logger;
import javax.ws.rs.core.MediaType;

@Path("/greeting")
public class GreetingResource {
    private static final String template = "Hello, %s!";

    private final static Logger log;

    static {
        log = Logger.getLogger(GreetingResource.class.getName());
    }

    @GET
    @Produces(MediaType.APPLICATION_JSON)
    @Timed(value="custom")
    public Greeting greeting(@QueryParam("name") String name) {
        pause();
        return new Greeting(String.format(template, name));
    }

    private void pause() {
        Span span = Span.fromContext(Context.current())
                .setAttribute("pause", "start"); ❶
        try {
            Thread.sleep(2000);
        } catch (InterruptedException e) {
```

```
            span.setStatus(StatusCode.ERROR, "Execution was interrupted");
            span.setAttribute("unexpected.pause", "exception");
            span.recordException(e); ❷
            log.severe("Thread interrupted");
        }
    }
}
```

❶ Attribute set to trace when the logic started.

❷ After recording the exception, set the attribute to trace the exception case.

Given the changes introduced, you can rebuild and push the container image, and deploy the Kubernetes resources generated at compile time by using the following:

```
mvn package -Dquarkus.container-image.build=true \
    -Dquarkus.container-image.push=true \
    -Dquarkus.kubernetes.deploy=true
```

To instrument end-to-end distributed tracing, you can use a tool like Jaeger (*https://oreil.ly/Kp09K*) (Figure 8-8). This top-level CNCF project (*https://oreil.ly/vZRTZ*) can easily integrate with Kubernetes. You can set up the value for `quarkus.open` `telemetry.tracer.exporter.otlp.endpoint` by using the Jaeger endpoint. Within the Jaeger UI, you can search traces by using the `pause` tag.

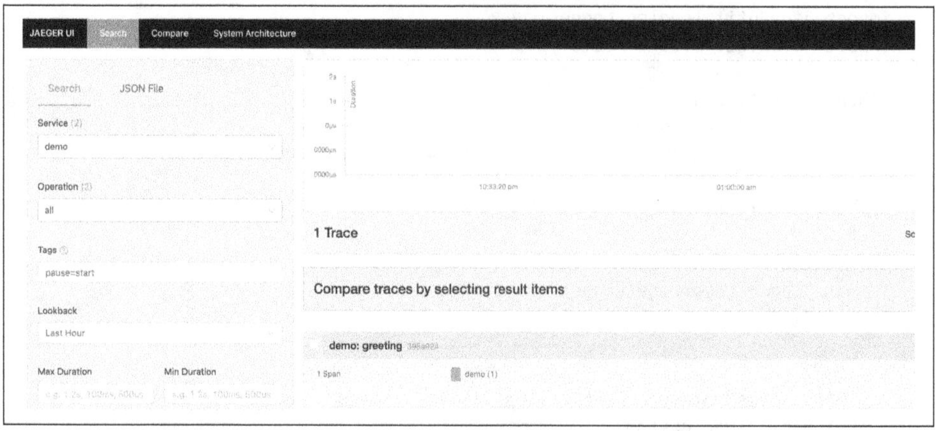

Figure 8-8. Filtering traces by tag with Jaeger

Furthermore, you can observe the requests that generated an exception as follows:

1. Search in the Jaeger UI for traces having `error=true` and `unexpected` `.pause=exception` tags.

2. Utilize the `Timer` named `custom` in a Prometheus query like the following one:
   ```
   avg(rate(custom_seconds_sum[1m])) by (exception)
   ```

3. Inspect logs for the message `Thread interrupted`.

Here are some recommended practices for tracing:

- Instrument a trace end-to-end, meaning forward the tracing headers to all the downstream services, data stores, or middleware part of your system.
- Report metrics related to request rate, errors, and their duration. The rate, errors, duration (RED) method is popular in the SRE world and focuses on instrumenting: request throughput, request error rate, latency, or response time.
- If you instrument your custom tracing spans, avoid using a lot of metadata.
- When searching for Java-compatible tracing solutions, look at the language-specific implementation of OpenTelemetry in Java (*https://oreil.ly/Df5RD*).

When designing systems for observability, remember that your metrics and logs should be available for a later analysis. As a consequence, regardless of where you deploy, always have tools and practices that can reliably capture and store metrics and logging data.

High Availability and Geographic Distribution

When working on a software system, you have probably received a nonfunctional requirement indicating that your application(s) should be available 24/7. In the industry literature, *availability* refers to the probability that a system is operational at a given time; this is expressed as a percentage of uptime in a given year.

High availability (HA) is the ability of a system to work continuously without failure for an established time. As developers, we create software with the intent to be always available for end users, but external factors like power outages, network failures, and underprovisioned environments can impact the quality of service received by consumers.

Small-size container images and successful deployments to Kubernetes are the first steps toward having an application available on Kubernetes. For example, let's assume you have to upgrade your worker nodes to a newer Kubernetes version. This operation includes that your nodes have to pull all the containers before working with the latest Kubernetes version. The longer it takes for each node to pull the containers, the lengthier it will be for the cluster to work as expected.

Different deployment strategies were explained in "Choose and Implement a Deployment Strategy" on page 219 because downtime, traffic routing between deployment versions, and the rollback process influence availability. In a failed deployment, a fast rollback process can save you from user discomfort, time, and compute resources. Moreover, you want your system to have a highly available state, and the way you define health checks and adjust resources for your containerized applications impacts its performance to work continuously without failure for an established time. Eventually, you can fine-tune your health checks, resource consumption, and deployments by observing your system's behavior through logs, metrics, and traces.

Availability is commonly defined as a percentage of uptime in a given year. Table 8-7 shows the connection between a given availability percentage to the corresponding amount of downtime per year. The table uses a year with 365 days, and for consistency, all times are rounded to two decimal digits.

Table 8-7. Connecting a certain availability percentage to downtime per year

Availability %	Downtime in a year
90%	36.5 days
95%	18.25 days
99%	3.65 days
99.9%	8.76 hours
99.95%	4.38 hours
99.99%	52.56 minutes
99.999%	5.25 minutes
99.9999%	31.53 seconds

Nowadays, service providers use service-level indicators (SLIs) to measure the goal set by a service-level objective (SLO). SLOs are the individual commitments made by the service provider to a customer. You can incorporate the percentages from Table 8-7 by setting a value for availability as part of the SLO. Tools like Prometheus (*https://prometheus.io*) and Grafana (*https://grafana.com*) can help you calculate the performance of your applications by incorporating the SLOs, querying metrics, and alerting when goals are endangered.

To create highly available systems, reliability engineering offers three principles of systems design:

- Eliminate single points of failure at the application, network, and infrastructure level. Because even the way you internally code your application can sometimes generate failures, you should properly test every software component. Observability and great deployment strategies help you eliminate the possible failures in your system.

- Detect failures as they occur. Monitoring and alerting help discover when a system reaches critical conditions.

- Have a reliable transition to a running component when a failure occurs to another one. An efficient rollback process in case of deployment issues, the

Kubernetes self-healing mechanism, and smooth traffic routing between Kubernetes resources help in this matter.

A good plan for failure involves following the preceding principles and implementing them using several best practices:

- Perform data backups, recovery, and replications.
- Set up network load balancing to distribute the traffic efficiently when increased workloads are received by the critical features of your applications. Load balancing helps you eliminate single points of failure at the application level while using the network and infrastructure available.
- When it comes to natural disasters that could affect your system, having it deployed in multiple geographical locations can prevent service failure. It is critical to run independent application stacks in each location so the others can continue running if a failure occurs in one place. Ideally, these locations should spread globally and not be localized in a specific area.
- If you are worried about a Kubernetes cluster performance when a component or its control-plane node goes down, you should choose to have highly available Kubernetes clusters (*https://oreil.ly/9iTgz*). Kubernetes high availability is about having a multiple control-plane setup behaving like a unified data center. A setup consisting of multiple control planes protects your system from losing a worker node to the failure of the control plane node's etcd. Managing Kubernetes clusters is not an easy task, but you should know that a wide range of cloud providers will share this type of configuration up-front when setting the clusters for you.
- Depending on your requirements, maintaining multiregion Kubernetes clusters can be unjustified. But you can still set up multiple namespaces to ensure availability across the same cluster.

Since one of the previous practices involved multiregional deployments, you should know that by using this technique, you can improve end-user experiences by keeping latencies low for a distributed user base. Your application architecture can achieve low latency because it would keep data close to end users distributed worldwide.

Another aspect to consider when having geographically distributed applications is the ability to comply with data privacy laws and regulations. As more and more social and economic activities occur online, the importance of privacy and data protection is increasingly recognized. In some countries, collection, usage, and sharing of personal information to different parties without notice or consent of consumers are considered illegal. According to United Nations Conference on Trade and Development (UNCTAD) (*https://oreil.ly/p0KH2*), 128 out of 194 countries have put in place legislation to secure the protection of data and privacy.

As you start to understand the requirements on your end to ensure the high availability of a distributed system, let's explore the cloud models that can help you achieve it.

Hybrid and MultiCloud Architectures

The *cloud* is a collection of technologies to approach challenges like availability, scaling, security, and resilience. It can exist on premises, on a Kubernetes distribution, or in a public infrastructure. Often, you will see the terms *hybrid cloud* and *multicloud* used synonymously. The most intuitive definition for a multicloud architecture is that this type of architecture requires at least one public cloud.

Hybrid cloud architecture differs from multicloud by including a private cloud infrastructure component and at least one public cloud (Figure 8-9). As a result, when a hybrid cloud architecture has more than one public offering, that architecture can be simultaneously a multicloud one.

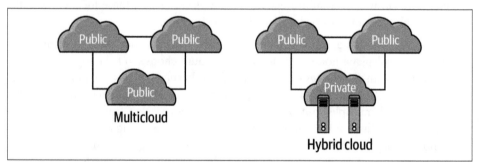

Figure 8-9. Multicloud and hybrid cloud

When deploying on hybrid or multicloud infrastructures, you should take into consideration these cross-team aspects:

- Having a unified view over what and where you deployed.
- Replacing provider-specific SaaS and IaaS services.
- Following a unified approach for mitigating security vulnerabilities across clouds.
- Scaling out and provisioning new resources seamlessly.
- When you port applications across clouds, you need to avoid disconnection of services. There is a time to recovery when moving workloads between infrastructures, but you can provide an end-user flawless transition using appropriate network configurations and deployment strategies.
- At such a large scale, automation helps when orchestrating processes. Besides, the orchestrations platform for containerized applications, you and your team will likely add an extra layer of tools and processes to manage workloads.

From a developer point of view, you can contribute to a hybrid or multicloud strategy by taking care of these elements:

- Your application's codebase should be the same regardless of the environment (namespace).
- Your local building and deployment practice should be reproducible when other colleagues attempt to work with your code.
- Avoid referencing local dependencies in your code or container image build.
- When possible, parameterize the container image through build-time variables or environment variables.
- If you need to support environment customizations, propagate them with environment variables from the orchestration platform toward container/application code parameters.
- Use dependencies and images from repositories and registries that your organization has previously validated as trusted sources.
- Prefer volumes to share information among containers.

When working toward a hybrid or multicloud architecture, always ask yourself how you and your colleagues will evolve the software piece you are currently building. A progressive software architecture starts with a forward-thinking developer mindset.

Summary

This chapter covered aspects of deployments that can concern a Java developer. Although the typical Java developer role does not involve infrastructure administration, you can influence the operational stages and processes of your application by doing the following:

- Building and pushing container images to container image registries by using Java-based tools like Jib and Eclipse JKube
- Generating and deploying Kubernetes manifests by using Dekorate and Eclipse JKube
- Implementing health checks and coordinating their execution at the infrastructure level
- Observing the behavior of the distributed system in order to know when to introduce changes and which resources to adjust
- Associating deployment aspects with high availability, hybrid, and multicloud architectures

Since you have a good understanding of deploying applications, the next chapter investigates DevOps workflows for mobile software.

## CHAPTER 9

Mobile Workflows

Stephen Chin

Program testing can be a very effective way to show the presence of bugs, but is hopelessly inadequate for showing their absence.
—Edsger Dijkstra

Coverage of DevOps wouldn't be complete without talking about mobile development and smartphones, which is the fastest growing segment of computer ownership. The past decade has seen a meteoric rise in smartphone usage, with billions of smartphones owned globally, as shown in Figure 9-1.

Smartphone ownership is expected to continue to rise since many large countries such as India and China have less than 70% ownership. With over 3.6 billion smartphones in the world today and an expected 4.3 billion smartphones by the year 2023, this is a market and user base that can't be ignored.

Smartphones also have another property that makes DevOps an essential practice: they fall into a class of internet-connected devices where continuous updates are expected by default, because they are targeted at consumers who are less technical and need to maintain their devices with minimal user involvement. This has been propelled by the app ecosystem built around smartphones, which makes downloading new software as well as receiving software updates easy and relatively low risk for end users.

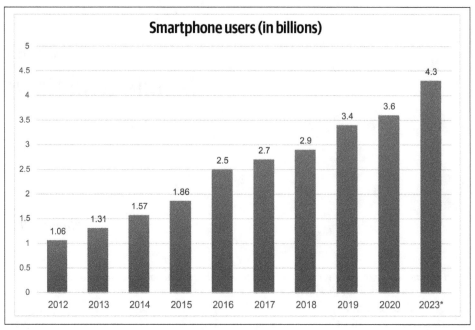

Figure 9-1. Number of smartphone users in the world from 2012 through 2023 according to Statista (https://oreil.ly/k8dk1) (prediction for 2023 marked with *)

You may want to update your app for several functional reasons:

Adding new features for users
> Most apps are released quickly and with a minimum viable set of features to reduce time to market. This allows for frequent small feature updates to add useful functionality for end users.

Fixing bugs and improving the stability of your application
> More mature applications have lots of updates that fix small bugs, stability issues, and user experience improvements. These changes are typically minor and can be released frequently.

Patching security vulnerabilities or exploits
> Mobile applications typically have a large attack surface that includes the locally installed app, the backend that supplies data, and user authentication workflows for app and cloud service logins.

In addition, a lot of app updates are driven by the need to increase market share and improve engagement with users. Some examples of updates that help to grow market share of your app include the following:

Aligning with major platform releases

Whenever a major platform release occurs, apps that are certified against the new version and updated to take advantage of new functionality will see an increase in downloads.

Raising visibility of your app in the store

App stores reward apps that frequently update by retaining user ratings between releases and highlighting new releases. The release notes also give you a chance to increase searchable content in the store. In contrast, if your app stagnates with no updates, it will naturally drop in search engine optimization.

Reminding current users about your application to increase utilization

Mobile platforms prompt users about updates to their existing apps and sometimes display badges or other reminders that will increase engagement.

The top applications in the app stores know the importance of continuous updates and update frequently. According to Appbot (*https://oreil.ly/CdW2A*), of the 200 top free apps, the median time since the last update was 7.8 days! With this pace of updates, if you do not use a continuous release process, you won't be able to keep up.

Java developers have great options for building mobile applications. These include mobile-focused web development with responsive web apps that adapt to constrained devices. Other options include dedicated mobile applications written in Java for Android devices. Finally, several cross-platform options for building applications work across Android and iOS devices, including Gluon Mobile and Electron.

This chapter focuses primarily on Android application development. However, all the same mobile DevOps techniques and considerations apply across these Java-based mobile platforms.

Fast-Paced DevOps Workflows for Mobile

Here are some of the business benefits you will realize from investing in mobile DevOps:

Better customer experience

With the easy and accessible rating systems available in the app store, customer experience is king. By being able to respond quickly to customer issues and test on a large variety of devices, you will ensure an optimal customer experience.

Faster innovation

By continuously releasing to production, you will be able to get new features and capabilities to your customers at a higher velocity than your competitors.

Higher software quality

With the large number and high fragmentation of Android devices, thoroughly testing your application manually is impossible. But with an automated mobile testing strategy that hits the key device characteristics of your user base, you will reduce the number of issues reported by end users.

Reduced risk

The majority of executable code in modern applications has open source dependencies that expose you to known security vulnerabilities. By having a mobile DevOps pipeline that allows you to test new versions of dependencies and update frequently, you will be able to quickly fix any known vulnerabilities in your application before they can be taken advantage of.

The same principles and best practices outlined in the rest of this book apply to mobile application development, but are amplified 10 times by the size and expectations of this market. When planning out a mobile DevOps pipeline for Android devices, here are the stages you need to consider:

1. Build.

   Android build scripts are usually written in Gradle. As a result, you can use any continuous integration server of your choice, including Jenkins, CircleCI, Travis CI, or JFrog Pipelines.

2. Test.

   Unit tests

   Android unit tests are typically written in JUnit, which can easily be automated. Higher-level Android unit tests are often written in some sort of UI test framework like Espresso, Appium, Calabash, or Robotium.

   Integration tests

   Besides testing your own application, it is important to test interactions between applications with tools like UI Automator that are focused on integration testing and can test across multiple Android applications.

   Functional tests

   Overall application verification is important. You can do this manually, but automated tools can simulate user input like the previously mentioned UI automation tools. Another option is to run robotic crawler tools like Google's App Crawler in order to inspect your application's user interface and automatically issue user actions.

3. Package.

   In the package step, you aggregate all of the scripts, configuration files, and binaries needed for deployment. By using a package management tool like

Artifactory, you retain all the build and test information and can easily track dependencies for traceability and debugging.

4. Release.

One of the best parts of mobile app development is that releasing mobile applications ends with the app store submission; the final deployment to devices is managed by the Google Play infrastructure. The challenging parts are that you have to prepare your build to make sure the app store submission is successful, and you'll be penalized for any mistakes in building, testing, and packaging by delays if you do not fully automate the submission process.

As you can see, the biggest difference in DevOps for Android development comes with testing. There is a lot of investment in UI test frameworks for Android apps, because automated testing is the only solution to the problem of testing across a highly fragmented device ecosystem. We will find out exactly how severe the Android device fragmentation is in the next section and talk about ways to mitigate this later in the chapter.

Android Device Fragmentation

The iOS ecosystem is tightly controlled by Apple, which limits the number of hardware models available, the variations in screen size, and the set of hardware sensors and features on its phones. Since 2007 when the first iPhone debuted, only 29 different devices have been produced, only 7 of which are currently sold.

In contrast, the Android ecosystem is open to a plethora of device manufacturers who customize everything from the screen size and resolution to the processor and hardware sensors, and even produce unique form factors like foldable screens. There are over 24,000 different devices from 1,300 different manufacturers, which is 1,000 times more fragmentation than for iOS devices. This makes testing for Android platforms much more difficult to execute.

When it comes to fragmentation, several key differences make it hard to uniformly test different Android devices:

Android version
Android device manufacturers do not always provide updates for older devices to the latest Android version, so users may be stuck on old Android OS versions until they buy a new device. The drop-off in use of old Android versions is gradual, with active devices still running Android 4.*x* releases that are more than seven years old, including Jelly Bean and KitKat.

Screen size and resolution

Android devices come in a wide array of form factors and hardware configurations, with a trend toward larger and more pixel-dense displays. A well-designed application needs to scale in order to work well across a range of screen sizes and resolutions.

3D support

Particularly for games, it is critical to know what level of 3D support you will get on devices, in terms of APIs and performance.

Hardware features

Most Android devices come with basic hardware sensors (camera, accelerometer, GPS), but support varies for newer hardware APIs such as near-field communication (NFC), barometers, magnetometers, proximity and pressure sensors, thermometers, and so on.

Android OS Fragmentation

Android version fragmentation affects device testing at two levels. The first is the major Android version, which determines the number of Android API versions you need to build for and test against. And the second is the OS customization done by original equipment manufacturers (OEMs) to support specific hardware configurations.

In the case of iOS, since Apple controls the hardware and the operating system, it is able to push out updates for all supported devices simultaneously. This keeps the adoption level of minor updates for performance and security fixes high. Apple also puts a lot of features and marketing into major releases to push the installed base to upgrade to the latest version quickly. As a result, Apple was able to achieve 86% adoption (*https://oreil.ly/3GYL8*) of iOS 14 only seven months after its initial release.

The Android market is significantly more complex since OEMs modify and test custom versions of Android OSs for their devices. In addition, they are reliant on system-on-a-chip (SoC) manufacturers to provide code updates for different hardware components. This means that devices created by major vendors are likely to receive only a couple of major OS version updates, and devices from smaller vendors may never see an OS upgrade even when they are under support.

To help you decide how far back you should support different Android OS versions, Google provides information in Android Studio on the device adoption by API level. The distribution of users as of August 2021 is shown in Figure 9-2. To achieve > 86% adoption comparable to the latest iOS version, you need to support at least Android 5.1 Lollipop, a release that came out in 2014. Even then you are still missing out on over 5% of users who are still using Android 4–based devices.

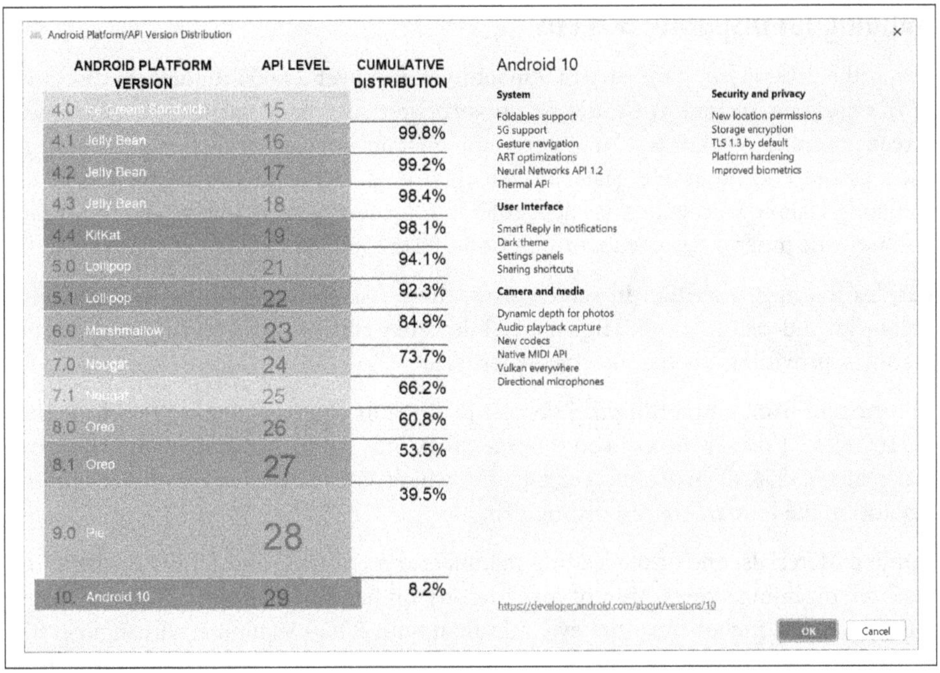

ANDROID PLATFORM VERSION	API LEVEL	CUMULATIVE DISTRIBUTION
4.0 Ice Cream Sandwich	15	
4.1 Jelly Bean	16	99.8%
4.2 Jelly Bean	17	99.2%
4.3 Jelly Bean	18	98.4%
4.4 KitKat	19	98.1%
5.0 Lollipop	21	94.1%
5.1 Lollipop	22	92.3%
6.0 Marshmallow	23	84.9%
7.0 Nougat	24	73.7%
7.1 Nougat	25	66.2%
8.0 Oreo	26	60.8%
8.1 Oreo	27	53.5%
9.0 Pie	28	39.5%
10. Android 10	29	8.2%

Android 10

System
Foldables support
5G support
Gesture navigation
ART optimizations
Neural Networks API 1.2
Thermal API

User Interface
Smart Reply in notifications
Dark theme
Settings panels
Sharing shortcuts

Camera and media
Dynamic depth for photos
Audio playback capture
New codecs
Native MIDI API
Vulkan everywhere
Directional microphones

Security and privacy
New location permissions
Storage encryption
TLS 1.3 by default
Platform hardening
Improved biometrics

https://developer.android.com/about/versions/10

OK   Cancel

Figure 9-2. Android Studio showing the distribution of users on different versions of the Android platform (Android 11 has < 1% adoption)

To further complicate the situation, every OEM modifies the Android OS it ships for its devices, so it is not enough to simply test one device per major Android version. This is a result of the way Android uses the Linux kernel to access hardware devices.

The Linux kernel is the heart of the operating system and provides the low-level device driver code to access cameras, accelerometers, the display, and other hardware on the device. To the Linux kernel that Android is based on, Google adds in Android-specific features and patches, SoC vendors add in hardware-specific support, and OEMs further modify it for their specific devices. Therefore, each device has a range of variation in performance, security, and potential bugs that could affect your application when a user runs it on a new device.

Google worked toward improving this situation with Android 8.0 Oreo, which includes a new hardware abstraction layer allowing device-specific code to run outside the kernel. This allows OEMs to update to new Android kernel versions from Google without waiting for device driver updates from SoC vendors, which reduces the amount of redevelopment and testing required for OS upgrades. However, other than Pixel devices that Google handles OS updates for, the majority of Android device upgrades are in the hands of OEMs, which are still slow to upgrade to new Android versions.

Building for Disparate Screens

Given the diversity in hardware manufacturers and over 24,000 models, as discussed in the previous section, it should be no surprise that a huge variation also exists in screen sizes and resolutions. New screen dimensions are constantly being introduced, such as the enormous HP Slate 21, which uses a 21.5-inch touchscreen, and the Samsung Galaxy Fold with a vertical 1680 × 720 cover display that opens to reveal a double-wide inner display with a resolution of 2152 × 1536.

Besides the huge variation in screen sizes, there is a constant battle over achieving higher pixel density as well. Higher pixel densities allow for clearer text and sharper graphics, providing a better viewing experience.

The current front-runner in pixel density is the Sony Xperia XZ, which packs a 3840 × 2160 UHS-1 display in a screen that measures only 5.2 inches diagonally. This gives a density of 806.93 pixels per inch (PPI), which is getting close to the maximum resolution the human eye can distinguish.

Applied Materials, one of the leading manufacturers of LCD and OLED displays, did research on human perception of pixel density on handheld displays. It found that at a distance of 4 inches from the eye, a human with 20/20 vision can distinguish 876 PPI (*https://oreil.ly/OecRt*). Therefore, smartphone displays are quickly approaching the theoretical limit on pixel density; however, other form factors like virtual reality headsets may drive the density even further.

To handle variation in pixel densities, Android categorizes screens into the following pixel density ranges:

ldpi, ~120 dpi (.75x scale)
Used on a limited number of very low-resolution devices like the HTC Tattoo, Motorola Flipout, and Sony X10 Mini, all of which have a screen resolution of 240 × 320 pixels.

mdpi, ~160 dpi (1x scale)
This is the original screen resolution for Android devices such as the HTC Hero and Motorola Droid.

tvdpi, ~213 dpi (1.33x scale)
Resolution intended for televisions such as the Google Nexus 7, but not considered a "primary" density group.

hdpi, ~240 dpi (1.5x scale)
The second generation of phones such as the HTC Nexus One and Samsung Galaxy Ace increased resolution by 50%.

xhdpi, ~320 dpi (2x scale)
One of the first phones to use this 2x resolution was the Sony Xperia S, followed by phones like the Samsung Galaxy S III and HTC One.

xxhdpi, ~480 dpi (3x scale)
The first xxhdpi device was the Nexus 10 by Google, which was only 300 dpi but needed large icons since it was in tablet form.

xxxhdpi, ~640 dpi (4x scale)
This is currently the highest resolution used by devices like the Nexus 6 and Samsung Galaxy S6 Edge.

As displays continue to increase in pixel density, Google probably wishes it had chosen a better convention for high-resolution displays than just adding more *x*s!

To give the best user experience for your end users, it is important to have your application look and behave consistently across the full range of available resolutions. Given the wide variety of screen resolutions, it is not enough to simply hardcode your application for each resolution.

Here are some best practices to make sure that your application will work across the full range of resolutions:

- Always use density-independent and scalable pixels:

  Density-independent pixels (dp)
  Pixel unit that adjusts based on the resolution of the device. For an mdpi screen, 1 pixel (px) = 1 dp. For other screen resolutions, px = dp × (dpi / 160).

  Scalable pixels (sp)
  Scalable pixel unit used for text or other user-resizable elements. This starts at 1 sp = 1 dp and adjusts based on the user-defined text zoom value.

- Provide alternate bitmaps for all available resolutions:

  — Android allows you to provide alternate bitmaps for different resolutions by putting them in subfolders named *drawable-?dpi*, where *?dpi* is one of the supported density ranges.

  — The same applies for your app icon, except you should use subfolders named *mipmap-?dpi* so the resources aren't removed when you build density-specific APKs, because app icons are often upscaled beyond the device resolution.

- Better yet, use vector graphics whenever possible:
  — Android Studio provides a tool called Vector Asset Studio that allows you to convert an SVG or PSD into an Android Vector file that can be used as a resource in your application, as shown in Figure 9-3.

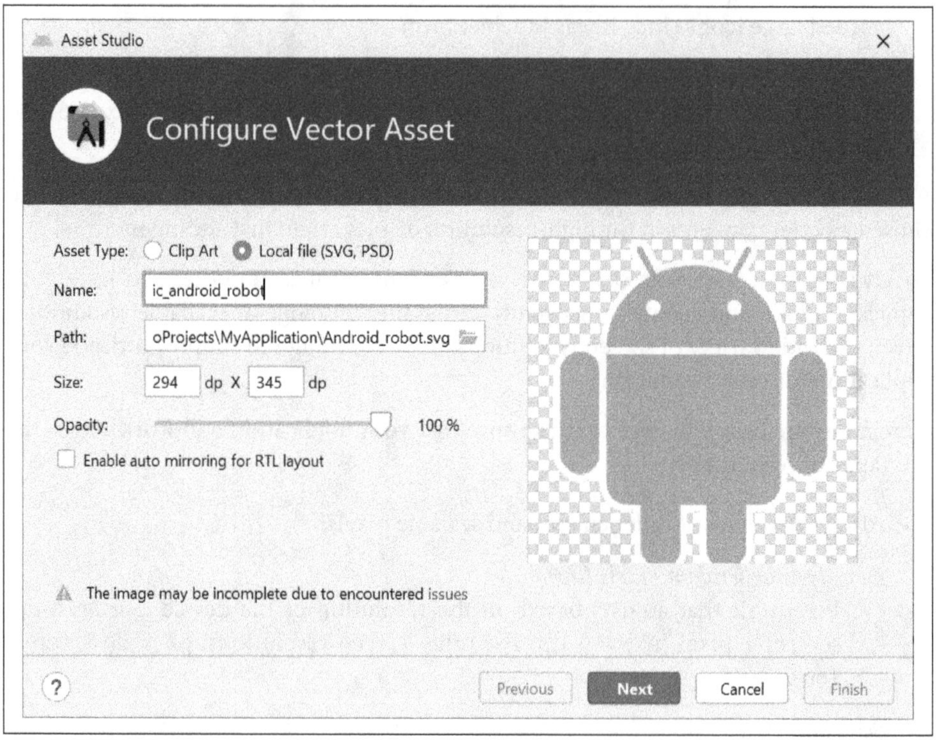

Figure 9-3. Conversion of an SVG file to an Android Vector format

Building applications that cleanly scale to different screen sizes and resolutions is complicated to get right and needs to be tested on devices with differing resolutions. To help focus your testing efforts, Google provides user-mined data (*https://oreil.ly/ Aqw18*) on the usage of different device resolutions, as shown in Table 9-1.

Table 9-1. Android screen size and density distribution

	ldpi	mdpi	tvdpi	hdpi	xdpi	xxhdpi	Total
Small	0.1%				0.1%		0.2%
Normal		0.3%	0.3%	14.8%	41.3%	26.1%	82.8%
Large		1.7%	2.2%	0.8%	3.2%	2.0%	9.9%
Xlarge		4.2%	0.2%	2.3%	0.4%		7.1%
Total	0.1%	6.2%	2.7%	17.9%	45.0%	28.1%	

As you can see, some resolutions are not prevalent and, unless your application targets these users or legacy device types, you can prune them from your device-testing matrix. The ldpi density is used on only a small segment of Android devices and with only 0.1% market share—few applications are optimized for this very small resolution screen. Also, tvdpi is a niche screen resolution with only 2.7% usage and can be safely ignored since Android will automatically downscale hdpi assets in order to fit this screen resolution.

This still leaves you with five device densities to support and a potentially innumerable number of screen resolutions and aspect ratios to test. I discuss testing strategies later, but you will likely be using a mix of emulated devices and physical devices to make sure that you provide the best user experience across the fragmented Android ecosystem.

Hardware and 3D Support

The very first Android device was the HTC Dream (a.k.a. T-Mobile G1), shown in Figure 9-4. It had a medium density touchscreen of 320 × 480 px, a hardware keyboard, speaker, microphone, five buttons, a clickable trackball, and a rear-mounted camera. While primitive by modern smartphone standards, it was a great platform to launch Android, which lacked support for software keyboards at the time.

Compared to modern smartphone standards, this was a modest hardware set. The Qualcomm MSM7201A processor that drove the HTC Dream was a 528 MHz Arm11 processor with support for only OpenGL ES 1.1. In comparison, the Samsung Galaxy S21 Ultra 5G sports a 3200 × 1440 resolution screen with the following sensors:

- 2.9 GHz 8-core processor
- Arm Mali-G78 MP14 GPU with support for Vulkan 1.1, OpenGL ES 3.2, and OpenCL 2.0
- Five cameras (one front, four rear)
- Three microphones (one bottom, two top)
- Stereo speakers
- Ultrasonic fingerprint reader
- Accelerometer
- Barometer
- Gyro sensor (gyroscope)
- Geomagnetic sensor (magnetometer)
- Hall sensor
- Proximity sensor

- Ambient light sensor
- NFC

Figure 9-4. The T-Mobile G1 (a.k.a. HTC Dream), which was the first smartphone (https://oreil.ly/ijUOh) to run the Android operating system (photo used under Creative Commons license (https://oreil.ly/GLSPZ))

The flagship Samsung phones are at the high end of the spectrum when it comes to hardware support, and include almost all of the supported sensor types. Phones meant for mass market may choose to use less powerful chipsets and leave off sensors to reduce cost. Android uses the data from the available physical sensors to also create "virtual" sensors in software that are used by applications:

Game rotation vector
Combination of data from the accelerometer and gyroscope

Gravity
Combination of data from the accelerometer and gyroscope (or magnetometer if no gyroscope is present)

Geomagnetic rotational vector
Combination of data from the accelerometer and magnetometer

Linear acceleration
> Combination of data from the accelerometer and gyroscope (or magnetometer if no gyroscope is present)

Rotation vector
> Combination of data from the accelerometer, magnetometer, and gyroscope

Significant motion
> Data from the accelerometer (and possibly substitutes other sensor data when in low-power mode)

Step detector/counter
> Data from the accelerometer (and possibly substitutes other sensor data when in low-power mode)

These virtual sensors are available only if a sufficient set of physical sensors is present. Most phones contain an accelerometer, but may choose to omit either a gyroscope or magnetometer or both, reducing the precision of motion detection and disabling certain virtual sensors.

Hardware sensors can be emulated, but it is much harder to simulate real-world conditions for testing. Also, much more variation occurs in hardware chipset and SoC vendor-driver implementation, producing a huge test matrix required to verify your application across a range of devices.

The other aspect of hardware that is particularly important for game developers, but increasingly is part of the basic graphics stack and expected performance of applications, is 3D API support. Almost all mobile processors support some basic 3D APIs, including the first Android phone, which had support for OpenGL ES 1.1, a mobile-specific version of the OpenGL 3D standard. Modern phones support later versions of the OpenGL ES standard, including OpenGL ES 2.0, 3.0, 3.1, and now 3.2.

OpenGL ES 2.0 introduced a dramatic shift in the programming model, switching from a functional pipeline to a programmable pipeline, allowing for more direct control to create complex effects through the use of shaders. OpenGL ES 3.0 further increased the performance and hardware independence of 3D graphics by supporting features like vertex array objects, instanced rendering, and device-independent compression formats (ETC2/EAC).

OpenGL ES adoption has been rather quick, with all modern devices supporting at least OpenGL ES 2.0. According to Google's device data shown in Figure 9-5, the majority of devices (67.54%) support OpenGL ES 3.2, the latest version of the standard released in August 2015.

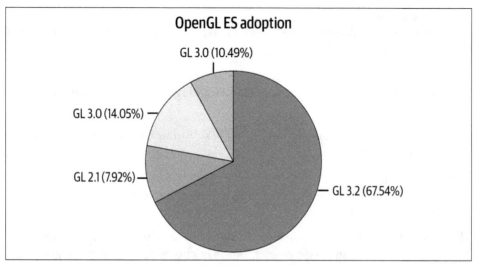

Figure 9-5. Percentage of Android devices adopting different versions of OpenGL ES from Google's Distribution Dashboard (https://oreil.ly/18xDQ)

Vulkan is a newer graphics API that modern graphics chipsets support. It has the advantage of being portable between desktop and mobile devices, allowing for easier porting of desktop code as computing platforms continue to converge. Also, it allows an even finer level of control over threads and memory management, and an asynchronous API for buffering and sequencing commands across multiple threads, making better use of multicore processors and high-end hardware.

Since Vulkan is a newer API, adoption has not been as quick as OpenGL ES; however, 64% of Android devices have some level of Vulkan support. According to Google's device statistics visualized in Figure 9-6, this is split between Vulkan 1.1, which is supported by 42% of devices, and the remaining 22% of devices that support only the Vulkan 1.0.3 API level.

Similar to hardware sensor testing, a large variety of 3D chipsets are implemented by different manufacturers. Therefore, the only way to reliably test for bugs and performance issues in your application is to execute device testing on different phone models, covered in the next section.

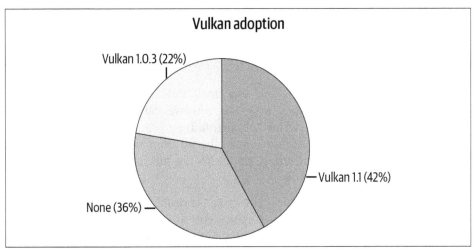

Figure 9-6. Percentage of Android devices adopting different versions of Vulkan from Google's Distribution Dashboard (https://oreil.ly/K9FZd)

Continuous Testing on Parallel Devices

The preceding section discussed the large amount of fragmentation in the Android device ecosystem. This is forced by technological factors like the Android OS architecture as well as the complex ecosystem of OEMs and SoC vendors. Also, the sheer popularity of the Android platform, with 1,300 manufacturers producing over 24,000 devices, creates a continuous testing and deployment challenge.

Device emulators are great for development and basic testing of applications, but cannot possibly simulate the complex interactions of unique hardware configurations, device drivers, custom kernels, and real-world sensor behavior. Therefore, a high level of manual and automated testing on devices is required to ensure a good experience for end users.

Two basic approaches are used for hardware testing at scale. The first is to build out your own device lab with shared devices. This is a practical approach to get started with testing, since you likely have a large collection of Android devices available that could be put to better use with proper infrastructure and automation. However, depending on the number of device configurations you want to support, this can be quite a large and expensive endeavor. Also, the ongoing maintenance and upkeep for a large device farm can be costly in both materials and labor.

The second option is to outsource your device testing to a cloud service. Given the advances in remote control of Android devices and stability of the platform, it is convenient to be able to select your matrix of devices and have your automated tests fired off in the cloud. Most cloud services offer detailed screenshots and diagnostic logs that can be used to trace build failures as well as the ability to manually control a device for debugging purposes.

Building a Device Farm

Building your own device farm, even at a small scale, is a great way to leverage Android devices that you already have and increase their utility for your entire organization. At scale, device farms can significantly reduce the run rate cost of Android development once you have made the up-front investment in hardware. Keep in mind, though, that running a large device lab is a full-time job and has ongoing costs that need to be accounted for.

A popular open source library for managing Android devices is Device Farmer (formerly Open STF). Device Farmer allows you to remotely control an Android device from your web browser with a real-time view of the device screen, as shown in Figure 9-7. For manual tests, you can type from your desktop keyboard and use your mouse to input single or multitouch gestures. For automated tests, a REST API allows you to use test automation frameworks like Appium.

Figure 9-7. Device Farmer user interface (https://oreil.ly/2MQpN) (photo used under Creative Commons (https://oreil.ly/bPhIL))

Device Farmer also helps you manage your inventory of devices. It shows you which devices are connected, who is using each device, and the hardware spec for your devices, and it assists with physically locating devices in a large lab.

Finally, Device Farmer also has a system for booking and partitioning groups of devices. You can split your device inventory into distinct groups that have owners and associated properties. These groups can then be permanently allocated to projects or organizations or they can be booked for a specific time period.

To set up a device lab, you also need hardware to support the devices. The basic hardware setup includes the following:

Driver computer
Even though Device Farmer can run on any operating system, it is recommended to run it on a Linux-based host for ease of administration and the best stability. A good option for getting started with this is a compact, but powerful, computer like the Intel NUC.

USB hub
Both for device connectivity and to supply stable power, a powered USB hub is recommended. Getting a reliable USB hub is important since this will affect the stability of your lab.

Wireless router
The devices will get their network connectivity from a wireless router, so this is an important part of the device setup. Having a dedicated network for your devices will increase reliability and reduce contention with other devices on your network.

Android devices
And the most important part, of course, is having plenty of Android devices to test against. Start with devices that are the most common and popular with your target user base and add devices to hit the desired test matrix of Android OS versions, screen sizes, and hardware support as discussed in the previous section.

Plenty of cables
You will need longer cables than usual for efficient cable management of devices to the USB hub. It is important to leave enough space between individual devices and hardware components to avoid overheating.

With a little bit of work, you will be able to create a fully automated device lab similar to Figure 9-8, which was the world's first conference device lab featured at the beyond tellerrand conference in Düsseldorf, Germany.

Figure 9-8. Open device lab (https://oreil.ly/QgEr9) at the beyond tellerrand conference in Düsseldorf, Germany (photo used under Creative Commons (https://oreil.ly/Xv18U))

Device Farmer is split into microservices to allow for scalability of the platform to thousands of devices. Out of the box, it easily supports 15 devices, after which you will run into port limitations with Android Debug Bridge (ADB). This can be scaled out by running multiple instances of the Device Farmer ADB and Provider services up to the limit of the number of USB devices that your machine can support. For Intel architectures, this is 96 endpoints (including other peripherals), and for AMD, you can get up to 254 USB endpoints. By using multiple Device Farmer servers, you can scale into the thousands of devices, which should be enough to support mobile testing and verification of enterprise Android applications.

One example of a large-scale mobile device lab is Facebook's mobile device lab at its Prineville, Oregon, data center, shown in Figure 9-9. The company built a customer server rack enclosure for holding mobile devices that is deigned to block WiFi signals to prevent interference among devices in the data center. Each enclosure can support 32 devices and is powered by 4 OCP Leopard servers that connect to the devices. This provides a stable and scalable hardware setup that allowed the company to reach its target device farm size of 2,000 devices.

Figure 9-9. The Facebook mobile device lab in its Prineville data center (photo by Antoine Reversat (https://oreil.ly/fbj35))

Running a large-scale device lab has challenges:

Device maintenance
Android devices are not meant to be run 24/7 for automated testing. As a result, you are likely to experience higher than normal device failure and have to replace batteries or entire devices every year or two. Spacing out devices and keeping them well cooled will help with this.

WiFi interference/connectivity
WiFi networks, especially consumer-targeted WiFi routers, are not highly stable, especially with a large number of devices. Reducing the broadcast signal power of the WiFi routers and making sure they are on noncompeting network bands can reduce interference.

Cable routing
Running cables among all the devices and the USB hubs or computers can create a tangled mess. Besides being hard to maintain, this can also cause connectivity and charging issues. Make sure to remove all loops in the cables and use shielded cables and ferrite cores as necessary to reduce electromagnetic interference.

Device reliability
Running a device lab on consumer devices comes with the general risk that consumer devices are not reliable. Limiting automated test runs to a finite

duration will help prevent tests from becoming blocked on nonresponsive devices. Between tests, some housekeeping to remove data and free memory will help with performance and reliability. Finally, the Android devices as well as the servers running them will need to be rebooted periodically.

 Starting on a small scale with devices you already own is easy and can improve the ability to test across a range of devices and fire off automated tests in parallel. At a large scale, this is an effective solution to solving testing across the fragmented Android ecosystem, but comes with high up-front costs and ongoing support and maintenance.

The next section talks about device labs that you can get started with today on a simple pay-as-you-go basis.

Mobile Pipelines in the Cloud

If the prospect of building your own device lab seems daunting, an easy and inexpensive way to get started with testing across a large range of devices is to use a device farm running on public cloud infrastructure. Mobile device clouds have the advantage of being easy to get started with and maintenance free for the end user. You simply select the devices you want to run tests on, and fire off either manual or automated tests of your application against a pool of devices.

Some mobile device clouds also support automated robot tests that will attempt to exercise all the visible UI elements of your application to identify performance or stability issues with your application. Once tests are run, you get a full report of any failures, device logs for debugging, and screenshots for tracing issues.

Many mobile device clouds are available, with some dating back to the feature phone era. However, the most popular and modern device clouds have ended up aligning with the top three cloud providers—Amazon, Google, and Microsoft. They all have sizable investments in mobile test infrastructure that you can try for a reasonable price and have a large range of emulated and real devices to test against.

AWS device farm

Amazon offers a mobile device cloud as part of its public cloud services. Using AWS Device Farm, you can run automated tests on a variety of real-world devices by using your AWS account.

The steps to create a new AWS Device Farm test are as follows:

1. *Upload your APK file*: To start, upload your compiled APK file or choose from recently updated files.

2. *Configure your test automation*: AWS Device Farm supports a variety of test frameworks, including Appium tests (written in Java, Python, Node.js, or Ruby), Calabash, Espresso, Robotium, or UI Automator. If you don't have automated tests, AWS provides two robot app testers called Fuzz and Explorer.

3. *Select devices to run on*: Pick the devices that you want to run your test on from a user-created pool of devices or the default pool of the five most popular devices, as shown in Figure 9-10.

4. *Set up the device state*: To set up the device before starting the tests, you can specify data or other dependent apps to install, set the radio states (WiFi, Bluetooth, GPS, and NFC), change the GPS coordinates, change the locale, and set up a network profile.

5. *Run your test*: Finally, you can run your test on the selected devices with a specified execution time-out of up to 150 minutes per device. If your tests execute more quickly, this can finish earlier, but this also sets a maximum cap on the cost of your test run.

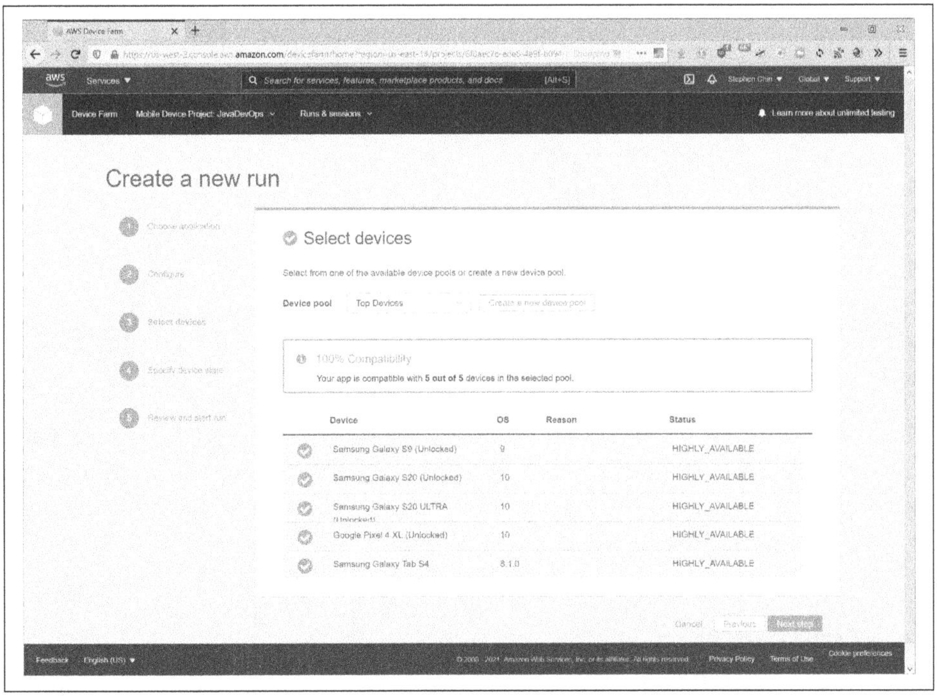

Figure 9-10. Selecting devices to run on in the AWS Device Farm wizard

AWS Device Farm offer a free quota for individual developers to get started with test automation, low per-minute pricing for additional device testing, and monthly plans to do parallel testing on multiple devices at once. All of these plans operate on a shared pool of devices, which at the time of writing included 91 total devices, 54 of which were Android devices, as shown in Figure 9-11. However, most of these devices were highly available, indicating that they had a large number of identical devices to test against. This means that you are less likely to get blocked in a queue or have a device you need to test against become unavailable.

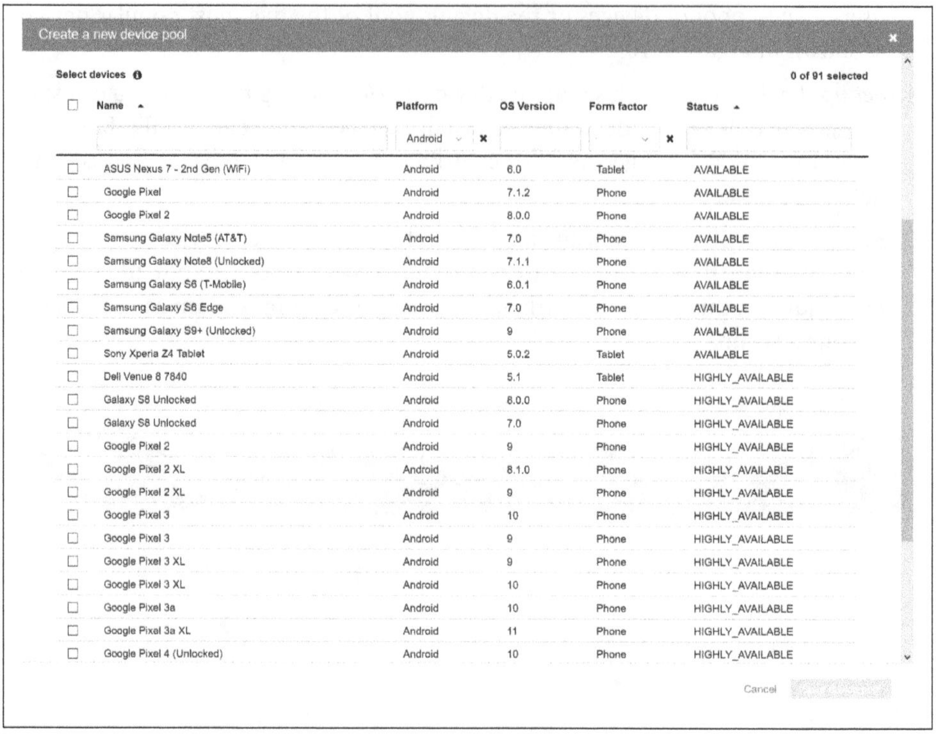

Name	Platform	OS Version	Form factor	Status
	Android			
ASUS Nexus 7 - 2nd Gen (WiFi)	Android	6.0	Tablet	AVAILABLE
Google Pixel	Android	7.1.2	Phone	AVAILABLE
Google Pixel 2	Android	8.0.0	Phone	AVAILABLE
Samsung Galaxy Note5 (AT&T)	Android	7.0	Phone	AVAILABLE
Samsung Galaxy Note8 (Unlocked)	Android	7.1.1	Phone	AVAILABLE
Samsung Galaxy S6 (T-Mobile)	Android	6.0.1	Phone	AVAILABLE
Samsung Galaxy S6 Edge	Android	7.0	Phone	AVAILABLE
Samsung Galaxy S9+ (Unlocked)	Android	9	Phone	AVAILABLE
Sony Xperia Z4 Tablet	Android	5.0.2	Tablet	AVAILABLE
Dell Venue 8 7840	Android	5.1	Tablet	HIGHLY_AVAILABLE
Galaxy S8 Unlocked	Android	8.0.0	Phone	HIGHLY_AVAILABLE
Galaxy S8 Unlocked	Android	7.0	Phone	HIGHLY_AVAILABLE
Google Pixel 2	Android	9	Phone	HIGHLY_AVAILABLE
Google Pixel 2 XL	Android	8.1.0	Phone	HIGHLY_AVAILABLE
Google Pixel 2 XL	Android	9	Phone	HIGHLY_AVAILABLE
Google Pixel 3	Android	10	Phone	HIGHLY_AVAILABLE
Google Pixel 3	Android	9	Phone	HIGHLY_AVAILABLE
Google Pixel 3 XL	Android	9	Phone	HIGHLY_AVAILABLE
Google Pixel 3 XL	Android	10	Phone	HIGHLY_AVAILABLE
Google Pixel 3a	Android	10	Phone	HIGHLY_AVAILABLE
Google Pixel 3a XL	Android	11	Phone	HIGHLY_AVAILABLE
Google Pixel 4 (Unlocked)	Android	10	Phone	HIGHLY_AVAILABLE

Figure 9-11. List of available devices in the AWS Device Farm

Finally, AWS Device Farm offers a couple of integrations to run automated tests. From within Android Studio, you can run tests on the AWS Device Farm by using its Gradle plug-in. If you want to launch AWS Device Farm tests from your continuous integration system, Amazon offers a Jenkins plug-in that you can use to start device tests right after your local build and test automation completes.

Google Firebase Test Lab

After Google's acquisition of Firebase, it has been continually expanding and improving the offering. Firebase Test Lab is its mobile device-testing platform that provides similar functionality to AWS Device Farm. To get started, Google offers a free quota for developers to run a limited number of tests per day. Beyond that, you can upgrade to a pay-as-you-go plan with a flat fee per device hour.

Firebase Test Lab offers several ways you can fire off tests on the service:

Android Studio

Firebase Test Lab is integrated in Android Studio and allows you to run tests in its mobile device cloud just as easily as you would on local devices.

Firebase Web UI

From the Firebase web console, you can upload your APK and will start by running your first app in an automated Robo test, as shown in Figure 9-12. In addition, you can run your own automated tests using Espresso, Robotium, or UI Automator. Game developers have the option to run an integrated game loop that simulates user scenarios.

Automated command-line scripts

You can easily integrate Firebase Test Lab into your CI system by using its command-line API. This allows you to integrate with Jenkins, CircleCI, JFrog Pipelines, or your favorite CI/CD system.

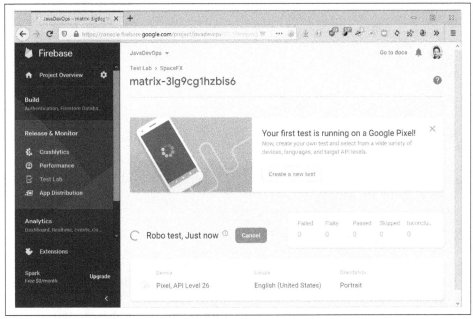

Figure 9-12. Firebase web user interface running an automated Robo test

At the time of writing, Firebase Test Lab offered a larger collection of Android devices than AWS Device Farm, with 109 devices supported, as well as multiple API levels for popular devices. Given the tight integration with Google's Android tooling and the generous free quota for individuals, this is an easy way to get your development team started building test automation.

Microsoft Visual Studio App Center

Microsoft Visual Studio App Center, formerly Xamarin Test Cloud, offers the most impressive device list of any of the clouds, with 349 Android device types for you to run tests on, as shown in Figure 9-13. However, unlike AWS Device Farm and Firebase Test Lab, no free tier exists for developers to use the service. Microsoft does offer a 30-day trial on its service to use a single physical device to run tests, and paid plans where you pay by the number of concurrent devices you want to use, which makes sense for large enterprises.

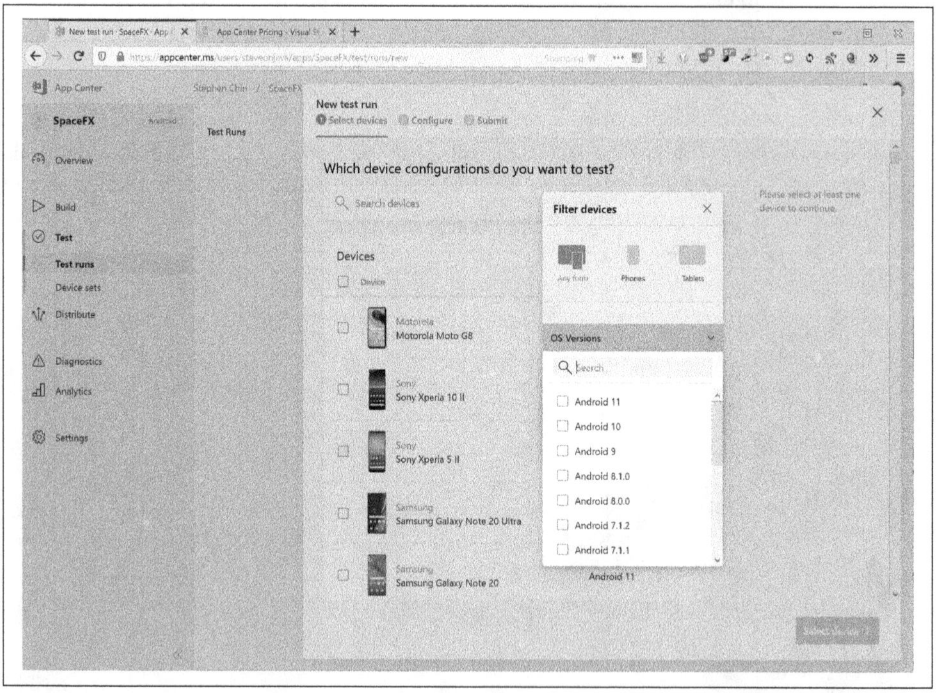

Figure 9-13. Visual Studio App Center device selection screen

Visual Studio App Center also is missing some of the user-friendly features like a robot tester and simple test execution via the web console. Instead, it focuses on the command-line integration with the App Center CLI. From the App Center CLI, you can easily fire off automated tests using Appium, Calabash, Espresso, or XamarainUITest. Also, this makes integration with CI/CD tools straightforward.

Overall, Visual Studio App Center wins on device coverage and has a clear focus on enterprise mobile device testing. However, for independent developers or smaller teams, it is less approachable and has higher up-front costs, but it will work well as you scale.

Planning a Device-Testing Strategy

Now that you've seen the basics of setting up your own device lab and leveraging cloud infrastructure, you should have a better idea of how these map to your mobile device-testing needs.

These are advantages of going with a cloud service:

Low startup costs
> Cloud plans often offer a limited number of free device tests for developers and utilization-based pricing for testing on devices. When starting out with device testing, this is the easiest and least costly way to begin exploring manual and automated device testing.

Large selection of devices
> Since cloud testing providers support a large installed base of customers, they have a huge inventory of current and legacy phones to test against. This makes it possible to precisely target the device types, profiles, and configurations that your users are most likely to have.

Fast scale-out
> App development is all about viral marketing and scaling quickly. Rather than investing in costly infrastructure up front, cloud services allow you to scale up the testing as the size and popularity of your application requires a larger device test matrix.

Reduced capital expenditures
> Building a large device lab is a costly up-front capital expenditure. By paying as you go for cloud infrastructure, you can delay the costs, maximizing your capital efficiency.

Global access
> With remote and distributed teams becoming the norm, clouds by design allow for easy access from your entire team, no matter where they are located.

However, even given all of these benefits, the traditional approach of building a device lab has unique advantages. Here are some reasons you may want to build your own device lab:

Reduced cost at scale
> The total cost of ownership for a device lab that you run and maintain at scale is much lower than the total monthly costs from a cloud provider over the device's usable lifetime. For a small team, this threshold is hard to hit, but if you are a large mobile corporation, this can be significant savings.

Fast and predictable cycle time

With control over the device farm, you can guarantee that the tests will run in parallel and complete in a predictable time frame to enable responsive builds. Cloud providers have limited device availability and queued wait times for popular configurations that can limit your ability to iterate quickly.

No session limits

Device clouds typically put hardcoded session limits on their service to prevent tests from hanging because of test or device failure. As the complexity of your test suite grows, a 30-minute hard limit can become an obstacle to completing testing of a complex user flow.

Regulatory requirements

In certain regulated industries such as finance and defense, security requirements can restrict or prohibit the ability to deploy applications and execute tests outside the corporate firewall. This class of corporations would require an on-premises device lab setup.

IoT device integration

If your use case requires the integration of mobile devices with IoT devices and sensors, this is not a configuration that cloud providers would provide as a service out of the box. You are probably better off creating a device lab with the IoT and mobile configuration that best matches your real-world scenario.

In some scenarios, it also makes sense to do a mix of both cloud testing and local device lab testing. Based on your specific requirements for cycle time, maintenance cost, device scale-out, and regulatory requirements, this can allow you to get the best of both approaches to testing.

Summary

Android is the most popular mobile platform on the planet, because of its huge ecosystem of manufacturers and application developers. However, this is also the challenge with Android development: an incredibly fragmented device market with thousands of manufacturers producing tens of thousands of devices. Given this scale of fragmentation and device inconsistency, having a fully automated DevOps pipeline for mobile development is a necessity for success.

The equivalent to DevOps for web application development would be if, instead of three major browsers, there were thousands of unique browser types. You would be forced to automate to obtain any level of quality assurance, which is exactly why there is so much focus in the mobile space on UI test automation running on real devices.

Using the tools and techniques you learned in this chapter, paired with the overall DevOps knowledge on source control, build promotion, and security, you should be ahead of your mobile DevOps peers to face the challenge of continuous deployments to millions of devices globally.

## CHAPTER 10

Continuous Deployment Patterns and Antipatterns

Stephen Chin
Baruch Sadogursky

Learn from the mistakes of others. You can't live long enough to make them all yourself.
—Eleanor Roosevelt

In this chapter, we will give you the patterns for continuous deployment that you need to be successful with implementing DevOps best practices in your organization. It is important to understand the rationale for continuous updates to be able to convince others in your organization about the change needed to improve your deployment process.

We will also give you plenty of antipatterns from companies that have failed to adopt continuous update best practices. It is good to learn from the failures of others, and plenty of recent examples exist in the high technology industry of what not to do and the consequences of ignoring best practices.

After completing this chapter, you will be armed with knowledge of seven best practices of continuous updates that you can start using today in order to join the top 26% of DevOps "Elite Performers" of the software industry (*https://oreil.ly/9MMwZ*).

Why Everyone Needs Continuous Updates

Continuous updates are no longer an optional part of a software development but are a best practice to be adopted by any major project. Planning for continuous delivery of updates is just as important as the functional requirements of the project and requires a high level of automation to execute on reliably.

It was not always this way. Historically, software was delivered on a much lower cadence and received only critical updates. Also, installation of updates was often a manual and error-prone process that involved tweaking of scripts, data migration, and significant downtime.

This has all changed in the past decade. Now end users expect new features to be added constantly, which is driven by their experience with consumer devices and continuously updated applications. Also, the business risk associated with deferring critical updates is significant, as security researchers constantly uncover new exploits that can be used to compromise your system unless it is patched. Finally, continually updated software has become a business expectation in the cloud age, as the entire infrastructure stack is constantly being updated to improve security, often with the requirement that you also update your application.

Not all software projects have been as quick to adopt continuous update strategies, especially in industries that are used to longer technology adoption cycles. However, the widespread use of common hardware architectures and open source technologies means that these projects are at an equal risk of exposure from critical vulnerabilities. When exposed, this can lead to catastrophic failures that are difficult or impossible to recover from. Like any other software, open source projects have bugs and security vulnerabilities, and those are fixed and patched faster than in proprietary projects, but if the organization won't update, what good will the patches do?

In the next few sections, we will dig into the motivation for continuous updates in more detail. If you do not already have a continuous update strategy, the material in this chapter will help you convince others in your organization to adopt one. If you have already embraced continuous updates, you will be armed with knowledge to reap the business benefits of having infrastructure and DevOps processes superior to those of your competitors.

User Expectations on Continuous Updates

The expectations of end users on release cadence of new features has dramatically shifted in the last decade. This is driven by a change in the way features and updates are delivered on consumer devices, but translates to similar expectations on other software platforms, even in the enterprise. Forcing users to wait for a long release cycle or to perform a costly migration to take advantage of new features will result in dissatisfied users and put you at a competitive disadvantage.

This change in user expectations can be seen in several consumer industries, including cell phones. When mobile communication first started to gain popularity, Nokia was one of the dominant hardware manufacturers of 2G cell phones. While primitive by today's standards, the phones had excellent hardware design with good voice quality, tactile buttons, and rugged design.

Small-form-factor mobile devices such as the Nokia 6110 accelerated adoption of cellular technology, but the software on these devices and users' ability to update them were extremely poor. This was a common problem with early consumer device companies in that they considered themselves hardware companies first and were slow to adopt modern practices in software development.

Like many emerging technologies, the software shipped with Nokia phones was bare-bones and buggy, requiring patches and updates to remain usable. While Nokia offered a data cable, this was limited to basic operations like transferring contacts from the device to a computer, but didn't allow maintenance features such as performing firmware updates. To get a feature update on your phone that contained important patches and mission-critical features (like the Snake game), you would need to take your phone into a service center to update your device.

It wasn't until the iPhone came out in 2007 that the phone industry took a software-first approach to mobile phone design. With the ability to update the firmware and entire operating system from an attached computer and later over-the-air updates, Apple could rapidly deploy new features to existing devices.

In 2008, Apple announced the App Store, which created a vibrant app ecosystem and laid the foundation for modern store features like security sandboxing and automatic application updates, which we will come back to later in this chapter with a longer case study. With the release of iOS 5 in 2011, Apple embraced over-the-air updates; you no longer even needed a computer to install the latest version of the operating system.

Now the process of updating software on your phone is seamless and automated to the point where most consumers have no idea which version of the operating system or individual applications they are running. As an industry, we have trained the general public that continuous updates are not only expected, but required for functionality, productivity, and security.

This model of continuous updates has become the norm for consumer devices of all types, including smart TVs, home assistants, and even newer self-updating routers. While the car industry has been slow to adopt a continuous update strategy, Tesla is pushing the industry with biweekly updates to your vehicle right on your home network. No longer do you need to drive to a vehicle service center for a recall or critical software update.

Security Vulnerabilities Are the New Oil Spills

Oil spills have had a tremendously detrimental effect on the environment over the past 50 years and continue to be an ongoing crisis. When running smoothly, oil drilling rigs are immensely profitable, but when accidents or natural disasters occur (particularly at sea, where environmental damage is amplified), the cost can be enormous. For large companies like BP, which can afford to pay or set aside tens of billions of dollars for fines, legal settlements, and cleanups, oil spills are just a cost of doing business. However, for drilling operations run by smaller companies, a single oil spill can spell financial disaster and put companies out of business with no means to address the aftermath.

This was the case for Taylor Energy, which lost an oil platform off the coast of Louisiana to Hurricane Ivan in 2004 and was leaking 300 to 700 barrels per day (*https://oreil.ly/3LOtN*). This disaster continues to haunt Taylor Energy, which is both the recipient and instigator of multiple lawsuits surrounding the oil spill and ongoing containment efforts. Taylor Energy has already spent $435 million to reduce the oil leakage in what has become the longest oil spill in US history, with the potential to keep leaking for the next century.

This is analogous to the risk that software vulnerabilities pose to the technology industry. Software systems have become increasingly complex, which means that there are more dependencies on open source software and third-party libraries, and it's a good thing. The problem is, old-school security audit approaches don't work anymore, making it virtually impossible to guarantee that a system is free of security vulnerabilities.

According to the 2021 "Open Source Security and Risk Analysis Report" by Synopsis (*https://oreil.ly/TFcnJ*), open source software is used in 99% of enterprise projects, and 84% of those projects contained at least one public vulnerability, with an average of 158 vulnerabilities found per codebase.

So how bad are these vulnerabilities that plague commercial codebases? The top 10 vulnerabilities allow an attacker to obtain sensitive information like authentication tokens and user session cookies, execute arbitrary code in the client browser, and trigger denial-of-service conditions.

Organizations' reactions to security vulnerabilities can be organized into three discrete steps that have to occur sequentially in order to respond:

1. Identify: first the organization must realize that a security issue exists and is currently or can potentially be exploited by an attacker.

2. Fix: once a security issue is identified, the development team must come up with a software fix to patch the issue.

3. Deploy: the final step is to deploy the software fix that addresses the security issue, often to a large set of end users or target devices that are affected by the vulnerability.

Going back to the Taylor Energy oil spill, you can see how difficult these steps are in the physical world:

1. Identify—six years

   The hurricane occurred in 2004, but it wasn't until six years later in 2010 that researchers observed a persistent oil slick at the Taylor site and brought it to public attention.

2. Fix—eight years

   The Couvillion Group won a bid for a containment system in 2018.

3. Deploy—five months

   In April 2019, the Couvillion Group deployed a shallow 200-ton steel box containment system. While not a permanent fix, this containment system has been collecting about 1,000 gallons of resalable oil per day and reduced the visible pollutants on the ocean surface.

Compared to a physical disaster like an oil spill, you would think that security vulnerabilities would be relatively easy to identify, fix, and deploy. However, as we will see in the following case studies, software vulnerabilities can be just as damaging and economically costly, and are by far much more common.

UK hospital ransomware

Let's look at another security breach. In 2017, a worldwide cyberattack (*https://oreil.ly/A7sPK*) was launched that encrypted the hacked computers and required a bitcoin "ransom" payment to recover the data. This attack had been exploited via the EternalBlue exploit on the Windows Server Message Block (SMB) service that had been previously discovered by the US National Security Agency (NSA) and leaked a year prior to the attack.

Upon infection, the virus attempted to replicate itself on the network and encrypted critical files, preventing their access, presenting a ransom screen. Microsoft had released patches for older versions of Windows that were affected by this exploit, but many systems were not updated because of poor maintenance or a requirement for 24/7 operation.

One organization critically impacted by this ransomware attack was the United Kingdom National Health Service (NHS) hospital system. Up to 70,000 devices (*https://oreil.ly/J0NLy*) on its network—including computers, MRI scanners, blood-storage refrigerators, and other critical systems—were affected by the virus. This also involved diversion of emergency ambulance services to hospitals and at least 139 patients who had an urgent referral for cancer that got cancelled.

The WannaCry ransomware attack resulted in an estimated 19,000 cancelled appointments and cost approximately £19 million in lost output and £73 million in IT costs (*https://oreil.ly/hx7OW*) to restore systems and data in the weeks after the attack. All of the affected systems were running an unpatched or unsupported version of

Windows that was susceptible to the ransomware. The majority were on Windows 7, but many were also on Windows XP, which had been unsupported since 2014—a full three years prior to the attack.

If we frame this with our vulnerability mitigation steps, we get the following timelines and impacts:

1. Identify—one year

   Both the existence of the vulnerability and an available patch were available for a year preceding the incident. NHS IT staff didn't realize its existence until the attack was launched on the world and affected the NHS.

2. Fix—existing

   Since the fix is simply to upgrade or patch systems with an existing fix, this was immediately available by the time the vulnerability was identified.

3. Deploy—multiple years

   While critical systems were brought back online quickly, there were enough affected systems that it took several years for the NHS to fully upgrade and patch affected systems with multiple failed security audits.

In this case, the security breach was at the operating system level. Assuming you are following industry best practices and keeping your operating system under maintenance and continually patched, you might believe you are safe. But what about application-level security vulnerabilities? This is by far the most common type of security vulnerability and is equally easy to exploit by an attacker—as happened to Equifax.

Equifax security breach

The Equifax security breach is a textbook example of an application-level security vulnerability causing massive financial damage to a high-tech company. From March through July of 2017, hackers had unrestricted access to Equifax's internal systems and were able to extract personal credit information for half of the total US population, or 143 million consumers.

This had the potential for massive identity theft, but none of the stolen Equifax personal data appeared on the dark web, which is the most direct monetization strategy. It is instead believed the data was used for international espionage by the Chinese government. In February 2020, four Chinese-backed military hackers were indicted in connection with the Equifax security breach.

For a credit agency to have a security vulnerability of this magnitude, the damage to its brand and reputation is incalculable. However, it is known that Equifax spent $1.4

billion on cleanup costs and an additional $1.38 billion to resolve consumer claims. Also, all of the upper executives at Equifax were quickly replaced after the incident.

Multiple compounded security vulnerabilities led to this breach. The first and most egregious was an unpatched security vulnerability in Apache Struts that allowed hackers to gain access to Equifax's dispute portal. From here, they moved to multiple other internal servers to access databases containing information on hundreds of millions of people.

The second major security vulnerability was an expired public-key certificate that impeded the internal system that inspects encrypted traffic exiting the Equifax network. The certificate had expired about 10 months before the breach occurred and was renewed only on July 29, at which time Equifax became immediately aware of the obfuscated payloads being used by the attacker to extricate sensitive data. Here's the Equifax timeline:

1. Identify—five months

   The initial security breach occurred on March 10, and while the attackers did not actively start exploiting this security breach until May 13, they had access to the system for almost five months before Equifax became aware of the data exfiltration. It wasn't until July 29, when Equifax fixed its traffic-monitoring system, that it became aware of the breach.

2. Fix—existing

   The Apache Struts security vulnerability (CVE-2017-5638) (*https://oreil.ly/ FiWeh*) was published on March 10, 2017 and fixed by Apache Struts 2.3.32 that was released four days prior to the CVE disclosure on March 6.

3. Deploy—one day

   The vulnerability was patched on July 30, one day after Equifax became aware of the breach.

The Equifax breach is particularly scary since it started with a vulnerability in a widely used Java library that affects many systems across the web. Even a year after the security vulnerability was identified, researchers at the SANS Internet Storm Center found evidence of exploitation attempts (*https://oreil.ly/ZCbXe*) looking for unpatched servers or new deployments that had not been secured. Continuous updates can help.

Widespread chipset vulnerabilities

Even if you are keeping up on security vulnerabilities in the application and operating system level, another class of vulnerabilities can affect you at the chipset and hardware level. The most widespread recent example of this are the Meltdown and Spectre exploits (*https://oreil.ly/z6E7i*) discovered by Google security researchers.

These flaws are so fundamental to the hardware platforms we use to run everything from cloud workloads to mobile devices that security researchers called them catastrophic. Both exploits take advantage of the same underlying vulnerabilities in how speculative execution and caching interact to get access to data that should be protected.

In the case of Meltdown, a malicious program can access data across the machine that it should not have access to, including processes with administrative privileges. This is an easier attack to exploit since it requires no knowledge of the programs you are trying to attack, but also it is easier to patch at the operating system level.

Upon the announcement of the Meltdown vulnerability, the latest versions of Linux, Windows, and Mac OS X all had security patches to prevent Meltdown from being exploited with some performance loss. In October 2018, Intel announced hardware fixes for its newer chips (*https://oreil.ly/bvCuh*) (including Coffee Lake Refresh, Cascade Lake, and Whiskey Lake) that address various variants of Meltdown.

In contrast, exploiting the Spectre vulnerability requires specific information about the process being attacked, making it a more difficult vulnerability to leverage. However, it is also much trickier to patch, which means that new exploits based on this vulnerability continue to be identified. Also it is more dangerous in cloud computing applications that use VMs, since it can be used to induce a hypervisor to provide privileged data to a guest operating system running on it.

The result is that Meltdown and particularly Spectre have opened up a new class of security vulnerabilities that break the principles of software security. It was assumed that if you built a system with the proper security protections in place and could fully verify the correctness of the source code and dependent libraries, that system should be secure. These exploits break this assumption by exposing side-channel attacks hiding in the CPU and underlying hardware that require further analysis and software and/or hardware fixes to mitigate.

So getting back to our analysis for the general class of chipset side-channel attacks, here's the timeline:

1. Identify—as fast as possible

   While there are generalized fixes for Meltdown and Spectre, exploits can occur at any time based on the architecture of your application.

2. Fix—as fast as possible

   A software fix for Spectre often involves specially crafted code to avoid either accessing or leaking information in misspeculation.

3. Deploy—as fast as possible

   Getting the fix into production quickly is the only way to mitigate damage.

Of these three variables, the one that can most easily be shortened is the deployment time. If you do not already have a strategy for continuous updates, creating one will hopefully give you the impetus to start planning for faster and more frequent deployments.

Getting Users to Update

We have now hopefully convinced you that continuous updates are a good thing, from a feature/competitive standpoint as well as for security vulnerability mitigation. However, even if you deliver frequent updates, will end users accept and install them?

Figure 10-1 models the user flow for deciding whether to accept or reject an update.

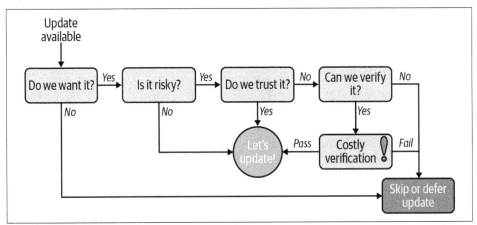

Figure 10-1. User model for update acceptance

The first question for a user is whether they really want the update based on features and/or security fixes. Sometimes the model for update acceptance is not a binary decision, because there is a choice to stay on a maintenance line with patches for security, but delay major upgrades that provide larger features but are riskier. This is the model that Canonical uses for Ubuntu release: long-term support (LTS) releases come out once every two years, with public support for five years. If you prefer riskier, but more frequent, updates, interim releases occur every six months with shorter support periods.

The second question is, how risky is the update? For security patches or minor upgrades, the answer is usually that it is low risk and safe to put in production with minimal testing. Typically, these changes are small, specifically designed to not touch any external or even internal APIs, and tested to make sure they address the security issue and don't produce undesirable side effects before release. Ability to perform local rollbacks (more on them later in the chapter) mitigates the risk.

Upgrading may also be safe when the party releasing the upgrade verifies that it is a safe upgrade, as shown in the third decision box of Figure 10-1. This is the model for operating system upgrades, such as iOS, where significant changes cannot be individually verified to be non-breaking. The OS vendor has to spend a significant amount of time testing hardware combinations, working with application vendors to fix compatibility issues or helping them upgrade their apps, and performing user trials to see what issues happen during an upgrade.

Finally, if it is both risky and the party producing the release cannot verify the safety, it is up to the recipient of the upgrade to do verification testing. Unless it can be fully automated, this is almost always a difficult and costly process to undertake. If the upgrade cannot be proven to be safe and bug free, the release may get delayed or simply skipped over in the hopes that a later release will be more stable.

Let's look at some real-world use cases and see their continuous update strategy.

Case Study: Java Six-Month Release Cadence

Java has historically had very long release cycles between major versions, averaging from one to three years. However, the release frequency has been erratic and often delayed, such as for Java 7, which took almost five years to be released. The release cadence has continued to decline as the platform has grown, due to several factors such as security issues and the difficulty of running and automating acceptance tests.

Starting with Java 9 in September of 2017, Oracle made the dramatic move to a six-month feature release cycle. These releases can contain new features and remove deprecated features, but the general pace of innovation was intended to stay constant. This means that each subsequent release should contain fewer features and less risk, making it easier to adopt. The actual adoption numbers of each JDK release are shown in Figure 10-2.

Given that 67% of Java developers never made it past Java 8, which came out in 2014, the new release model clearly has a problem! However, hidden under the data are a few issues.

First, the Java ecosystem can't handle six-month releases. As we learned in Chapter 6, virtually all Java projects are dependent on a large ecosystem of libraries and dependencies. In order to upgrade to a new Java release, all of those dependencies need to be updated and tested against the new Java release. For large open source libraries and complex application servers, this is almost impossible to accomplish in a six-month time frame.

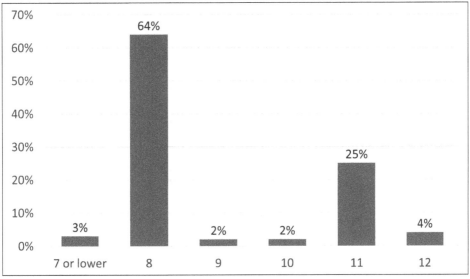

Figure 10-2. Developer adoption of recent Java releases[1]

To compound this, the OpenJDK support model provides public support for Java releases for only six months until the next feature release comes out. Even if you could upgrade every six months, you would be left without critical support and security patches, as detailed in Stephen Colebourne's blog (*https://oreil.ly/Axfki*).

The only exception to this is LTS releases that start with Java 11 and come every three years thereafter. These releases will get security patches and support from commercial JDK vendors such as Oracle, Red Hat, Azul, BellSoft, SAP, and others. Free distributions like AdoptOpenJDK and Amazon Corretto promise to provide Java releases and security patches at no cost. This is why Java 11 is the most popular release after Java 8 and none of the other six month releases have gained any traction.

However, in comparison to Java 8, Java 11 has not gained significant traction. The number of developers using Java 11, roughly two years after its release in September 2018, was 25%. In contrast, exactly two years after the release of Java 8, the adoption was 64%, as shown in Figure 10-3. This comparison is also biased in favor of Java 11, because anyone who adopted Java 9 or 10 would likely have upgraded to Java 11, providing three full years of adoption growth.

---

1 Brian Vermeer, "JVM Ecosystem Report 2020," Snyk, 2020, *https://oreil.ly/4fN74*.

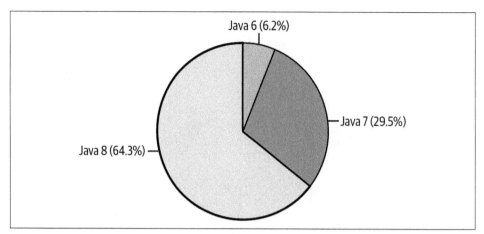

Figure 10-3. Developer adoption of Java 8 two years after release[2]

This brings us to the second reason for the poor adoption of Java 9 and beyond, which is a poor value/cost trade-off. The main feature of Java 9 was the introduction of a new module system. The idea of a modular Java Platform was first suggested by Mark Reinhold back in 2008 (*https://oreil.ly/22YFR*) and took nine years to complete in the release of Java 9.

Because of the complexity and disruptiveness of this change, it was delayed several times, missing both Java 7 and Java 8 as initial targets. Also Java 9 was highly controversial on release because it was initially incompatible with OSGi, a competing module system released by the Eclipse Foundation targeted at enterprise applications.

But perhaps the bigger issue with modularity is that no one really was asking for it. Modularity has many benefits, including better library encapsulation, easier dependency management, and smaller packaged applications. However, to fully realize these benefits, you need to spend a lot of work rewriting your application to be fully modularized. Second, you need all of your dependencies to be packaged as modules, which has taken a while for open source projects to embrace. Finally, the practical benefits for most enterprise applications are small, so even after upgrading to a module-enabled release, it is common practice to disable modularity and go back to the classpath model of Java 8 and prior. Figure 10-4 shows the simplified developer thought process on upgrading to Java 9 and beyond.

---

2 Eugen Paraschiv, "Java 8 Adoption in March 2016," last modified March 11, 2022, *https://oreil.ly/ab5Vv*.

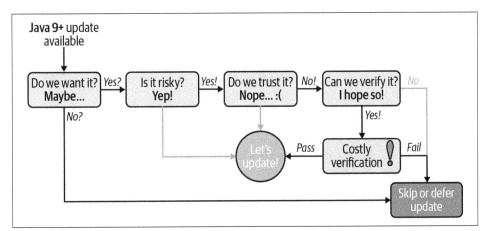

Figure 10-4. User model for java release acceptance

Clearly, choosing whether to upgrade comes down to comparing the value for you in modularity or other newly introduced features versus the cost to upgrade. And the upgrade cost is highly dependent on how difficult it is to test your application after upgrading, which takes us to our first continuous update best practice.

Continuous Update Best Practices

- Automated testing
  - — Problem: Manual testing is a major bottleneck in the software delivery process. This testing usually starts after the software was written and is time-consuming and error-prone.
  - — Solution: Automate, automate, automate. The more automated testing you have, and the quicker your tests run, the faster you can adopt new features safely and release into production.

Case Study: iOS App Store

We have had a very different update model for content since 1990, with the creation of the first web browser called WorldWideWeb by Tim Berners-Lee. Using a client-server model, content could be retrieved dynamically and updated continuously. As JavaScript and CSS technologies matured, this turned into a viable app delivery platform for continuously updated applications.

In contrast, while desktop client applications were comparatively complex and rich in their user interface, updates were infrequent and manual. This created a situation up to the mid-2000s of having to choose between either rich client applications that were difficult to update in the field or simpler web applications that could be continuously updated to add new features or patch security vulnerabilities. If you are a continuous update fan (which you should be by now), you know which one wins.

However, Apple changed all of this with the App Store on the iPhone in 2008, which was a game changer for deploying rich client applications to phones and other devices. Here is what App Store offered:

Update in one click
Updating a desktop application requires quitting the running version, following some sort of guided wizard to go through a seemingly dizzying array of choices for the common case (e.g., desktop shortcut, start menu, optional packages), and often rebooting your computer after installation. Apple simplified this to a single-button update, and in the case of many updates, a bulk option to update them all at once. The app update downloads, your mobile app quits, and the app is installed, all in the background with no user interruption.

There is only one version: latest
Do you know what version of Microsoft Office you are running? Up until 2011, when Office 365 was released, you had to, and had likely not upgraded in the past three to five years (or more). Apple changed all of this by providing only the latest version in the app store so the choice of which version to upgrade to is entirely removed. Also, you are not even provided a version number to reference, so all you know is that you are on the latest with a few notes from the developer on what you are getting. Finally, there is no cost to upgrade once you own an app, so the financial disincentive to upgrade that was the norm with paid desktop apps was entirely removed.

Security built in
While security vulnerabilities are the number one reason to install a patch, security concerns are also the number one reason *not* to upgrade. Being the first to upgrade puts you at risk if a vulnerability in the new software is discovered, which is why corporate IT policies typically forbid end users from upgrading their desktop apps for a certain period of time. However, Apple fixed this by integrating a sandboxed model in which the installed applications are limited in their ability to access data, contacts, photos, location, camera, and many other features without explicitly being given permission. This, combined with the rigorous app review process Apple instituted on store submissions for developers, reduced malware and app viruses to the point where, generally speaking, security is almost not a concern for consumers when upgrading their apps.

The availability of simple upgrades that are low risk makes the decision to update simple. Add to this the fact that releases are verified by a trusted authority, and users almost always make the decision to upgrade, as shown in Figure 10-5.

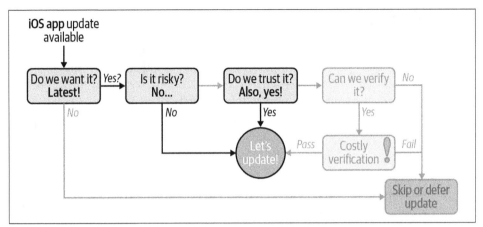

Figure 10-5. User model for iOS app update acceptance

The Apple App Store model is ubiquitous for not only mobile devices, but also desktop application installation. Google offered a similar model with its Android operating system in 2008, and both Apple and Microsoft introduced desktop app stores in 2011. Many of these app stores not only make it simple to upgrade to the latest version, but also offer an option to automatically upgrade.

As a result, self-updating applications are now the norm on mobile devices and have seen a resurgence on desktop computers, thanks to a few basic continuous update best practices.

Continuous Update Best Practices

- Automatic updates

  — Problem: Manual updates are often skipped or deferred because of risk or just time involved to evaluate risk.

  — Solution: The best type of update is one that requires no user interaction and just happens automatically (and safely). If the update is low risk and trusted, this eliminates the decision on whether the features are worthwhile, since it can happen without human intervention.

- Frequent updates

  — Problem: Lots of small and low-risk updates are better than a single large and infrequent one that is risky to end users.

  — Solution: Provide updates often and with small, low-risk changes. The store model encourages this by making small updates easier to get verified and released, and by the OS showcasing updated apps that increase engagement.

Continuous Uptime

In the cloud age, one of the most important measures for business success is service uptime. Rather than just delivering software, many companies are moving to a software-as-a-service (SaaS) model, where they are also responsible for the infrastructure the software runs on. Unexpected interruptions of service can be extremely costly, both in breach of service-level agreements and in customer satisfaction and retention.

While uptime is important for all business-provided internet services, there is no place where uptime is more important than in companies that build and support the very infrastructure the internet relies upon. Let's take a deeper look at one of the internet giants that runs global infrastructure underlying over 10% of the websites in the world and a myriad of applications and services that we rely upon on a daily basis.

Case Study: Cloudflare

As internet usage has exploded, so has the need for highly reliable, globally distributed, and centrally managed infrastructure like content delivery networks (CDNs). Cloudflare's business is providing a highly reliable content delivery infrastructure to businesses across the world with the promise that it can deliver content faster and more reliably than your own infrastructure or cloud computing servers can. This also means that Cloudflare has one job, which is *never* to go down.

While Cloudflare has had many production issues over the years involving DNS outages, buffer overflow data leaks, and security breaches, as its business has grown, the scale of the problem and resulting damage has gone up. Five of these outages occurred on a global scale, taking out an increasingly large portion of the internet. While many may secretly be happy to have a 30-minute break from the internet courtesy of continuous update failures (after which we promptly complain about them on Twitter), losing access to hundreds of millions of servers across the internet can cause major disruptions for businesses and huge financial loss.

We are going to focus on the three most recent global Cloudflare outages, what happened, and how they could have been prevented with continuous update best practices.

2013 Cloudflare router rule outage

In 2013, Cloudflare had 23 data centers across 14 countries serving 785,000 websites and over 100 billion page views per month. At 9:47 UTC on March 3, Cloudflare had a system-wide outage affecting all of its data centers when it effectively dropped off the internet.

After the outage commenced, diagnosing the problem took about 30 minutes, and a full hour for all services to be restored at 10:49 UTC. The outage was caused by a bad rule (*https://oreil.ly/oQ2LF*) that was deployed to the Juniper routers that sat on the edge of all its data centers, shown in Example 10-1. It was intended to prevent an ongoing distributed denial-of-service (DDos) attack that had unusually large packets in the range of 99,971 to 99,985 bytes. Technically, the packets would have been discarded after hitting the network, since the largest allowed packet size was 4,470, but this rule was intended to stop the attack at the edge before it impacted other services.

Example 10-1. The rule that caused Cloudflare's routers to crash

```
+    route 173.X.X.X/32-DNS-DROP {
+        match {
+            destination 173.X.X.X/32;
+            port 53;
+            packet-length [ 99971 99985 ];
+        }
+        then discard;
+    }
```

This rule caused the Juniper edge routers to consume all RAM until they crashed. Removing the offending rule fixed the problem, but many routers were in a state where they could not be automatically rebooted and required manual power cycling.

While Cloudflare blamed Juniper networks and their FlowSpec system that deploys rules across a large cluster of routers, Cloudflare is the company that deployed an untested rule to its hardware with no ability to fail over or roll back in the case of failure.

Continuous Update Best Practices

- Progressive delivery
  - Problem: In a distributed system, deploying new code to all production nodes (in this case, routers) simultaneously also breaks them all simultaneously.
  - Solution: Using a canary release design pattern (*https://oreil.ly/atq3W*), you can deploy the change to a few nodes first and test for issues before continuing the update. If an issue occurs, simply roll back the affected nodes and debug it offline.
- Local rollbacks
  - Problem: Reconfiguring edge devices can cause them to lose internet connectivity, making it difficult or impossible to reset them. In this case, an

additional 30 minutes of downtime was spent manually resetting routers across 23 data centers and 14 countries.

— Solution: Design edge devices to store the last known good configuration and restore to that in the case of an update failure. This preserves network connectivity for subsequent network fixes.

2019 Cloudflare regex outage

By 2019, Cloudflare had grown to host 16 million internet properties, serve 1 billion IP addresses, and in totality power 10% of the Fortune 1000 companies. The company had a very good run of six years with no global outages until 13:42 UTC on July 2 when Cloudflare-proxied domains started returning 502 Bad Gateway errors and remained down for 27 minutes.

This time the root cause was a bad regular expression (regex) (*https://oreil.ly/5Myhx*), shown in Example 10-2. When this new rule was deployed to the Cloudflare web application firewall (WAF), it caused the CPU usage to spike on all cores handling HTTP/HTTPS traffic worldwide.

Example 10-2. The regular expression that caused Cloudflare's outage

```
(?:(?:\"|'|\]|\}|\\|\d|(?:nan|infinity|true|false|null|undefined|symbol|math)
|\`|\-|\+)+[)]*;?((?:\s|-|~|!|{}|\|\|\||\+)*.*(?:.*=.*)))
```

Like any good regular expression, no human is capable of reading and understanding the series of unintelligible symbols, and certainly has no chance of verifying the correctness visually. In retrospect, it is obvious that the buggy part of the regex is .\ *(?:.*=.*). Since part of this is a noncapturing group, for the purposes of this bug, it can be simplified to .*.*=.*. The use of a double, non-optional wildcard (``.*``) is known to be a performance issue with regular expressions since they must perform backtracking that gets super linearly harder as the length of the input to be matched increases.

Given the difficulty of manually verifying bugs that get deployed to global infrastructure, you would think that Cloudflare would have learned from its 2013 outage and implemented progressive delivery. In fact, it had since implemented a complex progressive delivery system that involved three stages:

DOG point of presence
The first line of defense on new changes used only by Cloudflare employees. Changes get deployed here first so issues can be detected by employees before getting into the real world.

PIG point of presence

A Cloudflare environment for a small subset of customer traffic; new code can be tested without affecting paying customers.

Canary point of presence

Three global canary environments that get a subset of worldwide traffic as a last line of defense before changes go global.

Unfortunately, the WAF was primarily used for fast threat response, and as a result it bypassed all of these canary environments (as defined in the Canary Releases design pattern) and went straight to production. In this case, the regular expression was only run through a series of unit tests that did not check for CPU exhaustion before it was pushed to production. This particular change was not an emergency fix and thus could have done a staged rollout following the preceding process.

The exact timeline of the problem and subsequent fix was as follows:

1. 13:31—Code check-in of the peer reviewed regex.
2. 13:37—CI server built the code and ran the tests, which passed. Well, apparently, these weren't great. ¯_(ツ)_/¯
3. 13:42—The erroneous regex was deployed to the WAF in production.
4. 14:00—The possibility of an attacker was dismissed, and the WAF was identified as the root cause.
5. 14:02—It was decided to go to a global WAF kill.
6. 14:07—The kill was finally executed after delays accessing the internal systems.
7. 14:09—Service was restored for customers.

To recap, let's review the continuous update best practices that may have helped Cloudflare avoid another global outage.

Continuous Update Best Practices

- Progressive delivery
  - Problem: Canary deployments had now been implemented, but were not used for the WAF since this was used for fast threat response.
  - Solution: This particular rule was not an emergency and could have followed the canary deployment process.
- Observability
  - Problem: Some problems are hard to trace relying on user feedback only.
  - Solution: Implement tracing, monitoring, and logging in production. Cloudflare actually had specifically implemented a production watchdog designed

---

> to prevent excessive CPU use by regular expressions that would have caught this issue. However, a few weeks prior, this code was removed to optimize the WAF to use less CPU.

2020 Cloudflare backbone outage

A year after the previous Cloudflare outage, your author, Stephen, was sitting down to write about its 2019 outage when two peculiar things happened:

1. Around 2:12 P.M. PST (21:12 UTC), the family Discord channel stops, going off because of a Cloudflare outage, and I become incredibly productive.

2. A few hours later, all my searches for information on Cloudflare outages start turning up information on recent DNS issues instead of the articles from last year.

The nice folks at Cloudflare clearly recognized that good case studies come in threes and provided another antipattern for this chapter. On July 18, 2020, Cloudflare had another production outage for 27 minutes that affected 50% of its total network.

This time the issue was with the Cloudflare backbone, which is used to route the majority of traffic on its network between major geographies. To understand how the backbone works, it helps to understand the topology of the internet. The internet is not truly point-to-point but instead relies on a complex network of interconnected data centers to transmit information.

Cloudflare runs multiple centers in San Jose, Atlanta, Frankfurt, Paris, São Paulo, and other cities worldwide. These data centers are connected by a global backbone of direct, high-speed connections that allow them to bypass internet congestion and improve the quality of service between major markets.

It is the Cloudflare backbone that was the cause of the outage this time. The backbone is designed to be resilient to failures, such as the one that happened between Newark and Chicago at 20:25 UTC. However, this outage resulted in increased congestion between Atlanta and D.C. The attempted fix was to remove some of the traffic from Atlanta by executing the routing change in Example 10-3.

Example 10-3. The routing change that caused Cloudflare's network to go down

```
{master}[edit]
atl01# show | compare
[edit policy-options policy-statement 6-BBONE-OUT term 6-SITE-LOCAL from]
!       inactive: prefix-list 6-SITE-LOCAL { ... }
```

This routing change inactivates one line of a term script, shown in Example 10-4.

Example 10-4. The complete term the change was made on

```
from {
    prefix-list 6-SITE-LOCAL;
}
then {
    local-preference 200;
    community add SITE-LOCAL-ROUTE;
    community add ATL01;
    community add NORTH-AMERICA;
    accept;
}
```

The correct change would have been to inactivate the entire term. However, by removing the `prefix-list` line, the result was to send this route to all other backbone routers. This changed the `local-preference` to 200, which gave Atlanta priority over the other routes, which were set to 100. The result was that rather than reducing traffic, Atlanta instead started attracting traffic from across the backbone, increasing network congestion to the point where internet service was disrupted for half of Cloudflare's network.

There is a lot to say about configuration changes that can destroy your entire business. The core of the problem here is that Cloudflare is not treating the configuration of backbone routers as code that is properly peer reviewed, unit tested, and canary deployed.

Continuous Update Best Practices

- Automated testing
  - Problem: If you don't have automation around your code and configuration, manual errors will go into production uncaught.
  - Solution: All code (including configuration) needs to be tested in an automated fashion so it is repeatable.
- Observability
  - Problem: Detecting errors through observed behavior is error prone and time-consuming when seconds and minutes spell disaster. It took Cloudflare 27 minutes to identify a problem and trace it back to the Atlanta router.
  - Solution: Implement tracing, monitoring, and logging in production, especially for your key assets like the internet backbone.

The Hidden Cost of Manual Updates

Implementing continuous update best practices is not free, and often it can seem more cost-effective to delay automation and continual manual processes. In particular, doing automated testing, treating configuration like code, and automating deployment are all important, but also costly to implement.

However, what is the hidden cost of *not* automating your deployment? Manual deployments are fraught with errors and mistakes that cost time and effort to trouble-shoot and business loss when they negatively impact customers. What is the cost of having production errors that persist for hours as staff is brought in to troubleshoot the issue on a live system?

In the case of Knight Capital, where the answer turned out to be $10 million per minute of system failure, would you trust manual updates?

Case Study: Knight Capital

Knight Capital is an extreme case of a software bug going undetected, causing issues in production, and causing a huge amount of financial loss. However, the interesting thing about this bug is that the core issue was mistakes made in the deployment process, which was both infrequent and manual. If Knight Capital were practicing continuous deployment, it would have avoided a mistake that ended up costing it $440 million and control of the company.

Knight Capital Group was a market-making trader specializing in high-volume transactions, and throughout 2011 and 2012 its trading in US equity securities represented approximately 10% of the market volume. The company had several internal systems that handled trade processing, one of which was called Smart Market Access Routing System (SMARS). SMARS acted as a broker, taking trading requests from other internal systems and executing them in the market.

To support a new Retail Liquidity Program (RLP) that was set to launch on August 1, 2012, Knight Capital upgraded its SMARS system to add in new trading functionality. It decided to reuse the API flag for a deprecated function called Power Peg that was meant for internal testing only. This change was thought to have been successfully deployed to all eight production servers in the week leading up to the RLP launch.

At 8:01 A.M. EST, the morning of August 1 started with some suspicious, but sadly ignored, email warnings about errors on pre-market trading orders that referenced SMARS and warned "Power Peg disabled." Once trading commenced at 9:30 A.M. EST, SMARS immediately started executing a large volume of suspicious trades that would repeatedly buy high (at offer) and sell low (at bid), immediately losing on the spread. Millions of these transactions were being queued at 10 ms intervals, so even though the amounts were small (15 cents on every pair of trades), the losses piled up extremely quickly (*https://oreil.ly/w1a6K*).

In a business where seconds can be costly, minutes can wipe out weeks of earnings, and an hour is a lifetime, Knight Capital lacked an emergency response plan. During this 45-minute period, it executed 4 million orders for trading 397 million shares of 154 stocks. This gave the company a net long position of 3.4 billion and a net short position of 3.15 billion. After getting 6 of the 154 stocks reversed and selling the remaining positions, it was left with a net loss of around $468 million. This was a very tough period for Knight Capital.

Backtracking to the root cause of this problem, only seven of the eight production servers were correctly upgraded with the new RLP code. The last server had the old Power Peg logic enabled on the same API flag, which explains the warning emails earlier in the morning. For every request that hit this eighth server, an algorithm designed for internal testing was run that executed millions of inefficient trades designed to quickly bump up the price of the stock.

However, in troubleshooting this problem, the technical team erroneously thought that there was a bug on the newly deployed RLP logic and reverted the code on the other seven servers, essentially breaking 100% of the transactions and exacerbating the problem.

While Knight Capital did not go entirely bankrupt from this, it had to give up 70% of control of the company for a $400 million bailout of the company's position. Before the end of the year, this turned into an acquisition by a competitor, Getco LLC, and the resignation of CEO Thomas Joyce.

So, what happened to Knight Capital, and how can you avoid a disaster like this? See the next sidebar for some additional continuous update best practices.

Continuous Update Best Practices

- Frequent updates
  - Problem: If you only occasionally update your system, chances are that you are not very good (or efficient) at this and mistakes will be made. Knight Capital did not have the proper automation or control checks in place to reliably make production changes and was a continuous update disaster waiting to happen.
  - Solution: Update often and automate always. This will build the organizational muscle memory so that simple updates become routine and complex updates are safe.

- State awareness
  - — Problem: The target state (the flags in the Knight Capital example) can affect the update process (and any subsequent rollbacks).
  - — Solution: Know and consider target state when updating. Reverting might require reverting the state.

Continuous Update Best Practices

Now that you have seen the dangers of not adopting continuous update best practices from a variety of companies in different areas of the technology industry, it should be obvious why you should start implementing or continue to improve your continuous deployment infrastructure.

The following is a list of all the continuous update best practices along with the case studies that go into them in more detail:

- Frequent updates
  - — The only way to get good at updating is to do it a lot.
  - — Case studies: iOS App Store, Knight Capital.
- Automatic updates
  - — And if you are updating a lot, automating becomes cheaper and less error prone.
  - — Case study: iOS App Store.
- Automated testing
  - — The only way to make sure you are deploying quality is to test everything on every change.
  - — Case studies: Java six-month release cadence, 2020 Cloudflare backbone outage.
- Progressive delivery
  - — Avoid catastrophic failures by deploying to a small subset of production with a rollback plan.
  - — Case studies: 2013 Cloudflare router rule outage, 2019 Cloudflare regex outage.
- State awareness
  - — Don't assume that code is the only thing that needs to be tested; state exists and can wreak havoc in production.
  - — Case study: Knight Capital.

- Observability
  - — Don't let your customers be the ones to notify you that you are down!
  - — Case studies: 2019 Cloudflare regex outage, 2020 Cloudflare backbone outage.
- Local rollbacks
  - — Edge devices are typically numerous and hard to fix after a bad update hits, so always design for a local rollback.
  - — Case study: 2013 Cloudflare router rule outage.

Now that you are armed with knowledge, it is time to start convincing your coworkers to adopt best practices today, before you become the next Knight Capital "Knightmare" of the high-tech industry. Making headlines is great, but do it as an elite performer of the DevOps industry rather than on the front page of the Register. Don't try to boil the ocean, but small continuous improvement initiatives will, eventually, get your organization to continuous updates. Good luck!

Index

orchestration tools, 210
    (see also Kubernetes)
OS
    Android OS fragmentation, 256
    container definition, 56
    continuous updates (see continuous deploy-
        ment)
    Docker, 58
        Dockerfile, 204
    infrastructure as a service, 80
    metadata about, 135
    ransomware attack, 283
    VMs versus containers, 53
OWASP (see Open Web Application Security
    Project)

P

PaaS (platform as a service), 79
package management
    A/B testing, 132
    about, 131
    Android mobile workflow, 254
    artifact publication
        about, 162
        JFrog Artifactory, 167
        Maven Central, 164-167
        Maven Local, 162-164
        Sonatype Nexus Repository, 167
    dependency management
        about, 142
        Apache Maven, 142-155
        containers, 160
        Gradle, 155-160
        POM file metadata, 142-155
    metadata, 132
        capturing, 135-138
        dependency management, 142-162
        determining, 135
        insightful metadata, 133
        issues to consider, 134
        writing, 138-142
    version value format, 137
        tagging with SNAPSHOT, 137
parent images, 57
persistent data collections, 233
The Phoenix Project (Kim), 2
pixel density in mobile devices, 258
platform as a service (PaaS), 79
Podman, 204

Pods
    Kubernetes clusters, 211
    VerticalPodAutoscaler, 237
    workloads, 225
        Kubernetes resources, 225
        resource limit specification, 231
POM file (Apache Maven), 120-123
    Ant build file from, 123
    dependency metadata, 142-155
        direct dependencies, 143
        parent POM, 143
    Eclipse JKube plug-in, 208
privacy and metadata, 134, 135
progressive delivery, 9
    Cloudflare case study, 296
    continuous deployment best practices, 295,
        297
project management
    quality gate method, 193
    security expertise, 198
Prometheus
    metrics, 238-240
    performance of application, 246
    tracing, 242
provided dependency scope, 146
pull (Git command), 30
    book repository exercise, 22-26
    pull requests in central repository model, 38
push (Git command), 31

Q

quality gate method
    about, 191
    definition of done, 199
    implementing, 193
    practical application, 195
    project management, 193
    risk management, 194
    strategies
        flexible quality strategy, 193
        not reviews or milestones, 193
        uniform quality guideline, 192
quality via source code management, 16
Quarkus, 94-97
    about implementation, 83
        Java versus GraalVM Native Image, 83
    building container images
        Jib for, 206
        JVM base image customization, 207

X

About the Authors

Stephen Chin

Stephen Chin (*@steveonjava*) is VP of developer relations at JFrog and coauthor of *The Definitive Guide to Modern Java Clients with JavaFX 17*, *Raspberry Pi with Java*, and *Pro JavaFX Platform*. He has keynoted numerous Java conferences around the world including Devoxx, JNation, JavaOne, Joker, and Open Source India. Stephen is an avid motorcyclist who has done evangelism tours in Europe, Japan, and Brazil, interviewing hackers in their natural habitat. When he is not traveling, he enjoys teaching kids how to do embedded and robot programming together with his teenage daughter.

Melissa McKay

Melissa McKay (*@melissajmckay*) is a developer/software engineer turned international speaker and is a developer advocate on the JFrog Developer Relations team, sharing in the mission to improve the developer experience with DevOps methodologies. She's a mom, software developer, Java Champion, Docker Captain, huge promoter of Java unconferences, and she is active in the developer community. Given her passion for teaching, sharing, and inspiring fellow practitioners, you are likely to cross paths with her on the international conference circuit—both online and off.

Ixchel Ruiz

Ixchel Ruiz (*@ixchelruiz*) is a developer advocate on the JFrog Developer Relations team. She has developed software applications and tools since 2000. Her research interests include Java, dynamic languages, client-side technologies, DevOps, and testing. Ixchel is a Java Champion, Oracle Groundbreaker Ambassador, SuperFrog, Hackergarten enthusiast, open source advocate, public speaker, and mentor. She travels around the world (sometimes virtually) because sharing knowledge is one of her main drives in life!

Baruch Sadogursky

Baruch Sadogursky (*@jbaruch*) did Java before it had generics, DevOps before there was Docker, and DevRel before it had a name. Now Baruch helps engineers solve problems, and helps companies help engineers solve problems.

He is coauthor of *Liquid Software*, serves on multiple conference program committees, and regularly speaks at numerous prestigious industry conferences, including Kubecon, JavaOne, Devoxx, QCon, DevRelCon, DevOpsDays (all over), DevOops (not a typo), and others.

Ana-Maria Mihalceanu

Ana-Maria Mihalceanu (*@ammbra1508*) is a Java Champion, Certified Architect, cofounder of the Bucharest Software Craftsmanship Community, and a constant adopter of challenging technical scenarios involving Java-based frameworks and multiple cloud providers. She actively supports technical communities' growth through knowledge sharing on architecture, Java, and DevOps and enjoys curating content for conferences as a program committee member. Ana believes that every technical problem has various solutions, each with benefits and drawbacks, and that we can remediate any mistake as long as we hold the passion for our work.

Sven Ruppert

Sven Ruppert (*@SvenRuppert*) has been coding in Java since 1996 in industrial projects and is working as a developer advocate for JFrog with a focus on security and DevSecOps. He is a serial speaker at conferences worldwide and contributes to IT periodicals and tech portals as a domain expert. Sven has been working for more than 15 years as a consultant worldwide in the automotive, space, insurance, and banking industries, as well as the UN and World Bank. In addition to his primary expertise in DevSecOps, Sven is also a recognized expert in mutation testing of web apps, distributed unit testing, core Java, and Kotlin.

Colophon

The animal on the cover of *DevOps Tools for Java Developers* is a banded mongoose *(Mungos mungo)*. These small carnivores are found in much of sub-Saharan Africa, with the exception of the Congo and some parts of West Africa. They can live in a variety of habitats such as grasslands, brushlands, and woodlands, but they avoid the more arid climates of deserts and semideserts.

Banded mongooses can grow to lengths of 12 to 18 inches—not including a 6 to 12 inch tail!—and typically weigh between 3 and 5 pounds. The distinguishing feature of this breed is the dark stripes interrupting their coarse gray-brown coat from the base of the tail across the back. They have small, pointed faces, bushy tails that taper into a point, and long, curved claws on their front feet to allow for scratching and digging. Banded mongooses primarily eat insects, but they may also scavenge for crabs, earthworms, fruit, birds, eggs, rodents, scorpions, snails, and even snakes. They are very possessive and do not share food, and can travel more than five miles a day to forage.

Banded mongooses are more social than other mongoose species and usually live in packs of 10 to 20 individuals. These packs will hunt together, raise their young together, and even fight off predators by bunching together and moving as a group to create the appearance of a single large animal. Male banded mongooses court females by circling them with their tails head high. They are nonmonogamous and may sometimes synchronize reproduction so that all females in the pack give birth around the same time. Banded mongooses are born in litters of two to six, and are blind until they begin opening their eyes around 10 days later. The young may leave the den for short periods and begin accompanying the adults in foraging after four to five weeks. Banded mongooses are considered a species of "least concern" by the IUCN; they are widespread in their habitat and face no major threats. Many of the animals on O'Reilly covers are endangered; all of them are important to the world.

The cover illustration is by Karen Montgomery, based on a black-and-white engraving from Lydekker's *The Royal Natural History*. The cover fonts are Gilroy Semibold and Guardian Sans. The text font is Adobe Minion Pro; the heading font is Adobe Myriad Condensed; and the code font is Dalton Maag's Ubuntu Mono.

Printed in the USA
CPSIA information can be obtained
at www.ICGtesting.com
JSHW051658070823
46091JS00005B/60

9 781492 084020